LIVES AND TIMES OF SMITHILLS ESTATE

Smithills Estate Research Group

Edited by Helena Sanderson

First edition published 2022
by Smithills Estate Research Group
c/o The Woodland Trust, Smithills Hall, Smithills Dean Road, Bolton, BL1 7NP
smithillsresearch@gmail.com

Proceeds from the sale of this publication are being donated to the Woodland Trust for the furtherance of their work on Smithills Estate.

© 2022 Helena Sanderson for editorial matter. Individual contributions © the contributors (see individual chapters).

The right of the editor to be identified as the author of the editorial material, and of the authors for their individual chapters, has been asserted in accordance with sections 77 and 78 of the Copyright, Design and Patents Act 1988.

All rights reserved. No part of the book may be reprinted or reproduced or utilised in any form by any electronic, mechanical, or other means, now known or hereafter invented, including photocopying and recording, or in any information storage or retrieval system, without permission in writing from the publishers and copyright holders.

The authors, editor and publisher gratefully acknowledge the permission granted to reproduce the copyright material in this book. Every effort has been made to trace copyright holders and to obtain their permission for the use of copyright material. The publisher apologises for any errors or omissions and would be grateful if notified of any corrections that should be incorporated in future reprints or editions of this book.

First edition published by Smithills Estate Research Group 2022

British Library Cataloguing-in-Publication Data
A catalogue record for this book is available from the British Library

ISBN: 978-1-3999-4213-3

Typeset in Garamond Pro and Calibri
by Biskit Design, Registered office: 5 Granville Court, off Granville Mount, Otley, LS21 3PB
Printed and bound on 130gsm silk paper, by Minerva Print, King William House, 202 Manchester Road, Bolton, BL3 2QS

Main front cover: The old Halliwell Bleach Works chimney from Pendlebury's, looking over Bolton and Manchester © Tony Greenwood
Back cover: Sun sets on Two Lads and the lands of the Brigantes © Peter Ravald Photography and Drone Photography

This book is dedicated to the memory of all the ordinary people who lived, worked, and died on Smithills Estate. And also to those who seized a chance to migrate across the world, taking a little bit of Smithills with them, and leaving a little bit of themselves behind.

Without them all there would be no tales to tell, no songs to sing.

> *The years weave in, and the years weave out,*
> *And time like a shuttle flies,*
> *And weaves the web of day and night*
> *Across the eternal skies…*
>
> *…Oh, weave the days and weave the nights! –*
> *The shadow and the shine;*
> *The sun that hopes and the stars that dream,*
> *Through foul times and through fine.*

From 'The Handloom Weavers' Song', 1891

Contents

Biographies	viii
Acknowledgements	x
Notes	xi
Introduction to the First Edition	xii
Smithills Estate Plan	xiv

1. Karen Holroyd — 15
   Two Lads: The Myths and Legends

2. Tony Greenwood — 42
   Poaching on Burnt Edge, 1630 and 1864

3. Stephen Tonge — 46
   Chadwicks Close Farm

4. Linda Shaw — 53
   Women and Work from the Late 1780s to the Early 1850s

5. Barbara Winder — 69
   Who Killed George Henderson on Winter Hill?

6. Laura Kovaleva — 87
   Jack O' Nandies

7. Sam Holt — 92
   The Sutcliffes, Handloom Weavers at Walker Fold

8. Dotty Snelson — 104
   Slack Hall and Newfield

9. Tony Greenwood — 114
   Lost Cottages on Winter Hill: Newspaper Hall and Black Jacks

10. Laura Kovaleva   128
    The Freeman Sisters, Victorian Laundresses

11. Dawn Axon   134
    Leaving the Estate Far Behind

12. Lauren Pursey   142
    Women's Work on Deakins, Lomax Wives and Holdens Farms

13. Tony Greenwood   154
    Up the Sixty-three Steps to Twitchells Farm and the Brown Cow Beerhouse

14. Dotty Snelson   164
    Violent Attacks on Gamekeepers, and a Tragic Love Story

15. Laura Kovaleva   176
    Horwich Casanova

16. Phil Orth   184
    Old and New Colliers Row, and Colliers Row School

17. Laura Kovaleva   197
    The Story of Alice and William Stead

18. Sam Holt   203
    The Harts, Emigration to Canada

19. Dawn Axon   216
    Love Across the Continents: Putting Down Roots in the New World

References   ccxxx
Buildings Gazetteer   ccxl
Tenants and Occupiers, 1543-1902   ccxliv
Nineteenth and Early Twentieth Century Legislation   cclv
Index   cclvii

Biographies

Barbara Winder was born and brought up in Derbyshire, then moved around England in a variety of English and pastoral teaching posts. She made her home in Bolton over forty years ago, raising three children with husband Nigel. She obtained a Combined Honours degree at Birmingham University and a PGCE at Kings College London in the 1960s, and a MLitt at UCLAN in the 1990s, with a dissertation on crime fiction. She was a senior English examiner for AQA for over fifty years, and for ten years a local magistrate. She still enjoys painting, history, genealogy, and watching BWFC.

Dawn Axon was born in Bolton in 1959. She has lived in the Heaton area most of her life and credits her love of local history to her mother who was also born and bred in Bolton. She is particularly interested in the social history of the area and the lives of the people who worked in Bolton over the last two hundred years. She has found the book project fascinating as she walked around Smithills Estate as a child with her grandfather and has drawn on her research into her own family to provide personal details.

Dotty Snelson is a Chartered Librarian and later worked in the Civil Service for thirty-four years. She retired aged seventy and has since been able to indulge her love of writing. This project has enabled her to combine twin passions of writing and history. She has enjoyed the research involved and the interaction with the rest of the group. Dotty is a voracious reader and a lover of ballet, theatre, the outdoors, and walking. Caring responsibilities may restrict but never deter her.

Helena Sanderson dreams of time travel and immersing herself in history is the only way she can do it (for now…). She was born near Haslingden, and her family has lived in the Rossendale Valley for many generations going back to at least the 1650s. An oral historian, genealogist, and heritage project facilitator, she is also a non-executive Director at Farfield Mill Arts and Heritage Centre in Sedbergh. With a passion for letterpress, she is slowly building up a collection of typecases, indulging her ambition to recreate old posters, leaflets, and other ephemera.

Karen Holroyd is an intrepid adventurer. On explorations across the countryside with her children she retold folklore passed on to her by her uncle, Tom Leech, a local historian who shared his knowledge and enthusiasm with Karen from a young age, and sparked a lifelong love of history. Decades have passed, her children have grown up and, with free time to herself, she returned to the countryside for running, and peace and quiet. Finding echoes of memories past, her same youthful curiosity and sense of adventure drive Karen as she seeks answers and remembers those that came before.

Laura Kovaleva was a pupil at Moscow High School, with the dilemma of choosing between History and English for her main university subject. She chose English and after graduation began working as a teacher of English as a second language. In 2009 Laura moved to England where she continued working as an ESOL teacher and completed her PGCE in 2022.

Walking cobbled streets and reading date stones rekindled her interest in history and joining the Smithills Estate Research Group has inspired her to research the history of local farms and families.

Lauren Pursey was raised in Bolton and from a young age developed a strong interest in local history, particularly the history surrounding Barrow Bridge. In addition to collecting vintage postcards, she enjoys visiting museums and heritage sites, her favourite being Dunstanburgh Castle in Northumberland. Lauren is currently studying History at university and has written pieces on LGBTQ+ history for both her university's newspaper and their law journal.

Linda Shaw lives in Smithills and enjoys walking on the estate. Now happily retired, she has previously worked in adult and continuing education. Originally an historian, she was involved in the field of international development in both project management and research. Most recently Linda has worked with the co-operative movement in the UK and internationally. She has researched and written various publications on women, international development and co-operation.

Phil Orth is a retired primary school teacher who has lived on the edge of the Smithills Estate since 1976. He has always been interested in History and studied it at A Level and at college. Furthermore, he is keenly interested in the history of education and was eager to study the history of the school on Colliers Row, and also the history of the area in which he lives.

Sam Holt has lived on a farm near Smithills his whole life and has walked the paths round Barrow Bridge and Walker Fold Woods from a young age. Having always had a fascination with history, particularly the ancient world, he went on to study Classics and Ancient History at university. Since then, he has become increasingly interested in the history of his local area and his own family who have been farmers since at least 1765. This inspired him to research the lives of others who lived in farm dwellings across the nineteenth and early twentieth centuries.

Stephen Tonge - born and bred in Bolton. He is a family man, computer programmer, Camino hiker, mediocre guitarist and a keen local history researcher. He has published numerous transcripts and indexes of historical documents online, including abstracts of over 700 wills of Bolton people from the sixteenth to nineteenth centuries. He was the organiser of the Tonge Family DNA Project and author of Turton Local History Society's 2019 publication about the village of Egerton. He has a special interest in the Smithills Estate where his ancestors were once tenant farmers.

Tony Greenwood is a volunteer warden for the Woodland Trust. Tony helped organise the Winter Hill 125 march in 2021 and wrote the Trespass Trail Audio produced by local arts group Live from Worktown. He lives in Smithills, on the edge of the woodland and moorland that inspires his social history writing. After retiring from his career as a Charted Management Accountant, he became a Mountain Leader, taking people on expeditions around the world and training school children at local outdoor activity centres.

Acknowledgements

In an undertaking of this magnitude, where a group of people have come together to research and write the history of one of the most interesting and iconic places in the locale, there are of course many thanks to be given.

First, we'd like to thank the Woodland Trust for bringing us together in the form of the Smithills Estate Research Group. Particularly Dr Vicky Entwistle for enabling us to consider publishing our research and for allocating funding. Vicky has always been a positive and encouraging force. Likewise Roberta Gleaves whose enthusiasm and determination to elicit further funding led us to produce a full colour book. The book itself would never have happened without our facilitator and editor, Helena Sanderson. She helped us hone our research, finesse our writing and sourced many of the images. She has structured our chapters to provide a wonderful story of people and place, and we could not have done it without her encouragement and guidance. Also a great many thanks to Trust member Gillian Lonergan for the effort she has put in to provide the book with such an excellent index. And to Rachel Barker and Jim Turner for their respective writing and design workshops.

We have been assisted by a number of people and organisations. Terry Higginson and the late Margaret Koppens from the Halliwell Local History Society allowed us to visit their archive and were very helpful in pointing us in the direction of sources. Likewise, Julie Lamara and her staff at Bolton Archives. Julie led a study day where many of us gained valuable insight into the workings of the archives and were able to carry out important guided research. The Archives team were always informative and provided useful lines of enquiry. Derek Cartwright and everyone at Horwich History Centre gave enthusiastic help and guidance. As did Joan Dickinson of Chorley Historical and Archaeological Society, Bolton Archaeological Society, Bill Aldridge of Wigan Archaeological Society, and Ian Trumble of Bolton Museum. Beamish Museum provided us with old photographs.

On a more personal level, thank you so very much to our families and friends for their support, encouragement, proofreading, suggestions, and listening skills when all we seemed to want to talk about was our book. Thanks to Karen Holt for her wonderful artwork and to Mabel Sharples for her encouragement and support. To Elena Kovaleva and Vitaly Kovalev for being encouraging, supportive and inspirational. Nina and Matthew Pursey for encouragement and endless support. Nigel Winder was entirely focused in giving positive support, and often suggested useful adaptions.

Also thanks to Anna Pilgrim and Colin Murray for support and chapter proofreading. Photographer Yelena Overchenko for some great professional images. Peter Ravald for many of the photographs including the back cover. Andy Mallins for photography of Two Lads. Amy Ball for her wonderful photographs. Jake Gosling of Lug Design for his inspired CAD interpretation of the ancient Two Lads. Stuart Atkinson from South Pennines Park who helped interpret the landscape. Lee McCarren of Chadwicks Close Farm for providing photographs from his private collection. And regulars at the Ainsworth Arms for their stories of the school.

Finally, we would like to thank our fellow Research Group members for all their suggestions, advice, digital reading, newspaper articles, sharing of resources and all-round comradeship throughout the entirety of this project.

Notes

Dates
Prior to the introduction of the Gregorian calendar in 1752 the Julian year began on 25 March and the months January to March contained two dates (for example 23 January 1567/68). Due to discrepancies with the solar year, when the calendar changed 2 September 1752 was followed by 14 September 1752.

Currency
Decimalisation was implemented in the UK in 1971. All sources within this publication use pre decimal coinage where 12 pence (d.) = 1 shilling (s.), and 20 shillings (s.) = 1 pound (£).

Value of money
There are numerous ways of calculating how much an amount in the past is worth today. These include comparing the Retail Price Index, income, or net worth. Because there can be large differences in the resulting amounts direct comparisons are unhelpful. For instance, basing the calculation on RPI suggests that £1 in 1800 is worth £85.90 today, whereas basing it on income suggests it could be as much as £1158. Instead it is worth looking at what a particular amount would have bought in the past, or to compare it to a typical wage.

Census enumeration records
The censuses between 1841 and 1911 are mentioned regularly throughout this publication and are not referenced individually. Those interested in exploring further can view the records online at a variety of genealogy websites. The majority of the places mentioned fall within or near the current boundaries of Smithills Estate and can be found in the following record sets:

1841 HO107, Piece 541, Deane-Halliwell, Enumeration District (ED) 7; Deane-Horwich, ED 1
1851 HO107, Piece 2207, Halliwell, ED 2c; Piece 2207, Horwich, ED 1a
1861 RG9, Piece 2812, Halliwell, ED 3; Piece 2814, Horwich, ED, 1
1871 RG10, Piece 3925, Halliwell, ED 3; Piece 3927, Horwich, ED 1
1881 RG11, Piece 3823, Halliwell, ED 2; Piece 3826, Horwich, ED 1
1891 RG12, Piece 3101, Halliwell, ED 1; Piece 3104, Horwich, ED 1
1901 RG13, Piece 3606, Bolton-Halliwell, ED 1; Piece 3608-10, Horwich, ED 5
1911 RG14, Piece 23309, Bolton-Halliwell, ED 1; Horwich, ED 12

Owners of Smithills Estate

Radcliffe family 1335
Barton family 1485
Belasyse family 1659
Edward Byrom 1722/3
Peter Ainsworth 1801
Richard Ainsworth 1807

Peter Ainsworth 1833
Richard Henry Ainsworth (the Colonel) 1870
Nigel Combe Ainsworth 1926
Bolton Corporation 1938
Woodland Trust 2015/17

Introduction to the first edition

During the lockdown of 2020 I was working at Smithills Estate in Bolton, a site owned and managed by the Woodland Trust. The team there were mid-way through a Lottery-funded project which included a programme of community engagement, events, and volunteering. As you can imagine, most of our programme had been in-person events and activities. That changed overnight in March 2020, and by December of that year Bolton remained in local lockdown, one of the unfortunate places where some form of lockdown had been in place for most of the time since April. It was a tough year for the town.

Thinking of ways to connect people with the Estate from home, in December 2020 I talked to *The Bolton News* about a genealogy project and requested help from Bolton's community in joining our effort to chart the history of the people who lived and worked on Smithills Estate. We had a great response, and the Smithills Estate Research Group was born.

Over the months, it became clear that the group could do much more than list the various census results for Estate farms. We had completed that and many group members were keen to take our research further, and to look at the stories around the names we were finding. We began to look through the newspaper archives, visited Bolton Museum archive, and connected with local heritage societies. The group had writing sessions focussed on turning the facts they were finding into life stories, and design sessions looking at book layout. They learned about referencing and sourcing.

Stories began to emerge. Fascinating characters like Jack O' Nandies, tragic love stories, tough working lives, cruel accidents, possible miscarriages of justice, rumours of Saxon burials, and snippets of life lived in what was then a busy part of Bolton, with homes, pubs (legal and otherwise), mines, quarries, farms, and a school. Many Boltonians will have walked the routes mentioned in this book. Some of the buildings remain, others you may have walked past many times but not realised as they are now ruins. Landmarks such as Two Lads are very well known, the sites of the mines less so. But the stories you read here will make you see these routes and locations in a new light. Stop awhile on your next walk on the Estate and contemplate the lives lived here.

One of the joys of this project has been the way in which the Research Group have worked together, helping each other to find publications, connecting their findings to others in the group where stories overlapped (which they frequently did, with families intermarrying and people featuring in several of the stories), and encouraging each other. Remember, everyone in the group was researching and writing in their spare time. Some of the group are students, others working, others retired (but we know that can be even more busy than working!), and they are all historians. The dedication involved has been immense. Everyone brought distinct experience to the group, whether it was in creative writing, scouring archives, or genealogy. Where there were areas people wanted to get a bit of help with, members 'buddied up' to support each other.

I want also to shine a light on the skill of the group in researching the details surrounding the lives of the individuals on the census. In finding out what their jobs involved, and how that impacted day to day life. In picking up stories of emigration and finding out what that meant. What was the journey like? What did Smithills emigrants find when they got to their destinations? And in connecting the protagonists to the social and cultural situations of their times, focussing for example on women's work, on schools, on class differences and working conditions, and on social movements such as the Mass Trespass of 1896. By bringing these factors into the specific stories of Smithills Estate the group have connected the places and people of the Estate with wider historical topics, as well as enabling readers to get a real idea of what life involved for the Estate's residents.

There is some genuinely brilliant detective work in this book, too. As an historian myself I know the importance of checking sources and challenging old narratives. To highlight two examples (though there are more), Karen Holroyd's research into the origins of Two Lads cairns and Barbara Winder's review of the murder of George Henderson and the subsequent trial show what can be achieved with a keen eye and determination. They appraise stories which are well known amongst local historians, bringing new thoughts and possible conclusions which are well researched and compelling.

It's not easy to bring dry historical facts – census returns, birth, marriage and death certificates, tax and land documents – to life. Here, the group have done that with real skill. I hope you enjoy this selection of stories from the lives of Smithills Estate. From the laundresses to the gamekeepers, the miners and travellers, the woman farmers, the weavers, the intrepid families who made the move to Canada, America, Australia, New Zealand and Russia, the publicans, the schoolchildren, Saxon kings, medieval knights and the characters who defy description (see Jack O' Nandies!) there are stories of love, loss, courage, exploration, and endeavour.

Thank you to Barbara Winder, Dawn Axon, Dotty Snelson, Karen Holroyd, Laura Kovaleva, Lauren Pursey, Linda Shaw, Phil Orth, Sam Holt, Stephen Tonge, Tony Greenwood. It was such a joy to be a part of the group.

Dr Vicky Entwistle
Woodland Trust

Nineteenth Century Representation of Smithills Estate

- Industrial buildings
- Estate farms & cottages
- Other buildings
- Roads
- Old roads
- Footways
- Watercourses
- Reservoirs
- Current Estate boundary
- Cairns

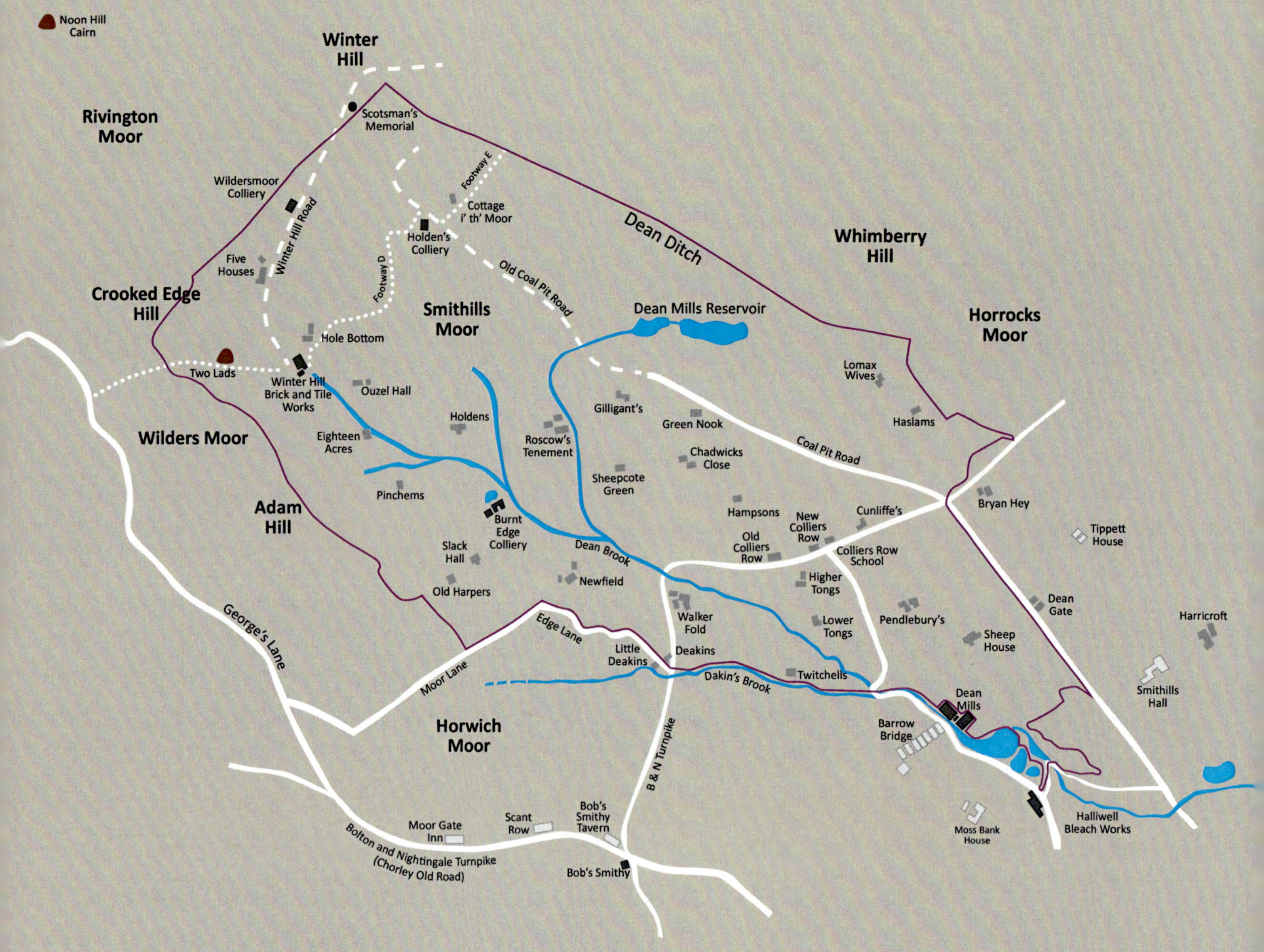

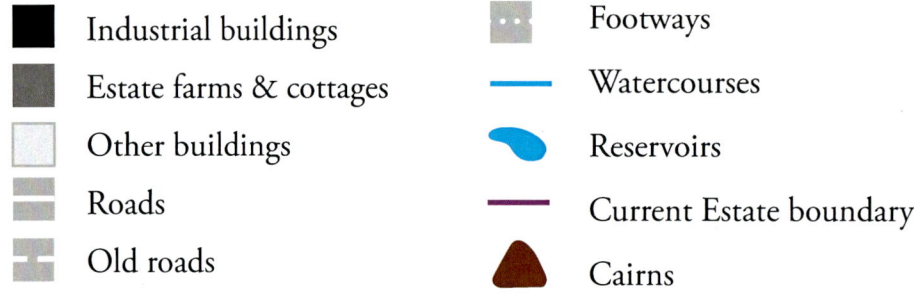

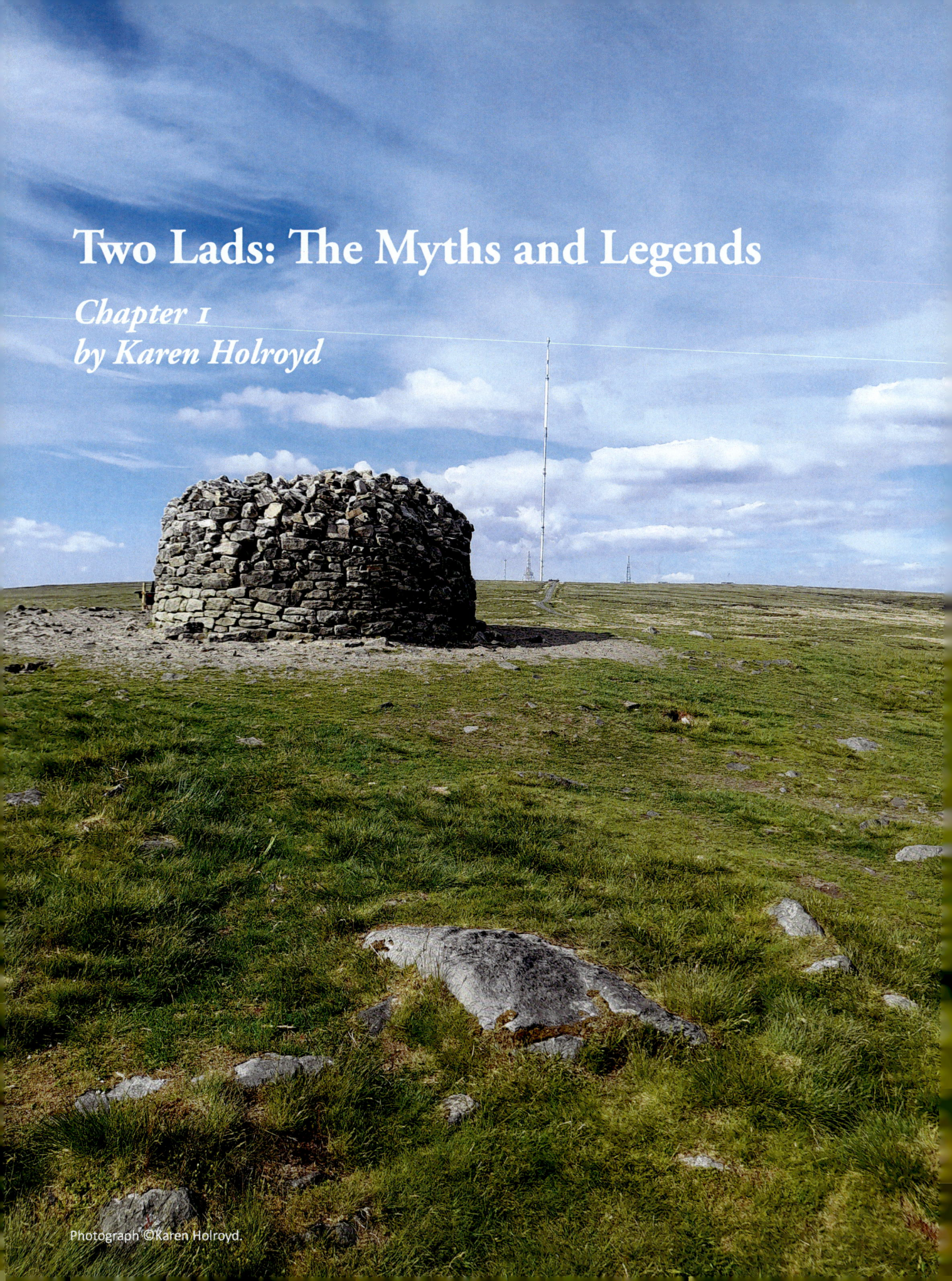

Two Lads: The Myths and Legends

Chapter 1
by Karen Holroyd

On the steep climb up to Winter Hill masts from George's Lane in Horwich sits Two Lads, on part of Wilders Moor called Crooked Edge Hill. It is a landmark that has been recorded on maps since 1787.[1] Whilst it lies within the Horwich town boundary, the land itself is part of Smithills Estate and currently owned by the Woodland Trust. On older maps it is shown as two cairns, but many local people will be familiar with just one large cairn until the 1970s when the second cairn was rebuilt. Since then, the cairn or cairns have been vandalised and rebuilt numerous times with a third one recently appearing. At the time of writing, there is one exceptionally large cairn, another demolished one, and a crudely built third one set some distance away. Although the site is acknowledged by Historic England Research Records, Monument Number 43445, it is not a protected Scheduled Monument and is described as, '"Two Lads", a confused heap of stones, seems to be the wreckage of one or more cairns'.[2]

Photograph
©Karen Holroyd.

Various articles have been written about Two Lads, and after collating all the theories I have tried to trace the origins of each source and verify accounts where possible. In modern times the most quoted author is respected local historian Thomas Hampson (1839-1918), but where did he get his information from, and is he right? In his book *History of Blackrod* published in 1882, he puts forward a very plausible argument originating from John Whitaker, who wrote in 1771 with intelligent reasoning, purporting Blackrod being the lost Roman town of Coccium.[3] However, this is now outdated and incorrect due to modern archaeological findings at Wigan.[4]

Two Lads Timeline

Various authors and surveyors have documented the site and we can put together this timeline:

c.1280: A grant of land deed from Cecily, widow of Roger de Worsley and daughter of William de Roynton, possibly includes Two Lads within the description of the land boundary.

'Beginning at "Kaldewell" below the house of William following under the bank as far as the Querin-stanes-clif and so following Querin-stanes-clif into Frid-broc and so ascending to the highway and so following the highway beyond Rounpik as far as "Stondandestan", thence going to the head of "Cringal-broc-heuyd", and so descending Cringal-broc as far as the foot of the cliff, and so following the cliff as far as Kaldewell, which is the first mete'.[5]

After tracking most of this route I have slightly different thoughts to the nineteenth century historian William Fergusson Irvine who suggests the modern places for these landmarks.[6] As I followed the route, I found the Querin-stanes-clif to be in the Terraced Gardens which is now filled in and Frid-broc no longer exists, it was probably rerouted during the building of the Terraced Gardens. The highway crosses over the shoulder of Rivington Pike and to follow this line to the Stondandestan would take you to Two Lads before turning to drop down to Cringal-broc-heuyd (the head of Crooked Edge Brook).

1776: Dorning Rasbotham describes the site of Two Lads, which is also drawn, and Edward Baines gives the description from Rasbotham's manuscript collections.

'To the right of the road from Bolton to Chorley, upon the summit of Horwich Moor, lie the Wilder Lads, two rude piles of stone, so called from the tradition of the country, that they were erected in memory of two boys, who were wildered (that is, bewildered) and lost in the snow at this place. They lie about three-quarters of a mile south-east by east from Rivington Pike, and may be distinctly seen, for considerable distance as you pass along the road, from which, at Horwich Chapel, they are something more than a mile distant.

They are undoubtedly of exceedingly high antiquity, and were originally united by a circular mound, above three-quarters of which as yet remains visible. Their circumference is about 26½ feet, and the passage betwixt them six and half feet. The remains of the mound is about four feet wide, but on the east side, for the space of 17 feet, is entirely levelled. The opening from the inclosure is exactly to the south. This account, and the drawing, were taken in the year 1776, but they have been lately raised, I imagine, by the proprietor of the common, with a view to their being more distinctly seen, perhaps at the place of his residence. September 14, 1787'.[7]

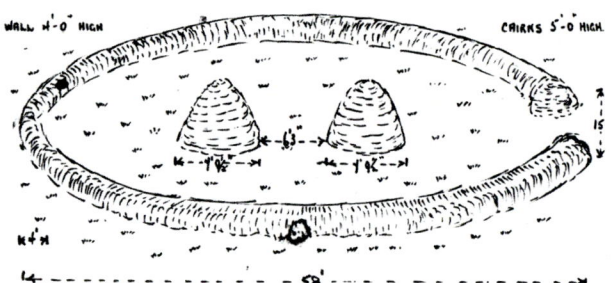

Two Lads drawing from 1776. Courtesy Horwich Heritage.

Using the same Imperial measurements, the diameter of the whole structure today is fifty-eight feet, and each cairn stands five feet tall with the base diameter of each measuring seven feet nine-and-a-half inches. The surrounding wall stands four feet high and four feet wide. The entrance is fifteen feet wide.

After this point in time, the retelling and passing on of information becomes a bit erratic with some anomalies and maybe some merging and mixing of characters and dates.

1787: Two Lads is drawn on the Lancashire map for the first time.[8]

1788 copy of William Yates' map showing Two Lads. Courtesy Lancaster University Library.

c.1800: 'The cairn on the summit has been built from two cairns and a surrounding wall about the year 1800 by a local Lord of the Manor so it could be discerned from his residence', according to historian Robin Smith.[9] After considering all the likely dwellings of someone of import, such as Wilderswood Manor House at Wilderswood, Colemans near Bottom o' th' Moor, and Rivington Hall, Ridgmont House is the only one visible from Two Lads that has a direct line of sight. A newspaper report in 1979 claims it was Joseph Ridgeway who dismantled the cairns and rebuilt one single cairn.[10] The Ridgeway family did indeed live at Ridgmont House from around 1801 but were not lords of the manor. They were notable industrialists though who created employment within their bleaching industry at Wallsuches. They played a pivotal part in the population growth that turned Horwich from a hamlet into a village.

However, the date of Rasbotham's diary entry is 14 September 1787 so the perpetrator may have been Richard Pilkington who sold the building now known as Ridgmont to the Ridgeways. Under Richard's occupation the house was called Whitehouse and he had also been involved in the textile industry.

1819: Bolton surveyor John Albinson drew two cairns without a wall. Each cairn is now standing at nine feet, taller than in 1776.[11] From this survey we can still see the same view today, the hill just to the right of centre is Rivington Pike. Standing with this frame in view we can still see the remains of part of the outer wall.

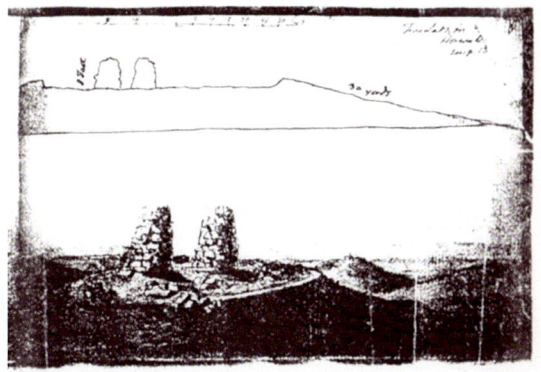 

John Albinson's 1819 survey, from *My Theory of Two Lads* by Robin Smith. Courtesy Horwich Heritage.

Roughly the same view as John Albinson's survey of 1819. The mound of grass to the left of Rivington Pike silhouette marks the perimeter wall. Photograph ©Andy Mallins Photography.

1844: In the *Pictorial History of the County of Lancaster* there is no mention of walls and a suggestion they had already been excavated.[12]

Early 1900s: Lord Leverhulme allegedly excavated and demolished the two cairns to build one larger one so it could be seen from his bungalow in the Terraced Gardens, according to local historian John Smith.[13] Please note this is the same story from 1800, so there may be a mix up of people or dates by the authors retelling the stories.

1970s: Someone had rebuilt the second cairn. I first learned the story about two boys perishing in the snow around 1975-1977 and at that time there were two cairns roughly the same size.

1986: Local historian Robin Smith rebuilt one of the cairns.

Photograph
©Karen Holroyd.

Durham Cathedral by
Arnold William
Brunner (1857-1925).
Public domain.

1988: Due to the damage caused by people climbing, the cairns were severely compromised and a mystery man who wished to remain anonymous, was rebuilding one cairn until he abandoned the task once the local press latched on to what he was doing. This work was continued by Robin Smith, who built it back up to twelve feet tall.[14] Bolton Council ordered the demolition of the cairn claiming it was a danger to children.[15]

1989: Robin Smith rebuilt one cairn much to the annoyance of Bolton Council who threatened legal action. Bolton Council then demolished it for the second time much to the outrage of locals who rebuild it, and the cairns become known as the yo-yo cairns.[16]

Right up until the present day, some visitors to Two Lads still cause damage by climbing on it and locals and walkers will still rebuild it.

The Folklore and Theories

Let us take a closer look at the stories that have been handed down from older generations and the theories that have been mentioned by previous historians.

Burial mounds or memorials for sons of James, Bishop Pilkington
This is a story which has endured, and claims that two sons of Bishop Pilkington were lost on Wilders Moor, perished in a snowstorm, and were buried where they were found, resulting in the two cairns being constructed in memoriam.

James, Bishop Pilkington was born about 1518 at Rivington and died on 23 Jan 1575/76. He was buried at Auckland, County Durham before his remains were reinterred at Durham Cathedral. He was a descendent of

Leonard Pilkington who was the Lord of the Manor of Rivington, and under the approving eye of Queen Elizabeth I, he founded Rivington Grammar School in 1566. With his wife Alice, daughter of Sir John Kingsmill of Sydmonton Court, Hampshire, he fathered four children: Deborah, Ruth, Joshua, and Isaac, with both boys dying young and without a church baptism. This suggests the boys died in infancy or suddenly prior to a church baptism being arranged. All the children were born in Auckland. Therefore, it is impossible for these boys to have perished on Wilders Moor.

But what about the idea that James, Bishop Pilkington had Two Lads built as a memorial? In his will dated 4 February 1571/72, James wished to be buried with 'as few popish ceremonies as may be, or vain cost'.[17] This suggests that James veered away from extravagance, and his homilies also preached against excess. Building a grand memorial for his sons seems a contradiction of his pious values. The only evidence we have that he may have returned to the Rivington area from Durham is for the founding of the grammar school, and Two Lads is in Horwich anyway, beyond the land boundaries of the Pilkington family in the sixteenth century.

In conclusion, this seems to be a tale handed down which has no substantiating evidence. Lieutenant-Colonel John Pilkington has extensively researched the Rivington branch of the family, and there is no mention of Two Lads or any memorial.[18]

Memorial mounds for two boys who perished on the moors on the way to or from work
To have child labour on the moors would likely be in one of the mines, so we can date this theory to between the late eighteenth century and approximately 1842 when the Mines and Collieries Act came into force, forbidding women and girls from working underground, and introducing an age minimum of ten for boys regarding underground working. However, they were allowed to work at the pit head. Not all collieries adhered to this Act though, and it was not always enforced, so it is possible boys were working in the vicinity, if not in the mines, then perhaps at the brick works, or one of the quarries. But would it be possible that two boys of whatever age could get lost and be out there long enough to perish?

Ruin of brick and tile works at Hole Bottom with Two Lads in the background. Photograph ©Karen Holroyd.

During this period there were two collieries on the moors, Wildersmoor Colliery and Holden's Colliery, plus numerous pits, with workers walking from the local areas to start their daily shifts. There would have been many people on the moors leading up to the shift start time, and a mass exit after work. In addition to this, there was a brick works extremely near Two Lads, and people lived on the moors at places such as Five Houses, with Garbutt's being a beerhouse frequented by travellers and locals alike. Mast Road almost as we know it today was part of a main thoroughfare for traversing Winter Hill, so the moors were a busy place and it is improbable that cries for help would not be heard by someone passing by.

Burial mounds for two princes, the sons of a Saxon king or chieftain who was called Edgar

This theory is also staged as boys perishing in a snowstorm and seems to have been embraced by modern historians. But how did the theory surface? The main source of this one comes from 1844 when Cyrus Redding describes his walk and the views from Rivington Pike. Regarding Winter Hill, Redding states:

'Properly enough is it named Winter Hill, on account of its wild appearance and of its attracting so much cold and so many heavy storms; but its ancient designation is Edgar Hill, so called from the circumstances of a petty Saxon king, of the name of Edgar, having hunted upon its sides. A part of the hill, however, we were tempted to mount, by the sight of two prominent objects. The way was longer than we had expected, confirming the common remark of the country, that it is three miles from Horwich to the top of this hill, and only two back. This part is termed Twa-lads-hill and stands on that side of Winter Hill which overlooks Horwich. Tradition reports that the name is derived from the fate of two lads who perished there in a snowstorm, and that the two heaps of stones on its top were erected to commemorate the catastrophe. These erections resemble huge cylinders. A gentleman assured us that he remembered them when they were of solid masonry, and that he knew the inside stones had been taken out and removed'.[19]

Photograph ©Amy Ball.

Thomas Hampson further embellishes this information:

'But a still older tradition, and one that we have elsewhere referred to ("The Two Lads"), exists in the more ancient unwritten history of the village, that here lie the bodies of two children of one of the early Saxon Kings, whose

parents died in battle; and when we remember that it was not uncommon custom for the ancients to bury their chiefs, Kings, and great warriors upon some towering elevation, and to mark the spot by some (to us) rude erection, sometimes a cairn of stones, a rude cross, or other symbol, our enquiry opens up a fair field for investigation, and delightful one for our imagination. This view may be strengthened by the surroundings, which tell of Saxon supremacy, in "Edgar's Den", and the inroads of the Danes in the "Danes' Ditch".[20]

A thorough search of all the maps yields that Winter Hill has never been listed as Edgar Hill or Edgar's Den. On the earliest documented land deeds from the thirteenth century it was called Wyntirheld, and variations of that name. Christopher Saxton's map of 1577 is the first Lancashire one to name land features and begin to show more detail than previous maps.[21] Rivenpike Hill is the first hill to be named on this map for this area.[22] In order to be named there must have been some significance of this hill; maybe it had just been a distinctly notable waymark for travellers through the preceding centuries, if not millennia. Or perhaps it held a specific feature that is lost to time, yet still a ghost on the peak in the form of a lipped circle. Could this ghostly circular imprint visible on Google Earth be the simple remains of the trig point that was erected there in the 1800s as shown on the Ordnance Survey map, or something far more ancient such as a Bronze Age ring cairn, or Roman activity? We may never know.

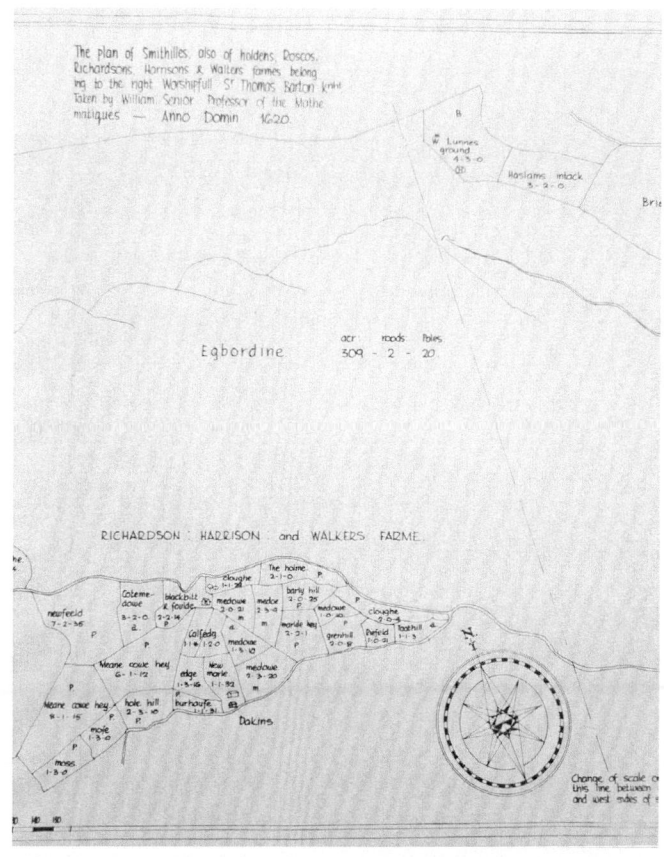

Section of a copy of William Senior's map for Sir Thomas Barton, 1620. John Albinson Collection ZAL/1231. Courtesy Bolton Council.

We find Winter Hill is named Egberden Hill on John Speed's map of 1610, then right through to the eighteenth century, settling back to Winter Hill in 1787.[23] In Old English, Egberden means the wooded valley belonging to Egbert. So which wooded valley does this refer to? Who was Egbert? And could he be the Saxon king we are looking for? William Senior's map drawn in 1620 for Thomas Barton of Smithills Hall shows that Egbordine covers quite a large area of the Smithills Estate moorland, not just Winter Hill.

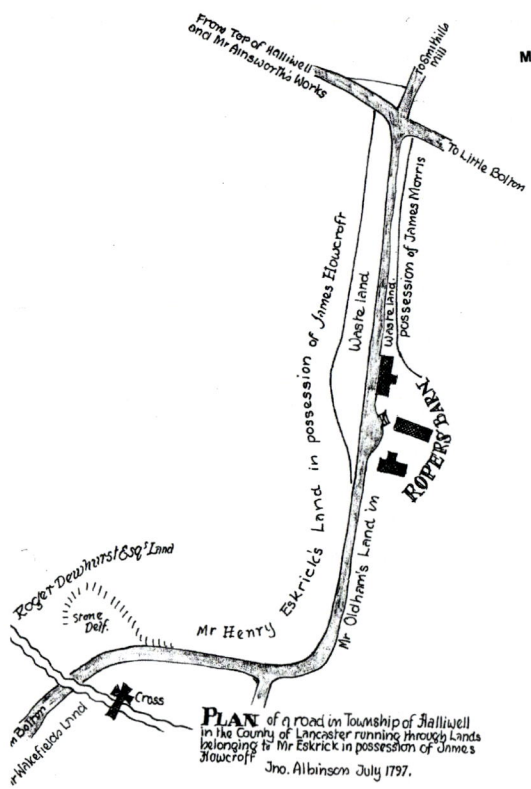

Copy of John Albinson's Map No. 954. Courtesy Halliwell Local History Society.

Halliwell Cross (also known as the Doffcocker Cross), St James the Great at Johnson Fold. Photograph ©Karen Holroyd.

There is not much recorded evidence to indicate any Saxon or Anglo-Saxon activities apart from some place names and stone crosses. One of these crosses had been used as a footbridge across Doffcocker Brook near what is now Vallets Lane. It may have originally been a wayside, boundary or preaching cross, and could have given rise to the naming of nearby Shepherd Cross Street.

It is certainly a huge size to have been moved far, currently standing seven feet two inches (over two metres) tall above ground with more buried. This cross could have been taken down during Henry VIII's dissolution of the monasteries and the period of church reformation, or during the Parliamentarian reign 1649-1660 after the Civil War, when bishops and the prayer book were abolished. Once rediscovered, the cross was taken to the school grounds for safekeeping and then moved again to St Mary's Church on Palace Street, Bolton where it remained until the 1970s. It was then removed to the garden at St James the Great, Johnson Fold. This cross is very plain compared to an elaborately carved eleventh century Anglo-Saxon cross which was discovered when rebuilding St Peters Church, near Bolton town centre.

Who would have constructed this cross in the first place, and how old is it? W D Billington said that it was, 'estimated to be about 1500 years old which would suggest it was erected in the heyday of the great monastic houses'.[24] We know the Knights Hospitallers of St John of Jerusalem were at Smithills, and that a grant of land was given to the Canons of Cockersands in the thirteenth century.[25] There is also the Holy Well from which the name Halliwell is derived, but there is little evidence either in documents or artefacts to say there was any kind of monastery or specific religious worship at Smithills. However, human bones have been unearthed in a cellar which suggests there was a burial vault that could belong to the ancient chapel to which this cross was linked.[26]

There is folklore that a king dwelled in the Smithills area:

'...mere tradition though it possibly may be – that as early as the sixth century Smithills Hall was a royal Saxon palace, occupied by Ella, King of the Deiri, and subsequently by many noble families; that in the year 680 Smithills was walled round to keep the wolves at bay, thus implying that it must then, at all events, have been a considerable residence, in which case we may be quite sure there would be "folds" or "thorps" – collections of dwellings or hamlets – not far off; and again that in the year 793 Eanbald, Archbishop of York, and Ethelbert, Bishop of Hexham, consecrated the Chapel of the Blessed Virgin, at Smithills'.[27]

This chapel would not be the current building at Smithills Hall, but an older structure. The Viking raid at Lindisfarne in 793 was the first attack on a British monastery, perhaps this event spurred the church elders to consecrate new chapels further inland.

Bolton, being close to the border of Mercia and Northumbria (combining Deira and Bernicia kingdoms) has spent time in both kingdoms. Looking at the kings we find Aelle (Ella) of Deira was peace-loving, living in harmony with his neighbours of Bernicia and Mercia. His daughter, Acha, married Aethelfrith, king of Bernicia who turned on Aelle and ousted him from his kingdom. Aelle sought refuge at several places and local historian Marie Mitchell believed Smithills was one of these refuges.[28] Aelle had died by 604.

Another King Aella of Northumbria fought the Viking raiders and, whilst his home was York where he died in 867, he could have had an ealdorman or thane overseeing this land close to the border of his Mercian enemies.

Maybe this king's name is wrong, and we should be looking for an Egbert. There were a few kings called Egbert and most of them can be ruled out due to location and fractious

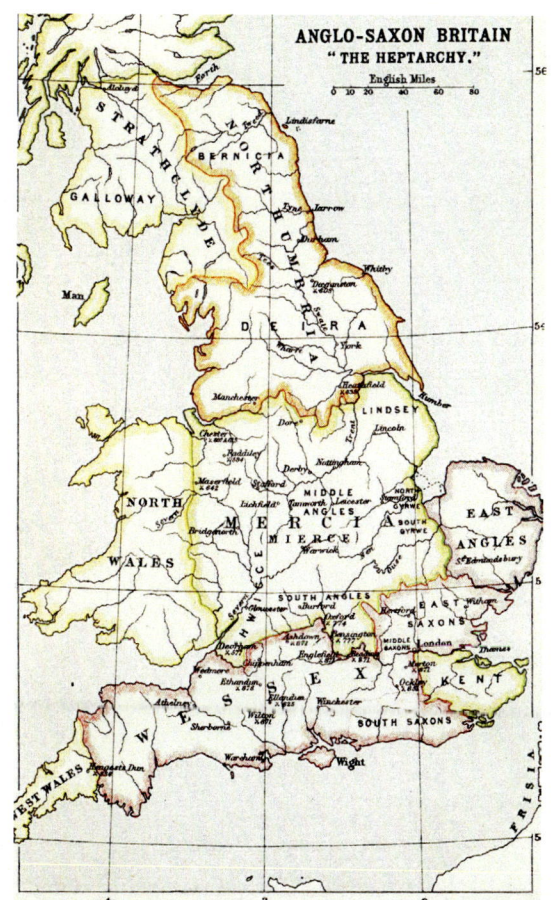

'The Heptarchy'. From J G Bartholomew's *A literary & historical atlas of Europe* (1914).

neighbours, such as Egbert of Kent who was pinned in his corner of England by the mighty King Offa of Mercia. We are left with Ecgbert I of Northumbria, a puppet king governed by the Danes after they won the battle of the Great Heathen Army at York in 866. Ecgbert II of Northumbria was also governed by the Danes. However it seems unlikely that they would name an area after a king they did not allow to rule by his own volition.

Ecgbert, King of Wessex, ruled 802-839, and was grandfather to Alfred the Great. Although Ecgbert defeated Beornwulf of Mercia at the Battle of Ellandun, there is no evidence that he ever set foot further north than Mercia. The Northumbrian kings submitted rather than fought. Egberden Hill could be named after this king who tried to unify England whilst fighting Cornwall, Devon, and Vikings too. And if it is named after a king at all, then I feel it would be this one who was acknowledged as Bretwalda: King of all England.

But perhaps Egbert was not a king at all, but someone else considered to have significant importance, perhaps someone from the Christian church. Christianity had been brought to Britain by travellers in the first century spreading tales about Jesus and God. The Romans at that time worshipped numerous gods and persecuted Christians due to their belief in one single god and their intolerance of other religions. Around 313, Emperor Constantine encouraged religious toleration and Christianity became accepted in Rome. By the late sixth century Pope Gregory sent Augustine to Britain to spread the Christian word. Many Anglo-Saxon and Saxon kings of Britain were baptised.

Ecgberht, son of Eata, was born into the Northumbrian royal family and was appointed the Bishop of York in 732 by his cousin Ceolwulf, king of Northumbria. The Venerable Bede urged him to deal with the corruption and disorder that ran through the northern diocese, to ordain more priests and to translate works into the Saxon tongue.[29] Ecgberht went on to obtain the pallium (a liturgical vestment) from Pope Gregory III at Rome and became the second Archbishop of York in 735. This gave him authority over the northern bishops, and once his brother Eadberht became King of Northumbria from 737 his power increased.

At that time, the See of York consisted of almost the whole of northern England and together the brothers formed a formidable force combining rulership and religion despite conniving families and warring neighbours. Archbishop Ecgberht reformed the parochial system and clergy, and founded and taught at the school of York, establishing a library there. He is seen as one of the most successful prelates, 'regarded as one of the great architects of the English church in the eighth century'.[30] Archbishop Ecgberht died in 766 and was buried in York Cathedral.

Surely this man is worthy to have Egberden Hill and Egbordine named after him.[31] The consecration of the chapel at Smithills in 793 was probably part of his new parochial system, the cross was linked to this chapel and the land probably belonged to the bishopric and remained holy land for centuries afterwards.

Returning to the original theory of two princes of a Saxon king called Edgar, we have ended up with an archbishop called Egbert who would certainly not have buried sons in unconsecrated ground under cairns. It seems a slip of the tongue by Cyrus Redding in 1844 when he said Edgar instead of Egbert, a slip that has sent contemporary writers looking for a person who never existed.

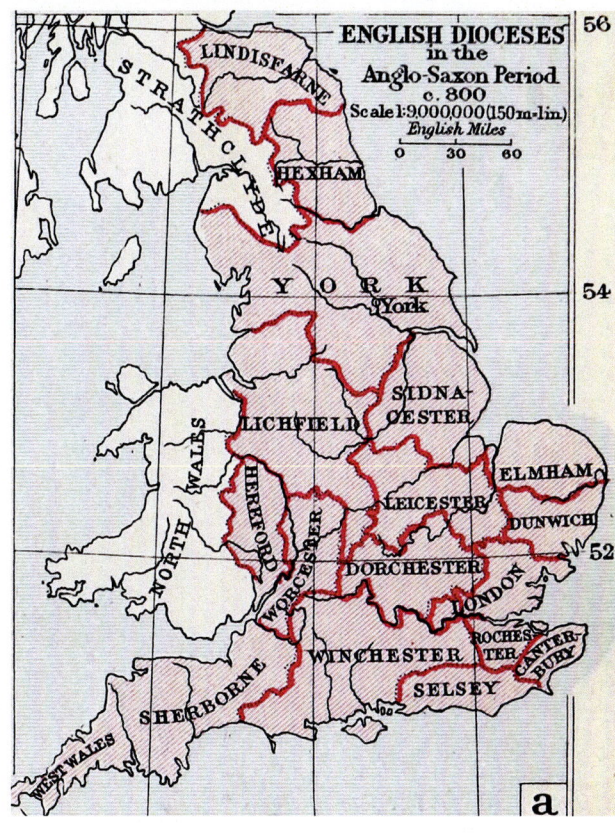

'English Dioceses during the Anglo-Saxon Period'. From Phillips' *New Historical Atlas*, CC BY-SA 4.0.

Photograph ©Amy Ball.

Bronze Age burial mounds

Looking around the area there is a wealth of pre-historic mounds, and many artefacts have been found. Could clues to the origins of Two Lads be found amongst them? Near the peak of Winter Hill was a composite round cairn Scheduled Monument, Listing 1008906. This cairn was sadly destroyed during the creation of the fire breaks when fighting the moorland fires of 2018, however walkers have recreated a cairn on this spot. It was initially investigated in 1957 by Chorley Historical and Archaeological Society and passed on to Dr John Bu'Lock of Manchester University in 1958. It was found to have previously been excavated at a date unknown and pollen analysis dates this cairn to the Bronze Age between 1600-1400 BCE.

Noon Hill also has a round cairn which was excavated by John Winstanley and Bolton and District Archaeological Society in 1958. In his trench book, John lists finding flint core, flint flakes and chippings, chert, a blade, thumb scraper, charcoal, a barbed tanged arrowhead, a notched flint, a knife, two sandstone balls with flattened ends, and another arrowhead, in quadrant A and C.[32] Further digging revealed post holes, thick layers of charcoal and at least four burials, including an adult male, adult female, a child and a cremation urn which is now in Bolton Museum. This is also a Scheduled Monument, Listing 1008905, and believed to be Bronze Age.

Both Winter Hill cairn and Noon Hill cairn are located close to the edge of a steep hill with breathtaking views. Anyone who has stood at Two Lads will note a similarity of the location for these sites. Horwich Moor barrow also shares the protection of being a Scheduled Monument, Listing 1008907. This barrow has not been excavated but is considered a funerary monument dating from the Bronze Age between 2000-700 BCE.

The Pike Stones at Anglezarke is the remains of a chambered long cairn. It stands alone as possibly being the oldest manmade structure in Lancashire dated around 3400-2400 BCE and built during the Neolithic Period when people started to settle in permanent dwellings and farming was just beginning. Quite rightly it is a Scheduled Monument, Listing 1009120.

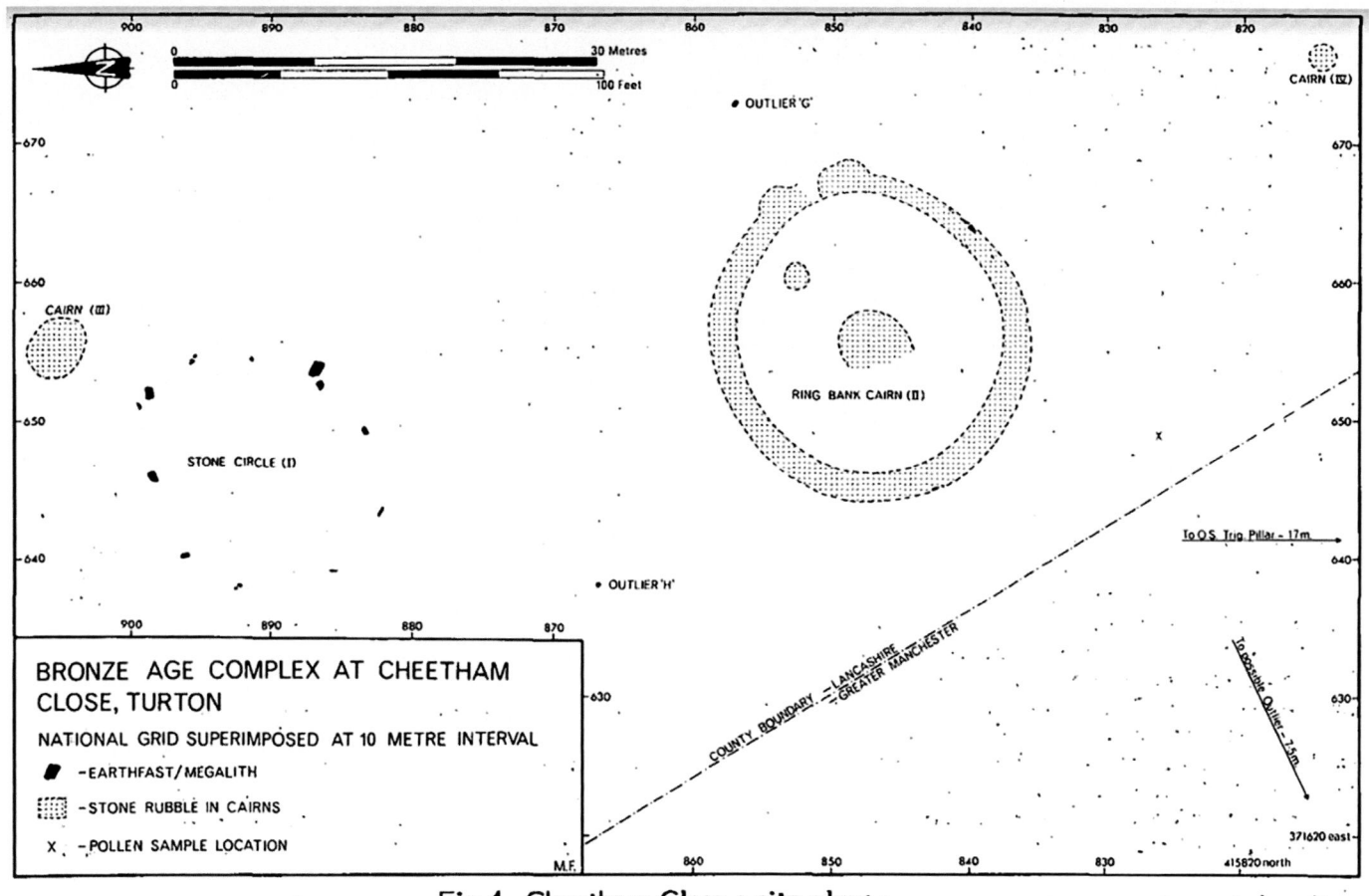

Fig 4 Cheetham Close : site plan

Site plan of Cheetham Close, from *The Bronze Age Complex on Cheetham Close: A New Survey* by M Fletcher.

Cheetham's Close at Turton has also been investigated, surveyed, and designated a Scheduled Monument, Listing 1009121. On this site is the remains of a stone circle, ringed cairn, and satellite cairns. It is believed this site was used by druids for religious purposes, and possibly a graveyard. When we look at the drawings of the survey, we can see a remarkable likeness to the Two Lads drawing of 1776 which is far too similar to ignore.[33] There is a four feet (over one metre) wide perimeter wall with an opening almost resembling gateposts, and inside is two cairns. This entire site has been dated to the Early Bronze Age between 2100-1500 BCE. Cheetham's Close is less than four miles away from Two Lads; perhaps this was the local style, and Two Lads' builders were a group who separated from the Cheetham's Close builders to form their own family group or tribe.

Does Two Lads belong in this elite club of monuments left behind by our ancient ancestors? It certainly ticks some of the boxes that should put it in this category but being so mutilated it has lost its historic value. Are there any clues from the surrounding land that may help us determine the purpose of the site?

Aerial view of Two Lads site alongside a graphic design showing how Two Lads would have looked in 1776. Photograph ©Peter Ravald Photography and Drone Photography. CAD Image ©Luke Gosling at Lug Design.

We can rule out the perimeter wall being part of a dwelling because the entrance is too close to the steep side and would present dangerous ground for toddlers running around. Houses may have had stone walls like they did at Grimspound on Dartmoor, but it was more common to have a wooden frame with wattle and daub style walls and a thatched or turfed roof. The post holes found in Winter Hill cairn would have held wooden posts for this type of structure.

A walk around the sides of Crooked Edge Hill studying rocks of the same form lying together the weathering and erosion proves to be inconsistent. These rocks may be glacial debris, but they have not lain undisturbed for 11,500 years. They have been moved and I can only think they have been cleared from the summit to make way for some structure being built.

Photograph ©Karen Holroyd.

John Winstanley was an amateur archaeologist who founded both Bolton and District Archaeological Society, and Chorley Historical and Archaeological Society. He found many artifacts on the moors, from neolithic microliths, arrowheads, and awls to Roman glass, pottery, and ochre, and has reported these finds to the Historic Environment Register. His diary from 1953-54 has been transcribed and is so descriptive that I have been able to retrace his footsteps to many of the sites he mentions.[34] Sadly, I have not discovered any prehistoric treasures, although John seemed to be quite prolific in his finds and other people have found spearheads, arrowheads, scrapers, axe and awls in the vicinity of Wilders Moor.

If we took a journey back in time to the Carboniferous Period 360-300 million years ago, we would see the moorland at the bottom of a shallow sea, the environment where coal is formed. Over time the constant shifting of tectonic plates, volcanic eruptions and multiple ice ages have shaped the world to what we recognise today. This land from the bottom of the sea is now Winter Hill and the moorland now pitted with bell pits and shafts, remnants from mining coal and clay. The glaciers towards the end of the last ice age around 11,500 years ago stripped land of vegetation, helped to shape hills and create valleys, and as they melted left a geographic smorgasbord of rocks collected and carried on the journey south. Across the moors is an assortment of glacial debris, and just below the peak of Winter Hill and Counting Hill huge slabs have been deposited. As the earth warmed, meltwater from the hills carved out the narrow and steep cloughs such as Tigers Clough and Roscow's Tenement Clough.

People of the Neolithic period then came to the hills, first living a nomadic hunter-gatherer lifestyle travelling around to the best seasonal hunting grounds. These people learned about animal husbandry and growing crops which meant they could have more permanent or seasonal dwellings. The building of barrows like Pikestones at Anglezarke showed care for the dead and these barrows would be local to the builders who still used tools of stone, bones, and wood. The hills were laden with trees and wild animals roamed.

The regional landscape as it could have looked during the Bronze Age. Illustration by Sharron Clayman.

The Bronze Age people arrived with a new toolkit and armoury made of bronze and alloys. These are the people who built the round cairns at Winter Hill and Noon Hill mentioned earlier. They left behind traces of their existence on these moors in the form of arrowheads, knives, flints, scrapers, and more. It is most likely that there was a settlement of some kind on the moors. Using their newly designed metal tools they could more easily cut down trees for building and fuel. As the upland trees disappeared peat formed and continues to form in the now seemingly barren wilderness.

Bronze Age arrowhead and spear tip found by John MacDonald in 1990. From the collection of Tom Leech.

As settled people increased from family groups to tribes, land ownership became important and squabbles or wars with neighbours could occur. People needed to mark their territory and often used existing landmarks as boundaries, such as streams, the ridge of a hill or a cluster of boulders left by glaciers. They also needed to keep their animals confined to an area for safekeeping from predators or thieving neighbours.

Earthworks

There is an earthwork ditch called Dean Ditch which runs along the top of Counting Hill and Winter Hill. It is named Danes Dyke on an archaeological survey map of 1896.[35]

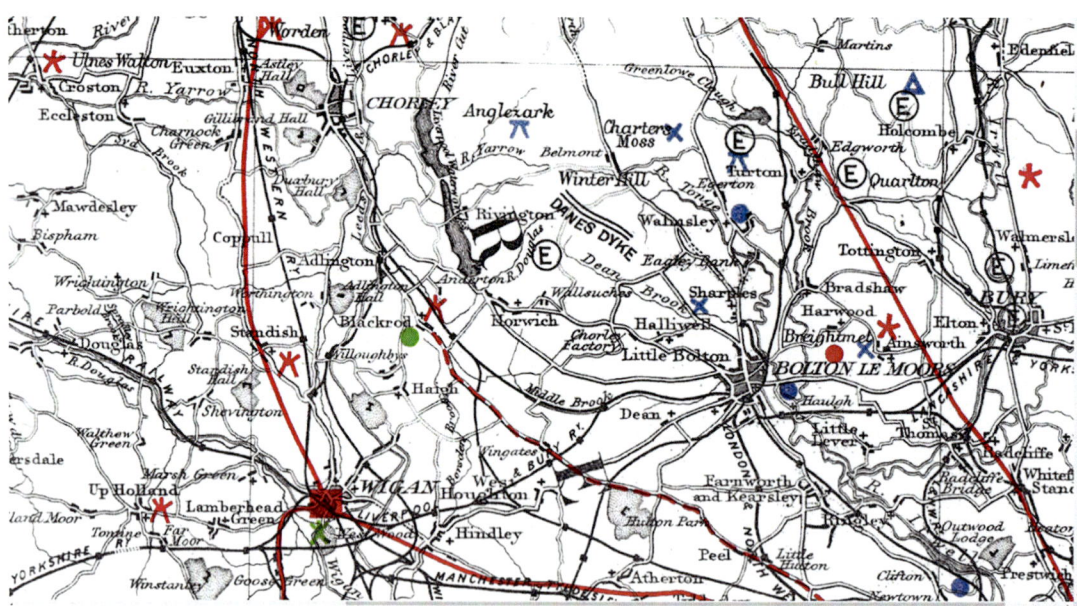

Danes Dyke on William Harrison's map of archaeological finds, 1896. From the collection of Karen Holroyd.

Surrounding Two Lads there is also a ditch and ridge earthwork which runs for over one and a half miles. Chris Atkinson, Heritage Consultant at South Pennines Park helped examine this earthwork. We concluded that it was not created by water flow, although water flows in it now. The ditch runs along the contour of the hill, not downhill which would be nature's course of action. It is not part of nineteenth century drainage to take water away from the mine shafts further up Winter Hill, because part of this ditch is completely cut through negating that suggestion. A stretch of the ditch has clearly been modified with a concrete pipe being laid across the path from Two Lads leading down to George's Lane. The ridge was eroded at this point and the pipe channelled the water along the ditch rather than flowing down the path created by walkers.

32

One end of this earthwork peters out and disappears going up towards the mast, running almost parallel with Crooked Edge Brook. The area between Two Lads and the mast had a great deal of mining activity and the land changed considerably during the eighteenth and nineteenth centuries. The earthwork probably continued up to the ridge and I hypothesise that it may have joined up with Dean Ditch at the top of Winter Hill. Just below Two Lads on the Horwich side, the ditch is a double ditch in the same style as Dean Ditch without the boundary wall. The earthwork continues to Mast Road and beyond into a natural gulley heading off towards Burnt Edge. I will note here that if this earthwork did link up with Dean Ditch it would encompass the whole area known as Egberden Hill and Egbordine. Looking at a dissection of the ridge we can see the different layers from when it was built. This earthwork had importance and people maintained it, but for what purpose?

Dissection of the ridge showing layers of maintenance. Photograph ©Karen Holroyd.

We need to consider that weathering and time will have reduced the size of this ridge. Robin Smith believed it was a defensive ditch meaning raiders would have to attack uphill, surmount the ridge, climb out of the ditch, and continue uphill to reach the defenders.[36]

John Smith, a local historian who was awarded the Horwich Civic Medal in 2001 for his voluntary services to the preservation of the history and heritage of the town, states:

'there are 1 mile and 1500 yards of earthworks enclosing an oval shaped area divided into three sections by two cross trenches with the cairn near the southern end. In some places the earthworks have been altered and adapted for water conservancy purposes but sufficient can be seen to lead one to believe that they were originally constructed to form a system of trench and breastwork defences. At the southern corner is a length of double trenching about eight feet apart which looks very much like an entrance. In the western side of the enclosed area the construction of the trench and breastwork is very interesting, the outside of the trench, that is the side which overlooks Horwich is much higher than the inner side, obviously the excavated material was all thrown up on this side also this side of the trench is almost vertical whilst the slope on the other side is very gradual. This is the type of trench which was dug around an area of land to enclose cattle, as the cattle straying into the trench would find the outer side impossible to climb and the easier slope on the inside would persuade them to return to the enclosed area'.[37]

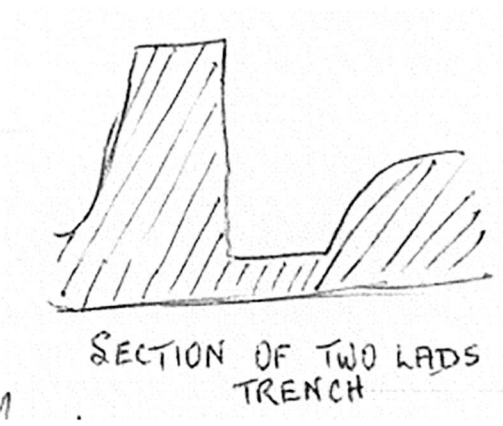

Drawing of the ditch and ridge from *Two Lads* by John Smith. Courtesy Horwich Heritage.

This earthwork forms the boundary to the modern Smithills Estate and probably has done for centuries. However, it is not a land boundary ditch from old times because the natural land boundary would be Crooked Edge Brook, not a feature at the top of a steep hill which would have taken months to dig. This earthwork serves a different purpose, and this depends on which side is the highest. For animal compounds the inside where the animals need to be slopes down into the ditch with the higher ridge on the outside making it impossible for the animal to get out. For defensive earthworks, the higher ridge would be on the inside nearest the defenders, so the enemies would have to go down into the ditch and then climb the higher side. A well-known example of a defensive earthwork is Offa's Dyke with the highest side in Mercia and the ditch side in Powys, designed to keep the Welsh out. With this principle in mind, it looks like this earthwork is for animal husbandry. There was probably at some point trees or hedgerows on top of the ridge. These type of earth enclosures were used from the Bronze Age all the way through to Medieval times which does not help narrow down a period. But it does tell us people were there keeping livestock and may have lived within the enclosure.

Manmade ditch and ridge curving round the contour line. Crooked Edge Brook and boundary wall run diagonally from George's Lane in the top left-hand corner. The second image shows a continuation of the ditch and ridge crossing the path. George's Lane is in the top left-hand corner. Photographs ©Andy Mallins Photography.

The Romans

I had not seen much written about the Romans utilising Two Lads or the area until reading the transcript of John Winstanley's diary from 1953-54:

> *'March 1953. In my opinion the near vicinity of the so called "two lads" is nothing more than the site of a Roman encampment. I have found proof so far in my statement by finding glass and pottery of Roman origin on the 7th and 14th March 1953, also flint tools dating back to the second glacial period of 3000 years ago. 15th March found good examples of Roman glass and uncovered the top slab of a Roman Tomb'.*[38]

John mentions that his friend Leslie Prosser, a local schoolteacher, had found a wooden pear-shaped object like a plumb bob hidden inside a Roman wall. Leslie had also found a blue ribbed bead and flint in the vicinity of Two Lads. John also relates finding two stone slabs, one a distance away from Two Lads mound, and the other on the mound. This latter slab may just be the foundation base of the trig point but is certainly of interest and not to be dismissed lightly.

John Winstanley's alleged Roman wall and the 1900s' culvert underneath George's Lane. Photograph ©Karen Holroyd.

Since studying the diary and meeting with Ian Trumble from Bolton Museum on the moors, we were able to dismiss some of John's conclusions regarding the Romans. The alleged Roman wall is a continuation of the boundary at Crooked Edge Clough. Whilst the section closest to George's Lane is different in style and structure to the rest of the boundary, it is like other dry stone walls in the area. It adjoins the culvert under the road from when Lord Leverhulme redirected the road near the junction with the path to Two Lads and is undoubtedly more modern than some of the other walls. There is a pottery fragment in Bolton Museum which was thought to be Roman and found on Winter Hill, but on close inspection it has Winberry Hill written on it. Also, the Roman glass and ochre that John found cannot be located to re-examine. Without these we are left with no physical evidence of Roman visitation to Two Lads, except perhaps the blue ribbed bead found by Leslie Prosser which was considered to be genuinely Roman.

The only other artefacts that have been recorded in the Bolton area are Roman urns uncovered in 1756 at Crompton Fold and in 1774 at Breightmet Hill near Cockey Moor.[39] It was once believed there was Roman activity at Blackrod. This theory comes from John Whitaker who was writing in the 1770s and further ingrained into local knowledge by Thomas Hampson saying there was a Roman fort at Blackrod. Wigan Archaeological Society have dismissed this because no Roman finds have been recorded and no evidence of any buildings, walls or roads have been found in Blackrod. When new estates are built such as Romans Green, it perpetuates this myth.

However, we know that the Romans were in the area at Wigan.[40] The remains of Roman buildings have been found at Millgate and the Wiend, two Roman roads leading to Ribchester and Manchester, coin hoards found at Standish, Market Place and Wigan Lane and an aureus (high value coin) found near The Mesnes. These Romans or Romano-British people would have lived, worked, and travelled in the surrounding area.

There are claims that Lord Leverhulme excavated a place called Will Narr, near the Rivington and Anglezarke boundary, and found Roman pottery which he donated to Liverpool Museum. Sadly, this museum was damaged during the bombing raids of World War II. Also, the very steep road leading from Sheephouse Lane, Rivington, past the car park and up to the Pigeon Tower, is alleged to have been built by the Romans. This is difficult to prove, but if it were such a road, where did it lead from and to? Geographically the likely place is either Rivington Pike or across the moors to Two Lads and maybe down to Halliwell.

The Brigante were the original Britons of the region who were pushed west by invaders, and historians put the Setantii tribe in the area from the Pennines to the Irish Sea. On the map of 1610 there is an area named Brigantes Hundred. Thomas Hampson goes as far as to say that Blackrod was the capital of the Setantii people, although I have been unable to find any further reference for this.[41]

The Romans were excellent military strategists; keeping an eye on the natives they had subdued with intentions of curbing any uprisings that may occur would be an ongoing task. Watchtowers were essential and there would be no better place than Two Lads and Rivington Pike. They were in general suitably placed so messages could be signalled from one to the next along a line. From both sites there is a clear view across most of the Brigante territory as much of the land is flat lowland all the way to the Cheshire and north Wales west coast, Cumberland, and Westmorland. Specifically, Manchester and Wigan are both easily visible from Two Lads. There was also an ancient tower at Blackrod:

> *'Close by the well delineated road is a knoll known as the highest spot in Blackrod, and there, within the memory of our informant, stood an old ancient tower or beacon, known in the district as "Chisnall's Summer House". From this spot, looking to the south-east, the city of Manchester is plainly discernible; while Liverpool, Preston, and the wide expanse of land bounded by the Ribble and Mersey are as an open book'.*[42]

View over Brigantes territory. Photograph ©Andy Mallins Photography.

John Smith notes, 'At the northern end of the summit of Two Lads there is a flattened circular place where the topsoil is very fine like a black dust as if at one period fires were burned here, perhaps a beacon site'.[43] This is difficult to check as there do not seem to be any signs of this now.

Could the perimeter wall drawn in 1766 be the remains of a Roman watchtower and the cairns added later? Robin Smith dug down to foundations and this suggests a solid structure. Barrows and cairns do not have foundations, although they sometimes have some infill of stones. These stones could have been compressed into the earth during all the episodes of vandalism and demolition and now seem like foundations. The traditional style of watchtowers was square with steps up the outside which would not fit the structure footprint at Two Lads. Could there have been circular watchtowers on Rivington Pike, Two Lads and across the valley at Blackrod? Whilst there is no hard evidence, this theory is worthy of further research because the Romans were far too tactical not to take advantage of this high ground.

Photograph ©Peter Ravald Photography and Drone Photography.

What does Two Lads mean today?

Whilst Two Lads can look forlorn and forgotten in the drizzly mist that often descends, it is by no mean unloved by locals and visitors. It is a steep climb to get there with a real sense of achievement on reaching the top, looking at the amazing views as you pause for breath. Amongst the stones, names of loved ones, scattered ashes, a birthday, and a proposal. A quiet place for memories and peaceful reflection. Far less crowded than Rivington Pike or Rivington Barn area, there is a sense of freedom for mountain bikers, runners, and hikers. Old and young stop by to take a rest, mission complete before turning back down the hill.

Journalist John Rawlinson writing in 1969:
'It is interesting to consider what a great deal of human activity has taken place on these uplands, generally thought to be desolate and deserted, burial mounds and flint chipping sites disclose the facts of prehistoric man's life here. Two Lads, nearby on Horwich Moor, has at separate times been a burial place, a hilltop camp, and a cattle compound, coal, iron, and fireclay deposits have been worked here and at one period the road across these moors was the quickest way from Wigan to Blackburn'.[44]

I doubt there will ever be any definitive answers regarding the origins of Two Lads, but hopefully in the future more evidence of the past will be found. Until then we can still treasure this special place which is neither a wreckage nor a heap of stones. When you are visiting, spare a moment for those whose ashes are scattered regardless of when they passed on, regardless as to whether it was three thousand years ago or yesterday.

Photograph
©Peter Ravald
Photography and
Drone Photography.

Poachers on Burnt Edge, 1630 and 1864

*Chapter 2
by Tony Greenwood*

Burnt Edge Photograph ©Tony Greenwood.

On 15 June 1630, Sir Thomas Barton, then owner of Smithills Estate, and John Bradshaw Esquire, 'his majesties justices of the peace within the county of Lancaster', examined poachers who had been caught on Burnt Edge.[1] According to the report of the trial in the archives, a group of four poachers: William Norris of Lostocke, husbandman; James Yate of Heaton, husbandman; John Seddon; and Adam Hulton Esquire of Parke, were caught poaching by two local farmers, Ellys Brooke and William Holden (the latter possibly of Holdens Farm which had permission from Barton to use Burnt Edge as pasture). They were on a 'certayne wast or Moore ground called the burnt Edge, and one other moore called the Wilders Ladds' (an old name for Two Lads).

An argument started with the farmers throwing stones at James Yate. 'What are you doing on our Master's Land and what have you in the bag', they asked. Yate opened his bag and pulled out nets. He said he was with Adam Hulton who had a setting dog (an English setter). The dog had made a sett (spotted a bird), so they spread the net and ran over the moor to catch more birds.
Norris said they took two moor game birds, 'a cocke and a henne'. They let the hen bird go but took the cock away with them.

William Norris had a fowling piece, a five-foot hunting gun, that he borrowed from Yate. Strangely, the witnesses do not mention the gun, but it was raised by Yate as an indication of his social status. Common people would not have been able to afford such an expensive item.

Yate also claimed that John Seddon and William Norris had also 'made a Sett with a Settinge Dogge and netts' on Mr Anderton's land (the land to the west of Burnt Edge). Another witness explained that James Yate was

Photograph ©Tony Greenwood.

'Chienne Blanche', Alexandre François Desportes. Courtesy Musée de la Chasse et de la Nature, CC PD 1.0.[4]

'Stalking Wildfowl in 17th Century' from *The Gentlemens Recreation*, Richard Bloom, 1686. From the collection of Tony Greenwood.

known as a poacher. John Meake, an innkeeper of Bolton, said Yate had previously come into his inn with some fowl in his linen bag. Meake saw the feet of the fowl hanging out of the bag and asked him what it was, to be told it was a black cock.

James Yate was asked if he had ever shot at 'Black Cock, Red Game, Partridge, Phesant, Pigeon, House Dove, Hare and other game'. He 'utterly denyth it!'[2] This list of game is a catch-all (if that is not an inappropriate phrase in the circumstances!) of game not to be taken, hence Yate's denial. But it is interesting to record that black and red grouse were on Burnt Edge in the seventeenth century and regarded as protected game at the time.

Poaching on Burnt Edge 1630: QSB 1/75/60, 'HORWICH - pursuit of game by setting-dogs on Horwich Moor'. Courtesy Lancashire Archives. Thanks also to local historian Alan Crosby who found this story in the Quarter Sessions records. Alan also wrote the report 'The Landscape and Industrial History of Smithills Estate'.

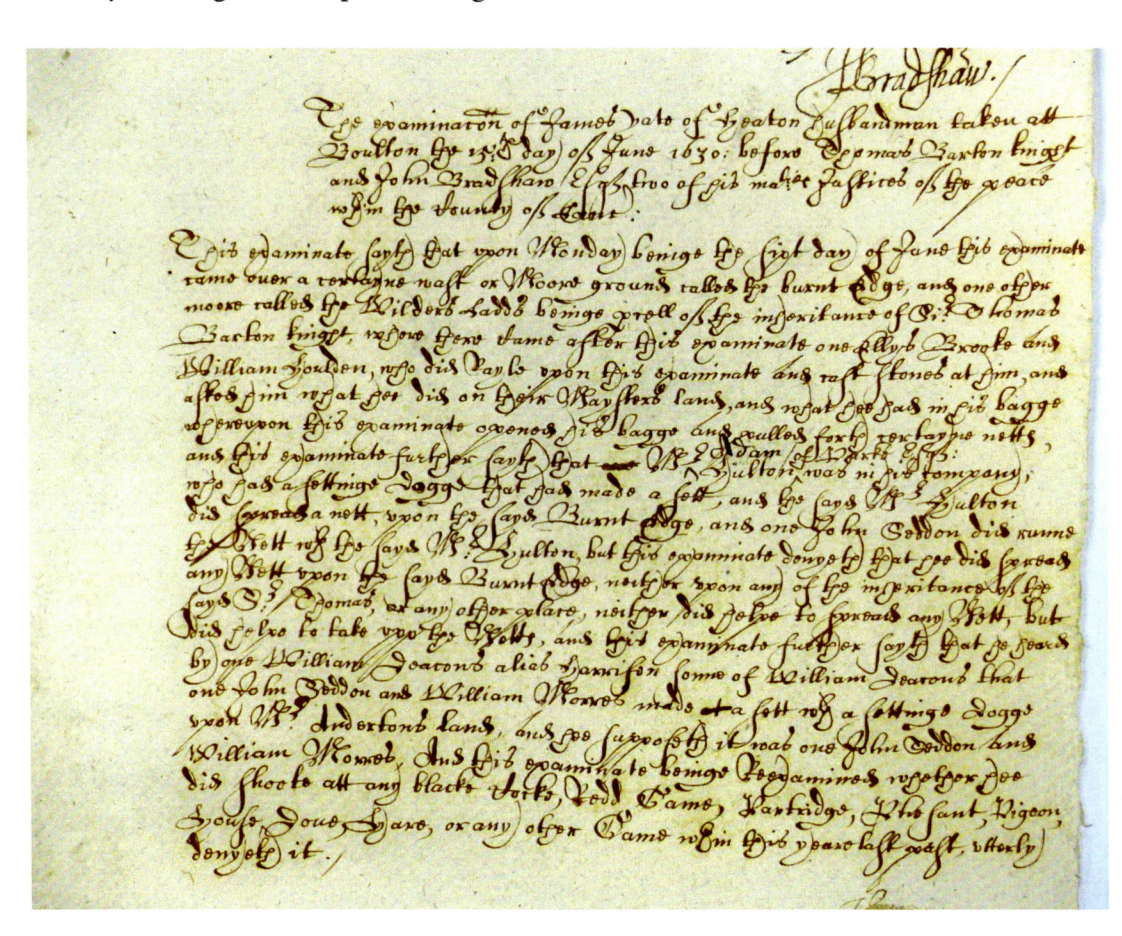

The archives do not show the verdict of this trial and it is unlikely the men were punished. Adam Hulton was a Gentleman and his fellow gentlemen on the magistrates' bench would be unlikely to take the case any further. The evidence that one of the poachers had a gun implies they were men of substance, and so were not to be treated as common criminals - class solidarity and all that! Whilst researching this, I came across another story of poaching in the same area, this time in 1864. A William Entwistle was charged with being in illegal pursuit of game in the township of Horwich.[3] Around four in the afternoon on the 15 August, he was out with a gun on the moors next to Edge Lane, the road between Ainsworth and Longworth land. Unfortunately for Entwistle he was spotted by his friend Thomas Fairhurst, a farmer at Deakins Fold, who saw him shoot and kill a hare in a field at Newfield Farm.

Fairhurst, who was in the next field on his own farm, ran up to his friend and asked what he had got under his jacket. Entwistle claimed it was 'only a tit-lark'. Fairhurst was not convinced, and he told his friend, 'It has long legs for a tit-lark; I'd keep those legs out of sight'. Somehow, this was reported to Henry Peachey, the Smithills Estate gamekeeper, who took Entwistle to court.

As Thomas Fairhurst knew Entwistle well he was accused by the defence of 'trotting' his friend. That did not help though, the magistrates convicted William Entwistle with a penalty of 20s. and costs, or one month in prison if he did not pay.

'...only a tit-lark': A sky lark hiding in the heather on Winter Hill. Photograph ©Tony Greenwood.

Map of the area, showing Burnt Edge, Newfield Farm, Deakins Farm and Twitchells Farm. Ordnance Survey six-inch map, surveyed 1892. Courtesy National Library of Scotland.

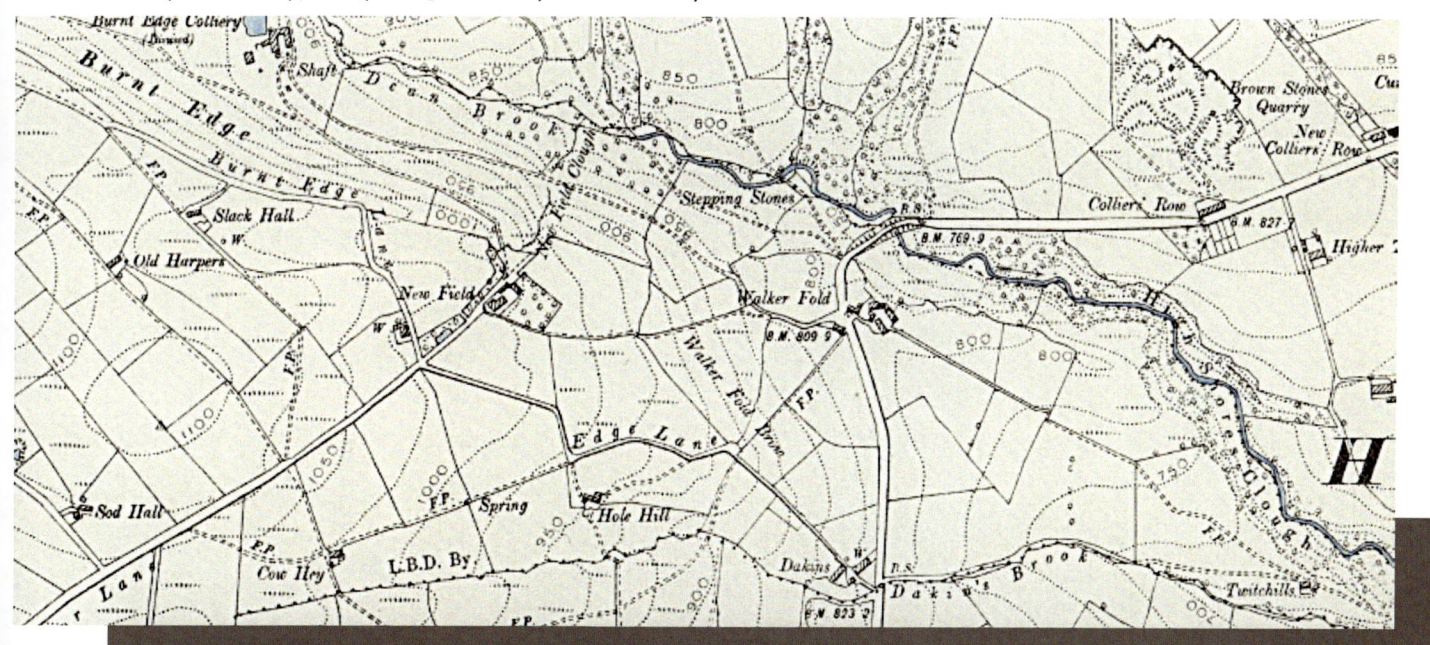

Thomas Fairhurst was part of a large family from Deakins, and three of his brothers lived at Twitchells Cottage at that time. William Entwistle was from a Winter Hill family and was born at Hole Bottom Cottage. He was a collier, probably working at Burnt Edge Colliery, and the son of Mary Entwistle, a witness at George Henderson's murder trial in 1838.

Chadwicks Close Farm

*Chapter 3
by Stephen Tonge*

Ordnance Survey six-inch map, surveyed 1845-47.
Courtesy National Library of Scotland.

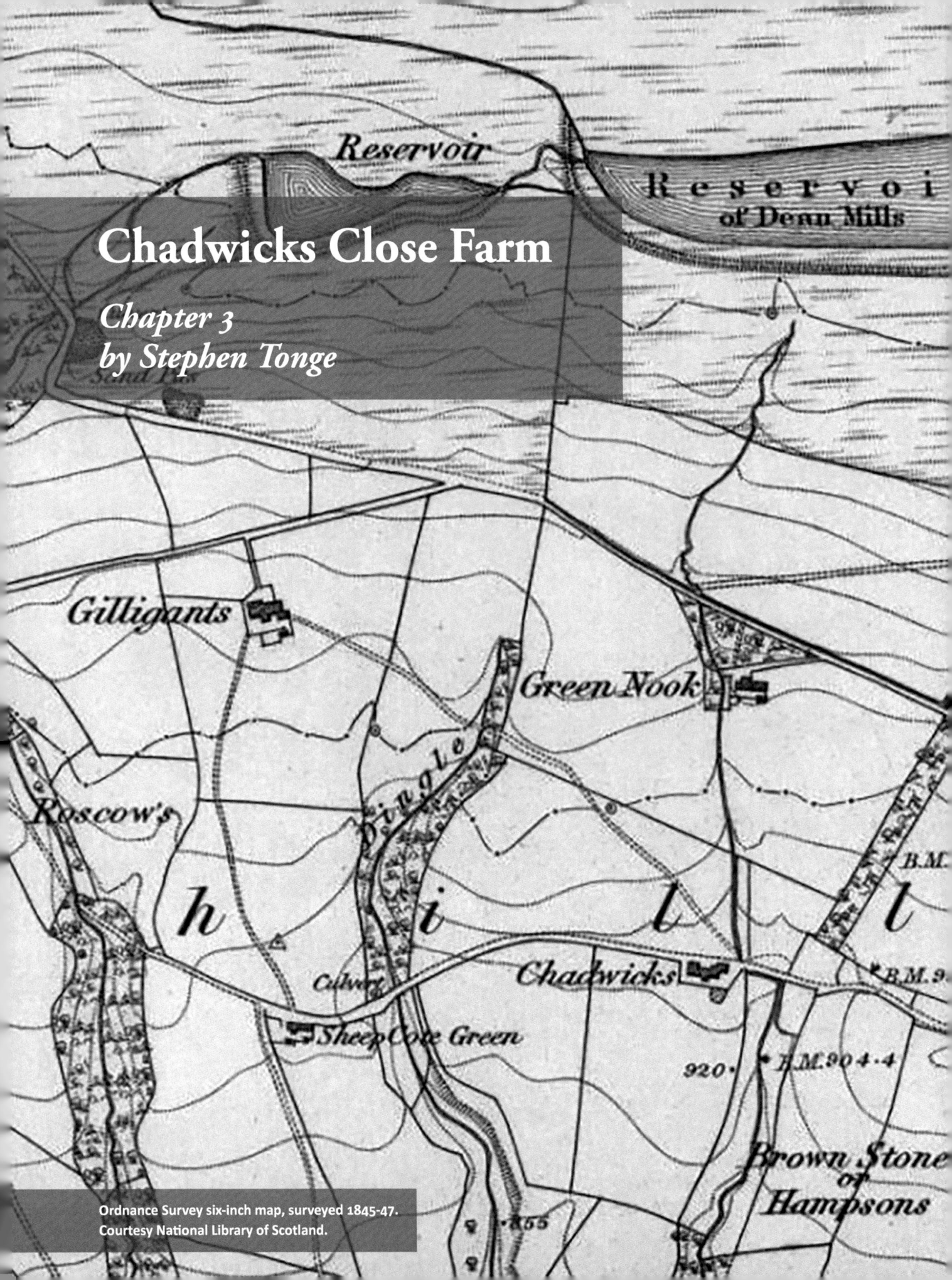

The Shuttleworth family at Chadwicks Close Farm, c.1900. From the collection of Stephen Tonge.

Chadwicks Close was one of the smaller of the twenty or so farms on Smithills Estate. It is situated off Coal Pit Road, on the south facing slopes of Smithills Dean. The farm did not exist in 1620 when William Senior drew up his plan of the estate, the land at that time being part of the 307 acres of unenclosed moorland called Egbordine.[1] The farm's name probably originated from an eighteenth-century occupier called Samuel Chadwick, or Chaddock. He was recorded as a tenant on the estate when it was sold in 1722/23 to Edward Byrom Esquire of Manchester. Little information has survived about Samuel, two possible glimpses being the baptism of a son named John at Deane in 1715, and a gravestone also at Deane, engraved with the words: 'ANN ye wife of SAMUEL CHADDOCK of Halliwell was here interred ye 17 day of Aug 1716'. In addition to Chadwicks Close, he probably also leased the farm now known as Cunliffe's on Colliers Row Road, which on the 1769 Estate map was named Chadwicks.[2]

Photograph ©Stephen Tonge.

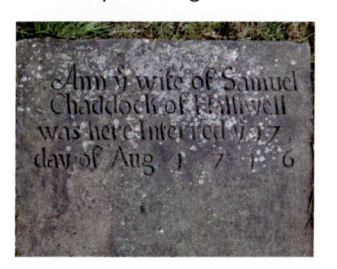

The Cunliffes

By the 1760s, the Cunliffe family held the leases on both farms. Stephen Cunliffe had Chadwicks (later renamed Cunliffe's), leasing the tenement from Edward Byrom on a term of lives, which included those of William Cunliffe and John Cunliffe, probably his sons. Stephen Cunliffe died in 1766 and was buried at Rivington Parish Church. Later that year his widow Elizabeth came to an agreement with John Cunliffe the younger of Halliwell (a party to the lease) to relinquish her rights to the farm, in return for an annual rental payment of £4 for the following twelve years. The money was to be used by Elizabeth to maintain two children, Robert Cunliffe, and another unnamed child, for 'meat, drink, washing, lodging and clothes'. The purpose of the arrangement seems to have been for John to provide income for the upbringing of his younger sibling, and another family dependent. The farm at that time was being subleased to a Robert Taylor.[3]

On the 1796 plan of Smithills Estate, Chadwicks Close was recorded as the 'lower house' of John Cunliffe, who also leased the neighbouring farm, Green Nook. The Cunliffe's tenure seems to have lasted at least half a century; the 1864 rental records show Robert Cunliffe holding Chadwicks Close at a rent of £6 per year, for a term of one life.

Plan of Chadwicks Close Farm and surrounding farms c.1769. Based on plan of Smithills Demesne by Hugh Oldham, Bolton Archives. Image ©Stephen Tonge.

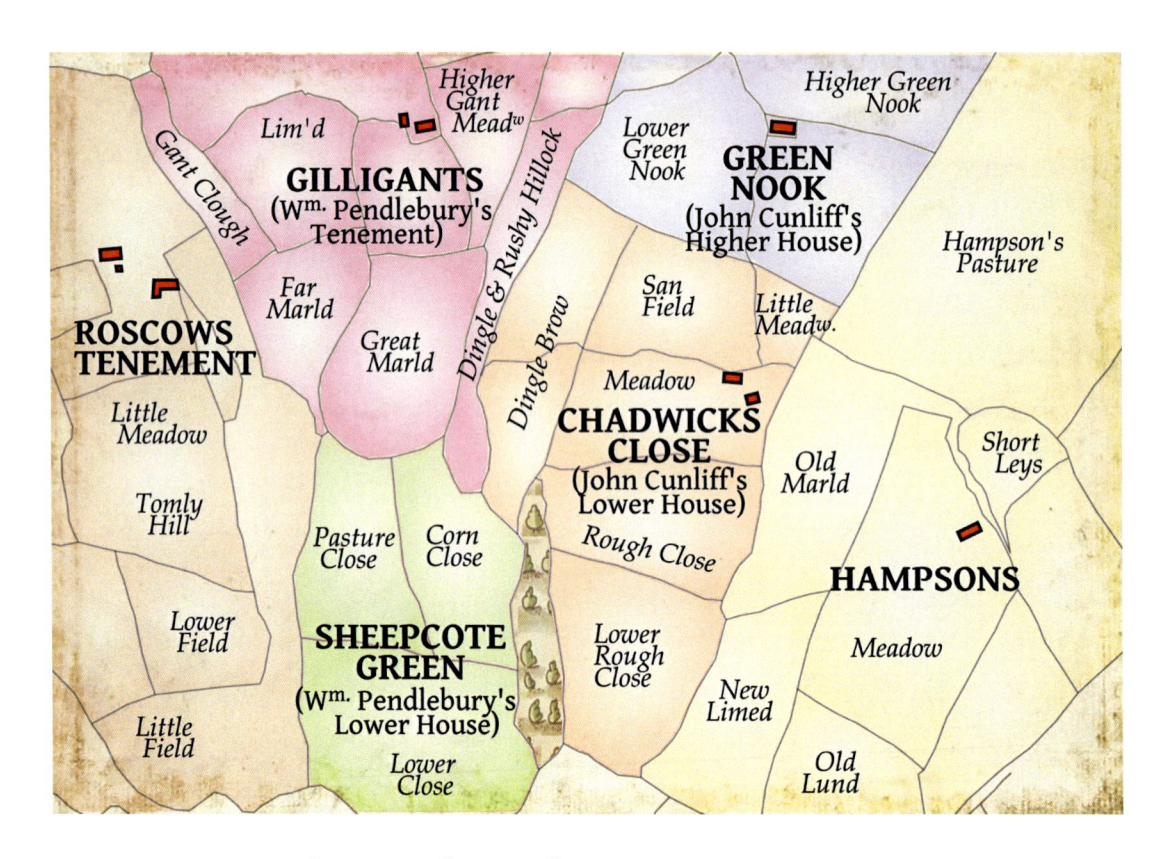

James Cooper's Death on the Moors

The land tax records suggest that Thomas Cooper was resident in Smithills from about 1802, shortly after the Ainsworths purchased the estate, so presumably subleasing Chadwicks Close from the Cunliffes.[4] He died in 1812, after which

James Cooper took over. James remained at Chadwicks Close for another thirty years or so, until his death in 1843, the unfortunate circumstances of which are related below.

On Friday 13 January, he left home at 3 o'clock, to go to the turnpike near the Waterloo (a former public house situated at the junction of Halliwell Road and Blackburn Road). He was going to see his wife's sister and get a pair of clogs mended. His wife Nancy met him there at 5 o'clock. She recounted events at the inquest:

> *'He went in the Waterloo, and after some time I went in, desiring him to come home with me. I got him away about seven o'clock; but he would call at John Settle's, a beer shop on the road. I would not stop, and there I left him. He was not drunk and I thought he would come to no harm. He had three glasses of ale at the Waterloo. I only saw him have one, but the landlady said he had two before'.*

Christopher Brownlow, the publican at the Ainsworth Arms, said he called in there at 8 o'clock. He appeared in good health but had some trouble on his mind. 'What's to do, James Cooper?' he asked. 'Least said is soonest mended,' Cooper replied. He had only one glass of beer, and a pennyworth of rum, said the publican, and left at 11 o'clock. Another witness saw him walking home between 11 and 12 o'clock, about a quarter of a mile from his house. His dead body was found the following day by three men, a few hundred yards from his home. It was covered in snow and sleet, with his head frozen to the wall; he had clearly been dead for several hours. The inquest concluded that he had died from exposure to the cold. One participant speculated that he had been struck by lightning.[5]

Photograph ©Tony Greenwood.

The Tonges & Shuttleworths

James Cooper's widow, Nancy, stayed on at the farm until she died of consumption there in 1852. The farm remained in the occupation of family members, and by 1861 Ralph Tonge was the farmer with his wife Susannah (née Cooper). When they came to Chadwicks Close, they had already been married for thirty years and had a large family. The small farm was insufficient to sustain the whole family, so while the parents tended the farm the children gained employment elsewhere. The girls worked as winders and doublers in local cotton mills, and the boys became coal miners as they grew older.

Their eldest son Elisha ran into trouble as a young man, when he was prosecuted in 1855 for assaulting the landlord of the Doffcocker public house, after being refused more drink at closing time.[6] In 1858 events repeated themselves, but this time took a more serious turn. He and his brother Robert were employed as colliers at Turton and had gone drinking at the Volunteer Inn on their way home. After being turfed out by a passing constable at closing time, they took umbrage, waited for him outside, and beat him badly.[7] They were each sentenced to six months imprisonment. Their wives appealed, but their tearful pleas were ignored. Robert eventually returned to live at his parent's farm with his wife Patience and their children, dwelling at Chadwicks Close Cottage until they retired to Horwich some time after 1871.

The Doffcocker Inn, c.1900. Courtesy Halliwell Local History Society.

William Cottam was the next tenant, but he quit farming and left in 1878. The following year, William Shuttleworth and his wife Fanny, natives of Wigan, moved in with their five children. They stayed for five years in total – William died of bronchitis at the farm in 1882, after which Fanny stayed on for another two years before moving elsewhere. Their son John would return twenty years later. The farm then spent several years empty, being occasionally let out to Elijah Lonsdale of Lower Tongs. In 1889, Thomas and Eliza Seddon took it on and stayed for ten years.

In the late 1890s, John Shuttleworth, son of William and Fanny, returned to the farm. He held the lease, but left the farming to his father-in-law, Robert Tonge (also previously resident), while John worked as a cotton carder in a local mill. Chadwicks Close had been his wife Margaret's home as a teenager and had been tenanted by her family for the best part of a century, on and off. Their youngest son Frank was born there in 1897, being the sixth generation of the family to have lived there, and the last. Their stay this time was relatively short-lived, and they moved away after a decade.

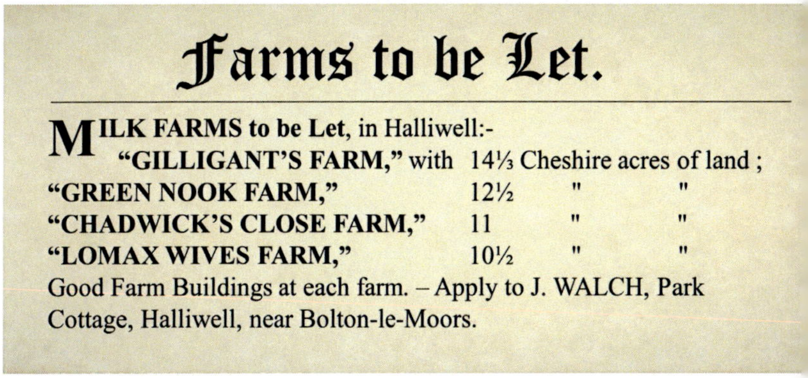

Farms to be Let.

MILK FARMS to be Let, in Halliwell:-
"GILLIGANT'S FARM," with 14⅓ Cheshire acres of land;
"GREEN NOOK FARM," 12½ " "
"CHADWICK'S CLOSE FARM," 11 " "
"LOMAX WIVES FARM," 10½ " "
Good Farm Buildings at each farm. – Apply to J. WALCH, Park Cottage, Halliwell, near Bolton-le-Moors.

Advertisement for the letting of several farms from the *Preston Herald*, 15 February 1885.[8]

Front row left: Seth Tonge (1859-1918) in India. The son of Robert & Patience Tonge, he spent his childhood years at Chadwicks Close Farm. After working at cotton mills in Bolton, he moved to Paisley in Scotland to be employed as a foreman, and then to India to act as a mill manager. From the collection of Stephen Tonge.

Frank Shuttleworth (1897-1961). Born at Chadwicks Close Farm on 14 December 1897. Emigrated to America. From the collection of Stephen Tonge.

Margaret Shuttleworth (1857-1919), formerly Tonge. Resident at Chadwicks Close Farm in the 1870s and again in the late 1890s. From the collection of Stephen Tonge.

John Shuttleworth of Chadwicks Close Farm c.1900. From the collection of Stephen Tonge.

Twentieth Century

During World War I, Frederick and Sophia Jackson were the tenants. Their two sons, Norman and Frank fought in France during this time. Norman was killed in the fighting on 25 April 1918, and was commemorated on Colliers Row School memorial, as well as Tyne Cot Memorial in West Flanders, Belgium. By 1922, Frederick Jackson expanded his area by also renting the land at the neighbouring farm, Green Nook.[9]

In a 1948 survey of the estate, ten years after its purchase by Bolton Corporation, the farm was recorded as having a house with two kitchens, sitting room, pantry, scullery and four bedrooms, as well as the barn, hayloft, cart shed, boiler house and pigsty.[10] Evidence of the lives that had been lived on the farm since the Chadwicks first tenanted it two hundred years earlier.

Aerial view of Chadwicks Close Farm in 1982. Photograph ©Lee McCarren. From the collection of Lee McCarren.

The present-day building has been significantly renovated, although is still easily recognisable from the old photograph. The many descendants of the tenant farmers who once lived at the farm are now numerous, both locally and overseas.

Chadwicks Close Farm, 2019. Photograph ©Lee McCarren. From the collection of Lee McCarren.

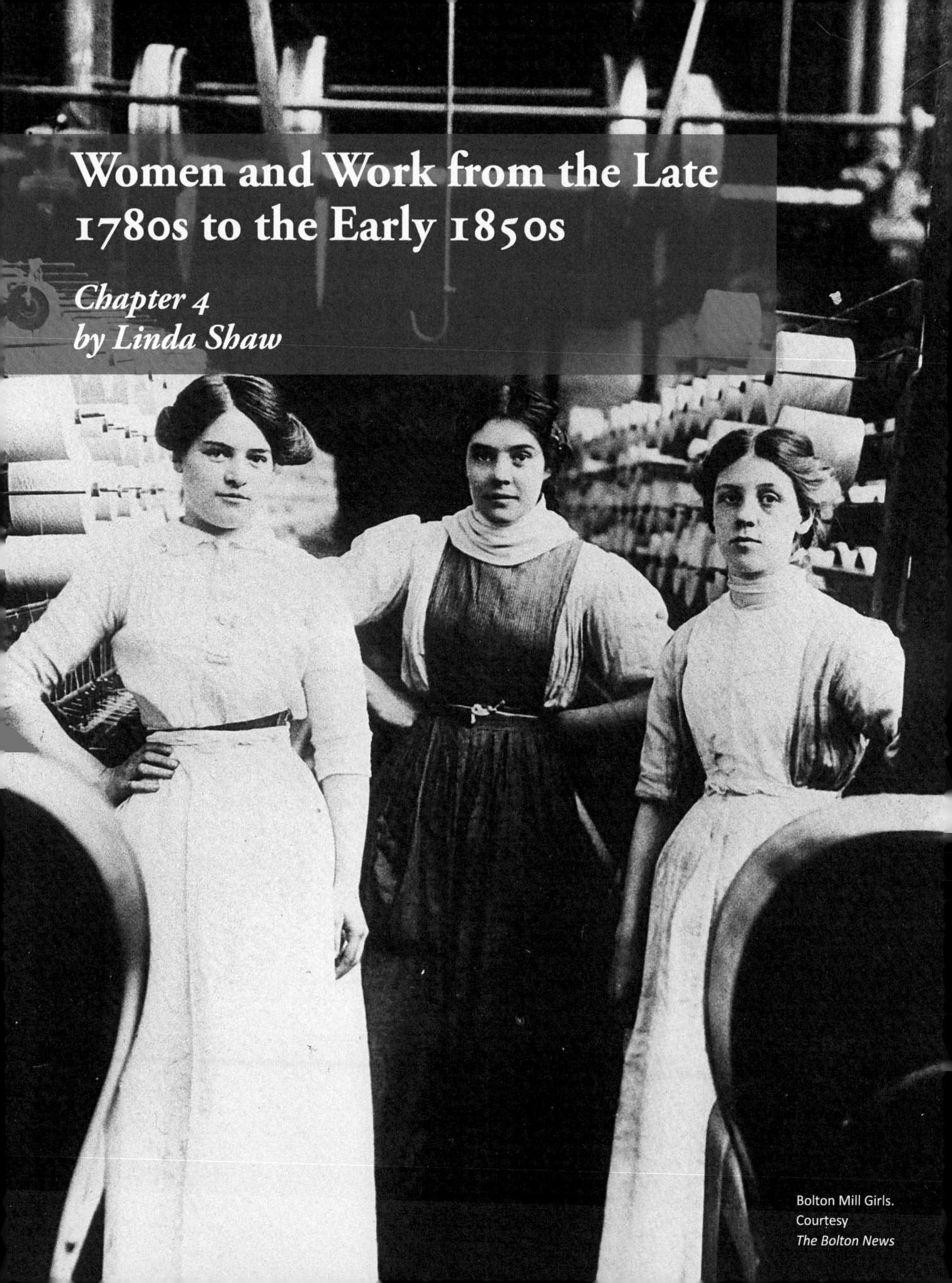

Women and Work from the Late 1780s to the Early 1850s

*Chapter 4
by Linda Shaw*

Bolton Mill Girls.
Courtesy
The Bolton News

This chapter looks at the kinds of work undertaken by women who lived on Smithills Estate and how this changed over time. Looking at the estate now, it is easy to imagine that most women would have worked in farming in addition to carrying out their domestic duties. But this was not the case. Many women were employed in the textiles industry. Indeed, far from living in a rural backwater, by tracing the changing nature of women's employment on the estate, we can learn not only how they worked in a trade with a global reach but also in one that was to drive the Industrial Revolution. 'King Cotton' provided jobs for thousands of women in Bolton and throughout the northwest for many decades. This chapter will show how, in a relatively brief period of around sixty years, women's working lives were transformed as they became the 'first industrial' women.[1]

'King Cotton'. Courtesy United States Board of Agriculture.

Making a living in the eighteenth century

Many women on the estate would have worked in agriculture on both large and small farms. Farmers' wives in the eighteenth century would have been actively involved, particularly in managing the dairy, pigs, and poultry. The dairy was an important source of income for many farms, and its success depended on the skill of the mistress, who usually ran the operation with no help from men. Even the wives of day labourers who had no land of their own contributed to their family income by keeping a cow or pigs, which were grazed on common lands. There they could also collect firewood. Access to common lands was particularly important for poorer women and their families as it provided a valuable income supplement.

Areas of Open Access in England and Wales, including Common Land, 2005. Courtesy Defra UK.

The rights of the common date back to at least the thirteenth century when local people were lawfully able to use commons as a collective resource for many activities, including grazing sheep, cows or horses (pasturage), keeping pigs (pannage), and collecting firewood and bracken (estovers). The Enclosure Acts that came into force between the eighteenth and twentieth centuries severely restricted the amount of common land, and in England today the area of land available has shrunk considerably, from around fifty percent before enclosure to three percent of land now.[2]

Most people who lived in the countryside were engaged in a mix of subsistence activities (such as growing food for their own consumption) and income earning labour.[3] Women and men worked alongside each other but typically carried out different tasks and received different wages for their work. One common source of income was to undertake daily paid work on farms, but this was very insecure and seasonally based with much less work available in winter. Children were often employed as bird scarers, whilst everyone worked at harvest time.

Many families also gained an income from the textiles industry in which production was based within the household. The work was largely divided along gender lines with women spinning and men weaving. Being household based enabled women to fit their spinning around all their other domestic and farming duties, and a spinning wheel could be seen in most houses and cottages.[4] The raw yarn was subcontracted, or 'put out', to the women, generally by agents employed by local manufacturers, who then had the spun yarn returned to them. The spinners received the yarn in two- or three-pound bundles. It was first washed before being carded into the right density for spinning on a wheel.[5]

From *Our Own Gazette*, 1877. Courtesy iStock/Cannasue.

It was estimated that women could walk up to thirty-three miles a week whilst spinning! The spun yarn was then woven into cloth by the weavers who worked on handlooms, also at home. Few traces of domestic spinning remain today but houses used for weaving can still be identified by the number and types of windows which were constructed to allow as much light in as possible. Most commonly in Lancashire, the loom was situated on the ground floor. Rows of windows with the central mullions removed typically indicate the location of the loom shop.[7] The cottages at Walker Fold housed James Sutcliffe, a weaver in 1841, and the rows of ground-floor windows characteristic of a loom shop can still be seen today.[8]

A domestic based textile industry was widespread throughout the UK and especially in Lancashire, including Smithills, by the eighteenth century. Although spinning was not especially well paid, it did enable women to make a significant

Ex-slaves working in a gang on a cotton plantation with a nearby overseer in 1875 ten years after emancipation. Wood engraving with modern colour, 1875. Courtesy Shutterstock/Everett Collection.

contribution to household costs. Demand for spun yarn greatly increased following the adoption of the flying shuttle in the 1730s which speeded up the weaving process. Following this invention, one estimate is that it now took eight spinners to supply one weaver with sufficient yarn.[9]

In much of the country, the yarn spun was wool but in south Lancashire women specialised in spinning cotton. The raw yarn for this was imported from India and the New World via British ports. Middlemen such as Henry Escricke from Bolton bought raw linen and cotton yarn in both Liverpool and Manchester. He sold it on to spinners, then sold the spun yarn to the weavers.[10] They produced several types of fabric including fustian which was a mixture of linen and cotton yarns.[11] Home spun cotton yarn was often not of sufficient quality to provide a good warp, so linen warps were used, typically imported from the Baltic.[12] These early cotton mixture fabrics were extremely popular in the UK and also sold well in overseas markets in the Americas, and to traders in the West African market supplying enslaved people.[13]

These high levels of demand for cotton fabrics and for cotton yarn stimulated the arrival of a series of technological developments in spinning. In the 1770s James Hargreaves' Spinning Jenny enabled women to spin multiple yarn threads at one time, though the preparatory carding and roving was still done by hand. Initially, the early jennies were used at home and by women.[15] However, from the 1780s, larger jennies were introduced in workshops, and these were more likely to be operated by men, arguably because of the heavier nature of the machinery.[16]

The warp thread was the thread which was held in place lengthwise on a hand loom and had to be strong enough to be held in tension. They were fastened to a beam at the rear of the loom, threaded through string eyelets called heddles, then tied to the front beam. The weft was then woven in from side to side using a shuttle.

Handloom showing warp attached to front and rear beams and threaded through string heddles. Courtesy Javier Carro, CC BY-SA.[14]

Samuel Crompton's Spinning Mule added rollers to the jenny, spun finer thread and was initially small enough for the domestic putting-out system, but it was more expensive. However, over time this new machinery not only increased production levels but also improved the quality of the yarn, and spinning mules became the main spinning machine in use until the turn of the twentieth century. They also became linked to machine carding, and small factories and workshops containing these machines spread very rapidly. A further incentive was the application of waterpower, greatly increasing productivity as it allowed the installation of mules in pairs, which could both be worked by a single spinner.[17] The first water powered cotton mill was introduced in Bolton in 1777 on the River Croal.[18]

Arkwright's Water Frame, c.1775. Courtesy Board of Trustees, Science Museum Group, CC BY-SA.

These early mills were often based on the outskirts of town as they needed to be situated near a suitable water supply.[19] Barrow Bridge, with its river and preexisting road, offered such a site. It provides a good example of this early transition from domestic to workshop to factory-based spinning. A carding mill was set up in the early 1790s by Thomas Whewell. This was on flat land opposite the Sixty-three Steps, and it may have included spinning jennies as well. There is very little evidence relating to this mill, but we do know by 1795 it was bought by Robert Lord, a local farmer and small-time textile entrepreneur who with his two sons had already built a small mill a short distance away in the Doffcocker area.[20]

The Lord brothers rapidly expanded production at Barrow Bridge and a local engineering works supplied them with several of the new mechanised mules each having 234 spindles. In 1798, they built a new mill, the Dean Cotton Works, further down the valley with a (fourteen-and-a-half metres) water wheel, and bought more machinery.[21]

Lord's Mill, 1802, from a series of engravings published by Dobson and Barlow Limited. Courtesy Horwich Heritage.

MR. ROBERT LORD'S MILL AT BARROW BRIDGE, NEAR BOLTON, ABOUT 1802.

The Dean Cotton Works

This new mill was four storeys in height, long and narrow with a sloping slate roof. It was typical of early cotton mills which tended to be long narrow buildings with regularly spaced windows to allow in light. Mills generally housed between 1000 and 2000 spindles: by 1816 there were around 10,000 spindles in the Lord's mill.[22] Carding and roving took place on the ground floor and spinning on the upper floors. The water wheel could be either internally or externally housed and would be fed via a series of reservoirs.[23] The Lord brothers initially constructed two reservoirs or lodges close to the mill (now the car parking area) and in 1826 higher up on the moor a third reservoir was constructed which is still there today.

There was a bell to summon the workers who would not otherwise have been able to arrive on time as few would have owned clocks or watches. In 1816, thirteen cottages were built for the workers and though the cottages are still there, the mill building was later demolished, and few traces now remain.[24]

What did all these changes mean for women's work? It's a mixed picture in terms of benefits. With the mechanisation of the spinning processes and their relocation in mills, women rapidly lost their domestic spinning work. This loss of income is likely to have had a devastating impact on household income. In the new mills, spinning was done by male workers who were relatively well paid.[25] They were sometimes described as the aristocrats of the mill workers. They were strongly unionised and guarded their status well with no women able to become spinners.

Dean Mills Reservoir showing the remains of old machinery. Photograph ©Peter Ravald Photography and Drone Photography.

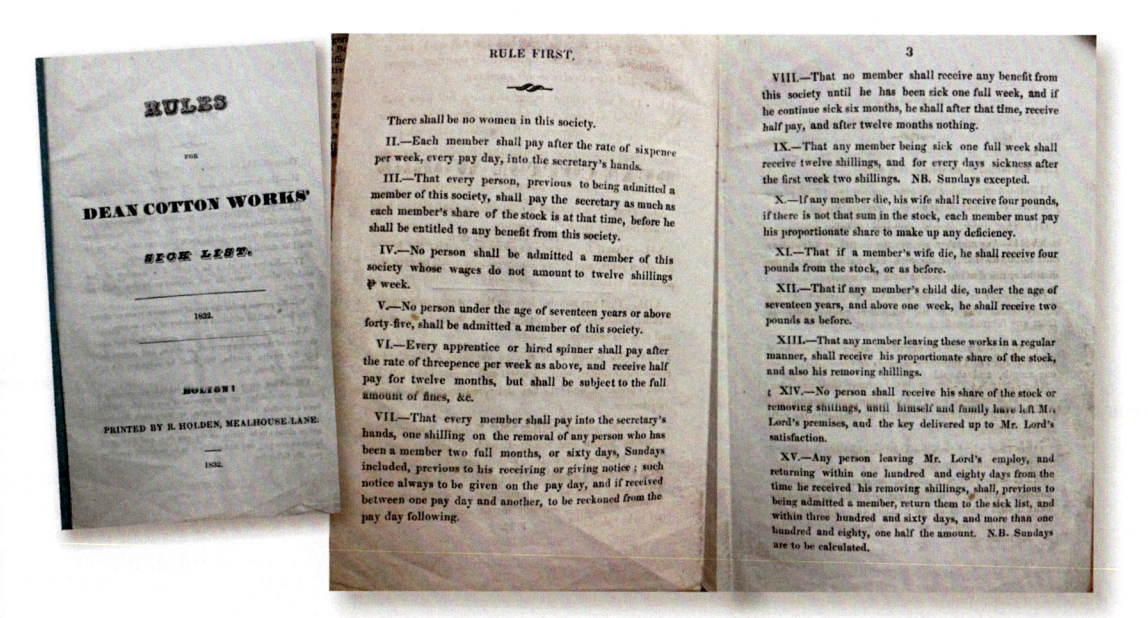

The first statement of the rules of the *Dean Cotton Works' Sick List* reveals that 'there shall be no women in this society'. These seem to be the rules of what was essentially a Friendly Society with a membership of spinners into which worker members paid weekly and could obtain sick pay if needed. Cover and pages 2-3 of *Rules for Dean Cotton Works' Sick List,* 1832. Courtesy Bolton Council.

However, women were not to be totally excluded from working in the new mills. By the 1840s, in Lancashire alone, a survey of 412 cotton factories found that just over half of the 116,300 workers were female. Around 10,700 of those were married women.[26]

In the spinning mills, they worked in the carding section where they prepared the loose cotton for spinners. This was a very dusty and dirty environment. There were several related processes involved in the preparation of yarn. Men would open the bales of cotton which fed into a series of machines which opened, cleaned, and blended the fibres. The fibres were then carried to the carding machines where it was fed through various machines by women card 'tenters' (those who tended machinery) until it was ready for the spinners.[27]

Women and children operating cotton carding machines in a factory. Coloured lithograph after J R Barfoot, 1804. Courtesy Welcome Collection.

Men and women's work was clearly segregated and women's wages were, on average, around only half (or less) those of men, according to the factory report of 1834.[28]

Hours were long for all mill workers especially before the reforms of the 1830s and 40s with twelve-to-fourteen-hour days being common. The Factories Act of 1844 limited the hours of women workers to twelve a day. Prior to that an Act of 1833 limited the working hours of children aged nine to twelve to eight a day and between twelve and eighteen to twelve a day. Importantly, this Act also established a number of factory inspectors to enforce the new requirements. Leonard Horner was the inspector for Lancashire and the owners of Dean Mills did, in fact, report to him in 1833 on the number of children and young people they employed.[29] This gives a fascinating snapshot of the situation that year.

		No2 Mill		No3 Mill	
Ages		Males	Females	Males	Females
between	10 & 11	2	12		6
"	11 & 12	5	3		4
"	12 & 13	6	12		4
"	13 & 14	6	35		12
"	14 & 15	8	13		8
"	15 & 16	4	7		6
"	16 & 17	7	12	1	13
"	17 & 18	1	9		6
"	18 & 19	2	12		5
"	19 & 20	1	9		5
"	20 & 21	3	3		0
Above 21		21	33	4	2
		66	160	5	71

Numbers of young people working at Dean Mills in 1838. From the Return to Leonard Horner, 30 October 1838. Courtesy Bolton Council.

We can see that a total of 231 females were employed at Dean Mills and seventyone males, of which sixty-six men and thirty-five women were over the age of twenty-one.[30] Many children were employed, some as young as ten. Sixty-two females aged fourteen and under were employed. The majority of these young workers would have lived locally, and their numbers would have included many young people living on Smithills Estate. Although their hours were now regulated, by today's standards they were extremely long. In this respect, Dean Mills was typical of the many cotton mills across the locality.

In 1830 the business was sold to Thomas Bazley and Richard Gardner who were, by the standards of the day, to prove good employers. They demolished the older water powered mill and built two new six-storey mills powered by steam engines. The latest mill construction methods were used to erect wider buildings built with iron frames to take the larger modern spinning and doubling machinery.[31]

Dean Mills, c.1901. From the collection of Lee Worsley.

In 1848, Bazley became the sole owner of the mills. They attracted national attention, not only because they were the largest doubling mills in the country producing fine cotton and lace thread, but also because of the activities of the owners in providing housing, and educational and recreational facilities for their workers. Bazley was also an early member of the Anti-Corn Law League, President of the Manchester Chamber of Commerce and was appointed one of the Commissioners to the Great Exhibition of 1851.[32]

In 1815, the Corn Laws had been enacted as a protectionist measure against the import of overseas grain. The laws were supported by many landowners as they kept cereal prices high. For ordinary people, however, the consequences were devastating. Based in Manchester, the nationwide Anti-Corn Law League was set up in 1838 by a number of individuals, including Richard Cobden, a Radical politician, and John Bright, an orator who spoke so well at meetings support for the League grew quickly amongst the working and industrialist classes. In 1846 legislation repealing the laws was passed by Robert Peel's Conservative government, a turning point in the drive for a free-trade economy in Britain.

'Corn Laws Repealed'. Petty, Ernst & Co., 1846. Broadside, GB127. Broadsides/F1846.3. Courtesy Manchester City Council.

In the same year, and probably prompted by their connection through working together on the Great Exhibition, Prince Albert paid a visit to the mills which occasioned much publicity. The prince visited not only the mills, but the rows of cottages built on the hillside to house up to three hundred workers. These are still present today.

The visit was covered in national newspapers such as the *London Illustrated News*, which contained an extensive description of the mills and surroundings as well as the model village.

> 'Dean mills……..are seated in a picturesque valley overlooked by the Horwich and Halliwell Moors – the haunt of the grouse…The waters of a stream which runs through the bottom past the Mills have been collected into an artificial reservoir, or lake, which contains abundance of trout and other fish, and forms a leasing connection with the Mill buildings, and village appended by the proprietors for the convenience of about 300 of the workpeople'. [33]

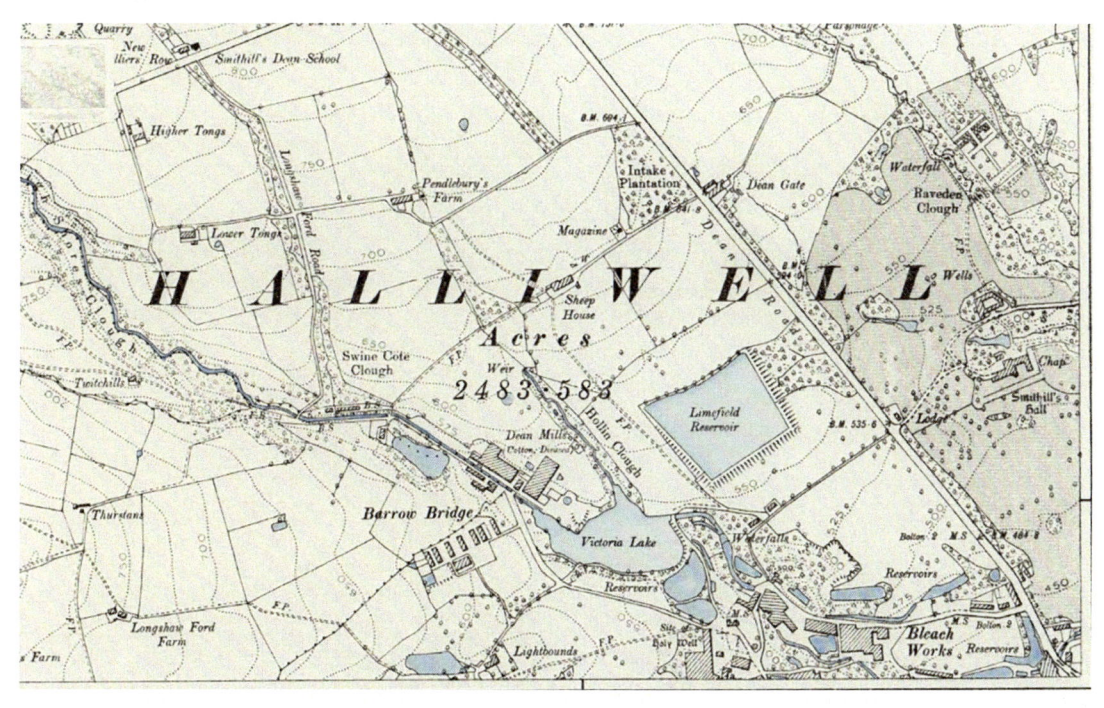

Ordnance Survey six-inch map, surveyed 1892, showing Dean Mills, reservoirs and the bleach works. Courtesy National Library of Scotland.

At the top of the hill was the Institute, erected at a cost of £4000. This contained on the ground floor a school which was not limited to children employed at the mill. They attended for three hours a day at a cost of around one-and-a-half pence a week, and other children could attend for three pence a week. On the first floor there was a large hall used for lectures that could hold over a thousand people. There was also a library.[34]

Women working in Dean Mill. *London Illustrated News,* 25 October 1851. Courtesy Bolton Council.

Dean Mills, 1851. *London Illustrated News,* 25 October 1851. Courtesy Bolton Council.

In 1848 Leonard Horner was to report that, 'Nowhere have I seen so admirable a school establishment as that lately founded by Messrs Gardner and Bazley for the benefit of their workpeople in their extensive factories… the internal fittings of the schools are of the most complete kind, and there is the most ample supply of books, maps and all other materials for teaching'.[35]

The workers also established a co-operative store managed by a committee of workmen that sold food and other provisions, with ovens for baking bread. The store was managed by a committee of workmen.[36] Benjamin Disraeli visited Barrow Bridge and it influenced the plot of his novel *Coningsby* with the village of Millbank being based on Barrow Bridge and the character Millbank, a cotton manufacturer, based on Gardner.[37]

Given the squalid conditions that most mill workers lived in during this period, Barrow Bridge does stand out as offering decent living conditions for the workers at the mills. A communal washhouse was built at the end of each row of cottages, all of which had running water piped in from a local reservoir, and gas for domestic as well as street lighting was piped in from the mill. For the women living in these houses, all these features must have made their domestic chores, especially washday, considerably easier and less time consuming.[38]

Dean Mills continued to provide employment for local women and men for much of the century.[39] Bazley retired from business in 1862 though he remained Liberal MP for Manchester until 1880, and the mills were then taken over by W R Callender who continued to run them along the same lines as before. However, the business struggled and the mills ceased operations by 1878.

The 1851 Census and beyond

The 1851 Census indicates just how important work in the textiles industry was for the women who lived on the estate. In Colliers Row alone, thirteen young women worked in the mills as doublers. Other families such as the Sewart family living at Lower Tongs reported a daughter working as a doubler while the Cooper family at Chadwicks Close reported two girls working as doublers. Doublers worked in the carding room operating a machine to twist together different stands of cotton in preparation for spinning.[40]

1851 Census	Women textile workers living on Smithills Estate (not including Barrow Bridge)
Finishers	2
Doublers	22
Cotton Mill Workers	5
Reelers	1
Winders	1

Women textile workers living on Smithills Estate, 1851.

It was difficult for women to combine mill work with family responsibilities especially given the long hours worked, so as elsewhere many young women working in the mills were unmarried. Their income must have made a substantial contribution to their families' finances and undoubtedly helped them achieve a higher standard of living. The Factories Act of 1844 limited the hours worked by children to six-and-a-half with three hours' schooling, and set a maximum twelve-hour day for young people between thirteen and eighteen. The twelve-hour rule also applied to women. In effect it was the first health and safety act in Britain. All dangerous machinery was to be securely fenced off, and failure to do so was regarded as a criminal offence. No child or young person was to clean mill machinery whilst it was in motion. The 1847 Act further reduced the hours of work in mills for women and young people to ten a day. But women's work in the carding room remained arduous and came low in the mill hierarchy. Women working there had the reputation for being amongst the toughest in the mill.[41] All workers in the carding room were susceptible to byssinosis (cardroom asthma) caused by breathing in too much of the cotton fluff from the air.[42] This disease eventually caused severe incapacitation, and commonly resulted in early death.

The 1851 Census also reports that two girls were working as finishers. They are likely to have been employed in the Halliwell Bleach Works which was owned and run by the Ainsworth family. Like cotton spinning, the bleach industry had grown from small domestic enterprises to mechanised and centralised production. The Ainsworths had bought land at what is now Moss Bank Park and grew their business. Initially cloth was first treated and then left out in the sun to dry, a process which could take several weeks and could only happen during the summer months. In the 1790s, working with the Valletts, a father and son from France, Peter Ainsworth (1737-1807) and his son Richard (1762-1833) introduced a much faster chemical bleaching process which did not involve leaving the cloth outside. The business expanded rapidly and with their new prosperity the Ainsworths built Moss Bank House, with extensive gardens. The gardens remain but the house suffered from dry rot and is now demolished. They also bought Smithills Hall and estate in 1801, partly because they were interested in the water catchment from the moors.

Halliwell Bleach Works chimney with Manchester in the background. Photograph ©Tony Greenwood.

Moss Bank House. Courtesy Halliwell Local History Society.

The Halliwell Bleach Works was also an important local employer. When Richard Ainsworth died in 1833 his eldest son, another Peter (1790-1870), took over the running of Smithills Estate whilst his younger son, John Horrocks Ainsworth (1800-1865), stayed in Moss Bank House and took over the running of the bleach works. His attitude to the workforce contrasted strongly with the views held by Bazley. Although he was responsible for the school on Colliers Row and provided much of the funding for St Peter's Church, Halliwell, he was against any form of government reform of employment conditions. He forced the Reverend Milton of St Paul's Church, Halliwell, out of his post for speaking out about child labour and poor working conditions in the bleach works. However Milton was able later to give testimony to a parliamentary committee about the poor working conditions there.[43]

Conclusion

During the period we have looked at, women living on Smithills Estate would have seen their working lives change hugely with the growth of mechanised production in cotton mills. The cotton industry had continued to provide an income and employment for many women. However, their working lives remained arduous, with long hours whether at home, on the land or in the mills. But working in the mills at least provided women and their families with an income. It offered an alternative to becoming a domestic servant that was often the only option for young women in many parts of the country. And the pay was better. The employment of young women in factories was a highly contentious issue, many commentators disapproved and asserted that the women were prone to unseemly behaviour, immodesty and worse.[44] As the century progressed, there was more acceptance of women mill workers. However, no other types of largescale factory employment for women developed until World War I.

Sarah Reddish (1849-1928) worked in cotton mills from a young age. She became an active suffragist and trade unionist as well a key figure in the Co-operative Women's Guild. Sarah is in the middle of the centre row. Courtesy *The Bolton News*.

It is surely no coincidence that given their mill work, Lancashire women led the way in the suffrage struggle. Locally, women mill workers formed their own Bolton Women Textiles Representation Committee which campaigned for the vote. And the regional Women Textile Workers asserted that 'What Lancashire and Cheshire women think today England will do tomorrow'.[45]

Who Killed George Henderson on Winter Hill?

*Chapter 5
by Barbara Winder*

Photograph
©Tony Greenwood.

Winter Hill

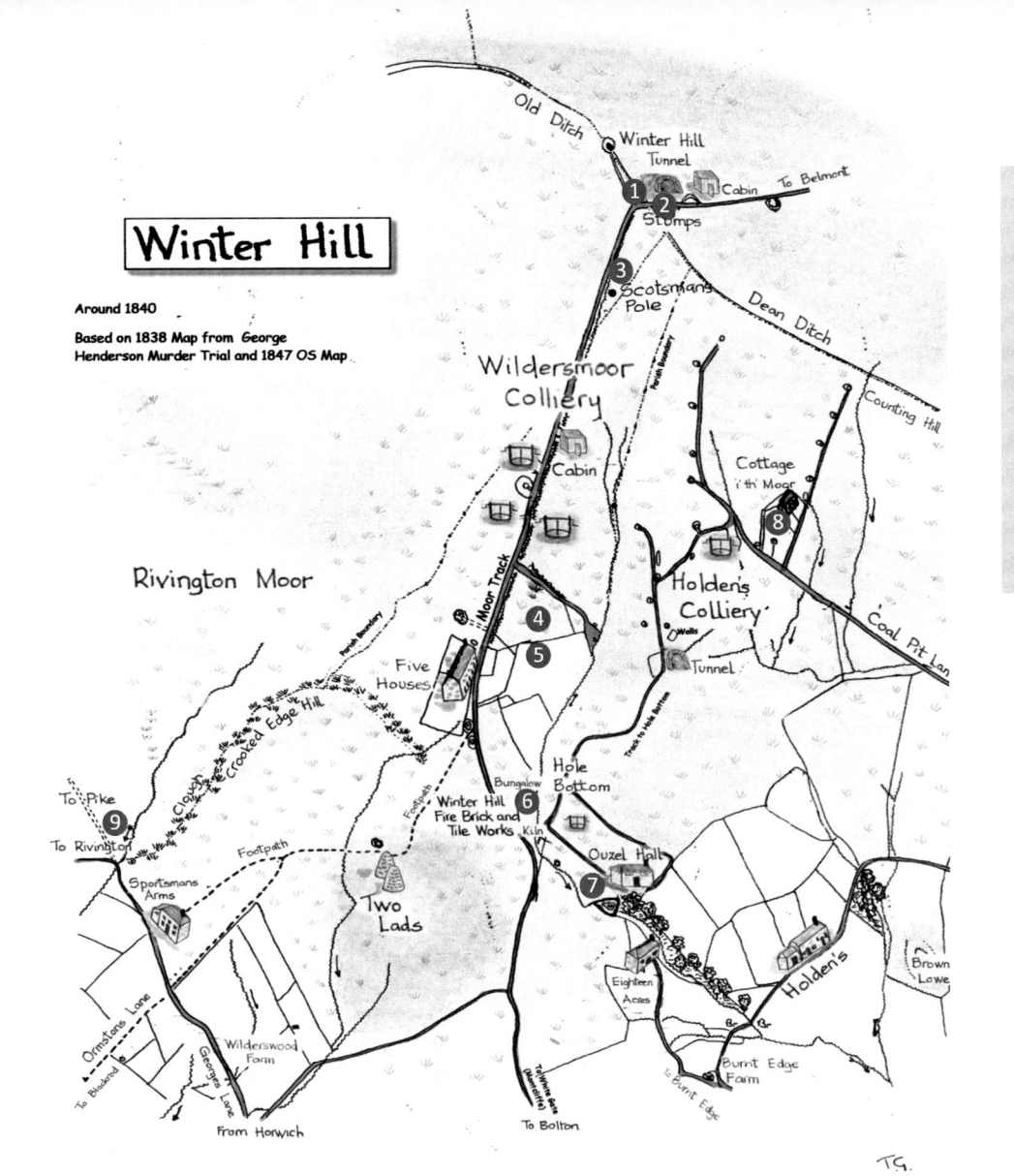

Around 1840
Based on 1838 Map from George Henderson Murder Trial and 1847 OS Map

Key to Map	
1	Stone Quarry
2	Winter Hill Gate
3	George Henderson found here
4	Turf Cess
5	Makinson Top
6	Quaker John's
7	William Heaton's
8	James Morris' farm
9	Brownlows Close

Map of the murder based on early Ordnance Survey and limited map given to jury and trial. Drawn by Tony Greenwood.

Many Boltonians have heard of the death of young George Henderson on Friday 9 November 1838 at around noon, commemorated over many years by the Scotsman's Stump memorial on the slopes of Winter Hill above the town. One local young man James Whittle was named at the inquest as the 'willful murderer', and arrested and tried in Liverpool in early April 1839, but acquitted.[1] Despite a gap of almost two hundred years, there is still evidence to be found which suggests a possible killer and subsequent cover-up for the killing, and many locals may have known who was responsible at the time.

The events of the killing

The victim George Henderson came from Annan in the Scottish borders to work as a Scottish draper for another Scotsman William Jardine. He was a wealthy draper of Blackburn, which had a growing Scottish community in an area of the town still known today as Little Scotland.

George's memorial suggests he was in his twentieth year, though estimates of his age vary between fifteen and twenty-four. He had only been working for five months and Mary Entwistle, mother of erstwhile poacher William Entwistle, describes him as 'the little Scotsman' in her evidence.[2] There is a birth record for a George Henderson on the Scotland's People website for 10 January 1823 to Joseph Henderson and Barbara Brown, which would make him almost sixteen at the time of his death. Kath Arkwright of Halliwell Local History Society says there was a partial Annan census for Hall Meadow showing a possible Henderson family with three daughters and son George. This record would make him twenty-two. The Prosecutor at Whittle's trial said Henderson was twenty-four!

Commercial travellers appeared in the eighteenth century at fairs, but from the nineteenth wholesale drapery merchants usually employed them. They would take samples of their wares to customers who placed orders with them and paid dues on delivery. Outside the main towns, this often involved walking long distances on a specified route each day. Many northern towns' drapery businesses employed young men from the Scottish borders looking for work. These men were known as Scottish drapers. Towns like Bolton and Blackburn still have areas where they lived and worshipped. Between 1871 and 1881 commercial traveller numbers almost doubled to 40,000.

It was in any case hard work, crossing the local hillsides on foot in all weathers, visiting local farms and taking in money and orders, but George was a conscientious respectable young man, rarely drinking alcohol, attending church, and even worrying about missed orders as he lay dying, when he talked about needing to send a parcel the following Monday.

On the last night of his life, Thursday 8 November, George stayed at the Old Cock Inn in Blackrod. The following morning was chilly and foggy, but he knew the road and had arranged to meet another Scotsman who he'd known in Annan, Benjamin Burrell, at Five Houses Beerhouse near the top of the moor, around eleven that morning. However, George was delayed and did not arrive till almost noon, and by then his friend had decided to go on, leaving a message that he would meet him for dinner at The Black Dog, Belmont that evening. This seems to have been a common arrangement; Mrs Lambert said in her evidence that on the afternoon of the murder James Whittle told her, 'There are two of them that make a point of meeting at Mr Garbutt's and going home together'.

Black Dog Inn, Belmont where Henderson and his friend Burrell planned to meet for dinner the day of the killing. Watercolour painting by Barbara Winder, 2006.

Five Houses. The Whittle family rented a cottage here. Henderson's body remained on a table in the beerhouse for several days after the killing and it was where the autopsy took place.
Watercolour painting by Barbara Winder, 2022.

A number of people were on the moor that day around noon, some taking a meal to their relatives at the mine, but the fog was increasingly thick, especially on Winter Hill's upper slopes, and none reported seeing Henderson being shot, although some heard shots at around half past twelve. Fourteen-year-old Thomas Whewell, who said it was 'a terribly rawky day-I could not see more than a yard or two before me', was taking his brother's dinner to the pit on his pony, and found George gravely wounded, lying moaning in a water-filled ditch at the right side of the road. Afraid for his own safety if the killers were near, he ran for help from two colliers eating their dinners in the mine tunnel entrance nearby: James Fletcher and Thomas Radcliffe. They carried Henderson back to the beerhouse on a chair, placing his wounded body on a long table in the main room, where he took two hours to die.

William Garbutt owned Five Houses and ran the beerhouse and the local pit that was owned by Peter Ainsworth. He sent out his colliers to look for likely killers, and they quickly arrested several men, one hiding in the outside privy with a gun, all members of a shooting party from Smithills Hall.

The Alehouse Act of 1828 and the Beerhouse Act of 1830 liberalised the regulations governing the brewing and selling of beer, partially to discourage the drinking of cheap spirits such as gin which had significantly more health implications.
The Acts allowed any rate payer to brew or sell beer for the annual payment of two guineas for a licence to sell on any day apart from Sunday. By 1841 some 45,500 licences had been granted. The applicant could brew and sell beer and cider in their own home, but not spirits or fortified wines. Beer was usually dispensed in a jug or from a wooden barrel. So profitable was it, that in some towns every other house became a beerhouse. It was not until 1869 that this growth was checked by a new Act and magistrates once more licenced all premises. Most beerhouse keepers like Garbutt at Five Houses did the work alongside their other jobs, and the beerhouse was part of their home. It may be that Garbutt's wife Anne did the majority of the serving and running of the place.

William Garbutt perhaps. London Characters by George Cruikshank, 1827. Published by Joseph Robins. Courtesy S P Lohia Collection.

The body remained on the table at the beerhouse after George died around half past two in the afternoon (although Garbutt refused to sell beer in that period), and an autopsy eventually took place there on the Monday following. The inquest jury also visited it on Tuesday, as did his sister, falling upon the coffin with tears and comforted by the Garbutts. Finally on the Wednesday, six days after the shooting, a sizeable funeral procession came to Five Houses, led by his employer Jardine, who took the body to Blackburn for a service of burial. Over a thousand people attended, and Jardine offered a reward for the apprehension of his employee's killer.

Wright, a local landowner, sent some of his men to help with the funeral and carry the oak coffin and twelve locals, including Whittle's father, helped to put the coffin in the carriage. There is no evidence of Peter Ainsworth, owner of Smithills Hall and organiser of the shooting party, involving himself or his servants in the proceedings.

Reward Notice from the *Blackburn Gazette* of the time. Offered by William Jardine, Henderson's employer, on 11 November 1838 for information leading to the detection of his killer. Public domain.

The evidence against James Whittle

James Whittle was twenty-two at the time of the killing. The family rented a cottage at Five Houses from the Garbutts and comprised: father John, a small farmer and labourer looking after fields on the top of the moor; mother Alice; brother Charles also a collier; and sister Ruth, a washerwoman. He was thus local to the crime, and on the day of the murder had taken the day off from his work as a collier at Ainsworth's mine, close to the area of the shooting.

Whittle also had a reputation as an effective poacher on Smithills Estate and the surrounding moorlands and had access to shotguns. His friend Matthew Lambert's evidence at the inquest makes clear that Whittle borrowed shotguns regularly from him, no doubt allowing Lambert to benefit from a regular supply of game birds at his inn (then the Moor Gate Inn and now the Blundell Arms).

It was common in those times for innkeepers to sell locals freshly caught game. He said on 8 November he had lent Whittle a single-barrelled fowling piece with percussion cap and some shot. Mary Cross, Lambert's niece who worked at his inn, said she had seen Whittle bringing back the gun and two warm dead grouse between half past twelve and one o'clock on the day of the murder. However,

Moor Gate Inn, now Blundell Arms, the pub run by Whittle's friend Matthew Lambert, and place of the inquest. Public houses were frequently used for inquests in this period, and this old inn seems to have the remains of a courthouse attached. Courtesy Horwich Heritage.

Whittle worked regularly down the mine and was arrested there on the day after the shooting. Both Peter Ainsworth and Wright, whose land abutted Ainsworth's, had complained to his father about his poaching. Mrs Lambert said at the trial that Mr Orrell, steward of Wright's estate, had been sent to his father to complain. Additionally, Ainsworth believed James to be workshy, asking him as he led his arrest, how 'he gained a living not attending to his work more than he did'. William Garbutt testified that he had seen Whittle firing at birds that morning between eight and ten o'clock, but then Whittle said to him 'it was not worth shooting', presumably because of the increasingly misty conditions. It is clear from this and many other witness statements that James lied about not taking a gun out on the morning of the murder, but as his lawyer said at his trial this may be because he feared being charged with poaching, which had some severe legal penalties.

The fact that he appears to have been an excellent shot, there are suggestions he was known to win prizes at local fairs for his prowess, may indeed be seen as a mark in his favour, since the close-range shooting of the victim was brutally and clumsily done. Some witnesses said the body showed signs of the gun being placed against Henderson's ear where there were clear powder burns. An expert on shotguns and the surgeon at the autopsy both testified at his trial that the shot used to kill Henderson was all No. 3 shot (the surgeon George Wolstenholme weighing the six pieces he found in the brain and bringing examples to show the jury). Lambert's gun contained No. 4 shot, with No. 2 in his bag. Lambert's gun seems to be the only one on the moor that day that was looked at closely, although James Corliss the gamekeeper leading the shooting party, at the trial said he used 'no 3 shot when the birds are wild' but 'some persons in the group used no 2 or 3'. If this evidence is to be accepted, the only guns we know of on the moor that lunchtime with No. 3 shot were those of the shooting party.

Photograph ©Tony Greenwood.

In addition, there are no local testimonies that place Whittle near the scene of the crime at the right time, and his behaviour after the shooting does not suggest a guilty man. He went to visit his friend Lambert for the afternoon where he discussed the rumours of the killing sensibly, and he went to work as usual the next day.

We also have the few words of the dying man, who had enough remaining sight to recognise James Fletcher who came to help him and probably knew James

Whittle: 'Oh Jamie, Jamie, they have robbed me. Damn them'. This suggests both a motive for the killing and the plurality of the attackers. The words were confirmed at the inquest by Whewell and Fletcher, who were both with Henderson. There were also signs of Henderson's pockets being emptied, though not his pack. It is one of the interesting differences between the trial and the inquest evidence that the use of the plural is lost at the trial. Garbutt for example changes Mary Entwistle's words in his trial evidence from 'Run Mr Garbutt *they* have shot the Scotsman!' to '*somebody* has killed the Scotsman'. Although many witnesses suggest that Whittle was shooting on the moor that morning, at around the time of the killing between twelve-fifteen and twelve-thirty he seems to be nearer Five Houses than the mine. He was seen at noon by Sarah Lomax, whose cottage was next door to the Whittles, and at ten past twelve by Anne Garbutt crossing in front of their windows, so going in the other direction from the killing. Garbutt also said that when Mary ran down the road shouting for help, having found the body, 'Whittle was at my right hand'.

Two witnesses' evidence remain problematic for Whittle. Burrell, Henderson's friend, gave clear and impressively honest evidence of an encounter with a young man with a gun who he met on the road, after he left the beerhouse but before the killing. The young man offered to show him a better track down the hill, and when he refused and looked back the man appeared to be levelling the gun at him. However, although he said the man was similar to Whittle, he was not sure it was him, and he probably knew James since his father John Whittle was one of his customers.

The other problem witness, Joseph Halliwell from Skipton, who was working in Bolton at the time of the killing, was brought specially to the trial at some expense and gave some very confused evidence of a ride over the moors to buy a heifer, in which he claimed he saw the body in the ditch and Whittle running away with a gun. He did identify Whittle at the inquest after his arrest, but this was not a line up; presumably he was just asked if the

Detail from 'Episodes in the trial of Dr G H Lamson at the Central Criminal Court', 1882. Wood engraving. Courtesy Wellcome Collection.

single prisoner was the man he saw running away. Whittle's lawyer's cross examination at the trial made great play of Halliwell's belief that he could see green buttons on the man's waistcoat, even though he said he was thirty yards away and the fog distance was only ten yards!

There were many signs Halliwell was drunk at the time, and he told no one of what he had seen when he visited the beerhouse on his horse later for more drink. It was also odd that he apparently carried so much money with him that day (he said he had £304 on him which he claimed was part of his business buying and selling cattle, but this was an enormous sum that could have bought sixty or more cows). He also had a piece of Henderson's skull which he said was given to him by a young Irish couple he met on the road, although no other witnesses reported seeing them. Both claims make him seem rather a suspicious character, and possibly one more intimately involved in the shooting and its possible cover up than he claimed. Generally, his evidence was laughed at and dismissed by the Liverpool trial jury, who announced in their verdict specifically that they did not believe him.

'Men of the Day No. 4' by Alfred Thompson. *Vanity Fair* 5 March 1870. From the collection of Tony Greenwood.

Finally, Whittle was wearing his holiday best blue clothes that morning, not his black dirty collier's outfit. He wore them also for the inquest and trial. They were the only good clothes he owned. The killing was at close range, but no one at the trial or inquest remarked on any blood damage or splatter on the outfit, or indeed evidence of green buttons. There is little doubt that if evidence of blood spatter were there, it would be mentioned.

The defence statement by Whittle's lawyer Mr Wilkins at the end of the trial, and noted in the *Liverpool Mail* of 4 April 1839, suggests for the following reasons he was not guilty: the lack of any real motive; the behaviour of Whittle after the murder; the shot recovered from the head of Henderson at the autopsy did not match those in Whittle's borrowed gun; that if he lied about his movements that morning it was because he was afraid of being arrested for poaching; that Halliwell's evidence was difficult to believe and why did he have over £300 on him on the day of the murder; and finally that Burrell did not make his identification certain, and even if it was Whittle, he did not seriously threaten Burrell.

It was almost eleven in the evening when the jury returned to deliver their verdict, after only a few minutes' deliberation. Whittle's other lawyer Taylor describes the court in a later memoir as unusually crowded with candles burning. The trial jury felt that there was sufficient reasonable doubt not to convict Whittle, the evidence being mainly circumstantial. When the jury announced not guilty 'a tumultuous round of approval resonated through the court'. The lawyer wrote, 'The prisoner's father, an old man, got within the dock, and father and son were locked in each other's arms'.[4] Afterwards, 'father and son and friends hastened out of court together'. Significantly the judge agreed with the verdict, saying to the jury before their deliberations that if they felt the evidence was wholly circumstantial they could acquit Whittle, and after the verdict he said that they had taken the 'safer side'.

The shooting party

The term 'shooting party' on the moor on the day of the murder suggests it was a group of wealthy friends of Peter Ainsworth being entertained for the weekend; going out to shoot game with his gamekeeper and possibly with some beaters to set up the birds, and perhaps also a superior picnic lunch sent out from the Hall. In many of these cases the local paper would afterwards publish their names and the number of birds each member shot. The gamekeeper Corliss said in his questionable evidence at the trial that the party were 'not local men but shooting guests of Mr Ainsworth'. However, when we look closely at the individuals in the party, the evidence suggests that they were far from wealthy friends and visiting dignitaries, and many were based and working in the Bolton area.

Photograph
©Tony Greenwood

First it was an unusual choice of day to go game shooting. By the time the group walked up the hill from Smithills Hall around noon, the fog had really descended, and there is no evidence in the testimonies that any birds had been shot by them. James Fletcher at the inquest said that 'it was not such a day as a sportsman would select for shooting, it was so misty'. This also calls into question Corliss' evidence that he had acted as their beater and could see all the shooting party all the time.

He was the only one of the party to give evidence, to be briefly questioned or officially attend the inquest and trial. His evidence was very contradictory. He was questioned by Whittle's solicitor about Roger Horrocks, the man hiding in the turfcess. The only explanation Corliss gave is barely creditable: 'they were meeting in low places until the birds came over'. It is reported in inquest evidence that Fletcher pointed out to his daughter, 'It's rare game for the poachers today, for the keepers can't see them'. So why did the shooting party go on the hillside that day, and what kind of men were they?

> The Turf Cess. The term seems to be old English in origin and links two terms. 'Turf' being usually used to describe the cutting of peat which was dried and used on house fires and for cooking. 'Cess' as in cesspool seems likely to have links with an outside toilet for the use of nearby dwellings. It is doubtful Five Houses had such facilities indoors, and it was common in this period to have some basic facilities for communal use in poorer housing. It is not clear exactly what such facilities contained but it is likely they might have included a seat over a pit and possibly some kind of cover for inclement weather, thus providing Horrocks with somewhere to hide.

Nineteenth century nightwatchman with his usual stick to deter wrong doers. 'Watchman' from London Characters by George Cruikshank, 1827. Published by Joseph Robins. Courtesy S P Lohia Collection.

There were five men that met with Corliss that morning and their names were recorded later by William Garbutt: Roger Horrocks; Wright Crompton; John Ridings; Isaac Ireland; and Bartholomew Ince. However, to these five names we might add a possible sixth man. In his trial evidence Corliss talks of taking a party of six on the hill, but we have only five names and no one appears to have clarified the comment. In his booklet on the Ainsworth family, Bill Jones writes that Peter Ainsworth was on the hill with the party that morning.[5] If Ainsworth were the sixth man, it would explain why he appeared so speedily to remove the party from being questioned. When we look at their backgrounds all of the five appear to be working-class men, and probably all would have been paid to attend. The *Bolton Chronicle* of 9 June 1838 gave an account of Horrocks, a member of the Bolton Watch, being loath to attend court as a witness on another matter, even at the request of a magistrate, unless he was paid to do so.[6] Both he and John Hardman, another member of the Watch, had witnessed a robbery and in the end only Hardman attended court.

Most of the shooting party had associations with keeping the peace in Bolton. In 1838, new police forces were beginning to be set up in major towns and cities, but many of the new urban centres still relied on watchmen at night to prevent theft and trouble. They were either private ones employed by local businesses, or public ones set up by the councils. Isaac Ireland and Roger Horrocks were both employed as nightwatchmen in Deansgate, Bolton, and John Ridings became a new policeman there. Ireland never married and was so proud of this position that it is noted on his burial stone in Tonge Cemetery: 'for 27 years was a night watchman in Deansgate'. He died on 20 October 1861 aged seventy-two.

Added to this information, it is clear by looking at local newspaper archives, that some of the party may have been suspected of being involved in violence and dishonesty. Horrocks is remarkably interesting in this regard. The *Manchester Times* of 17 November 1838 particularly comments on him. 'Roger Horrocks was one of the Bolton Watch found in a turf cess with a gun by his side in very suspicious circumstances'.[7] An article in the *Bolton Chronicle* of May 1838, some few months before the killing, saw him charged with an assault on William Norman, 'a respectable looking man', in Deansgate at midnight.[8] Asked twice where he was going, Horrocks did not like his answer (Norman was on his way home with two companions), and struck him in the eye with a club, felling him to the ground where he lay senseless for several minutes. The surgeon who attended said the blow was extremely dangerous, and the newspaper pointed out that Horrocks' reputation was to treat others in a similar manner. It is interesting that the magistrate said at the time that had Horrocks been a public not private watchman, he would have sent him to trial in Liverpool with a possible more serious sentence. As it was, he was cautioned with a £3 fine and costs of 16s. The reference in the *Manchester Times* to Horrocks being 'a member of the Bolton watch' makes clear they are almost certainly the same man.

Photograph
©Barbara Winder.

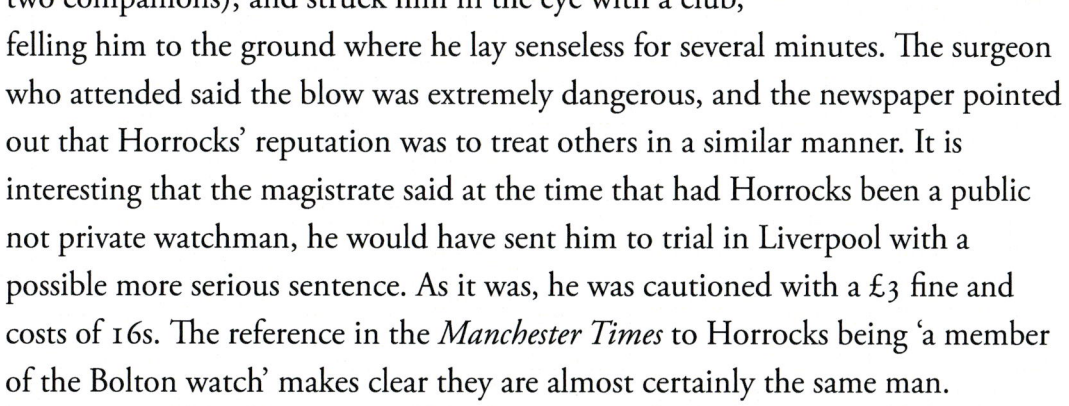

In August 1846, the *Bolton Chronicle* reported another case involving Horrocks. Two witnesses saw him with Thomas Greenhalgh, a collier from Westhoughton, in a public house in Deansgate. Greenhalgh said he had one sovereign and a half sovereign in his waistcoat pockets when leaving the public house, and a man 'like a policeman' came behind him on Oxford Road, pushed him across the road and down a narrow lane into some stumps.[9] The man tried to take his money and eventually succeeded, but in the struggle Greenhalgh was pushed down 'the brow and into the brook'. Greenhalgh identified Horrocks as the man, as did others present. Horrocks denied knowing any of the witnesses or being present but was committed for trial in Liverpool later that year on highway robbery.

A policeman from the Metropolitan Police in the 1840s. Illustration by Sharron Clayman.

John Ridings is described as 'a new policeman' in a *Bolton Chronicle* article of Saturday 17 August 1843.[10] He was in court charged by Lambert Heaton, 'a teetotaler', of obtaining money under false pretences. The article says that Ridings went to Heaton's house pretending to be the real Sergeant Beech of the police force, and took him to the lock up, but on the way he offered to let him go for five shillings and then dropped it to three shillings, which Heaton paid. In the end the case was dismissed because of lack of witnesses. Ridings seems also to have been a blacksmith suggesting he was strong and muscular, and later also became a spinner in the mills. The *Bolton Chronicle* of 7 February 1852 has him living in Crook Street with his family and young baby. One Saturday night he arrived home drunk, kicked over his hot meal in a temper and scalded his baby to death.[11] The inquest decided it was an accidental event as the baby was already extremely ill. Wright Crompton is also associated with affrays. In the *Bolton Chronicle* of Saturday 17 December 1836, we find an account of a beating he received from two men who objected to him assaulting a seventy-year-old man, John Stott.[12]

An early version of a truncheon with local coat of arms which acted as a warrant card. This has Whitbury, a village in Hampshire on it. Courtesy Science Museum Groups and Sir Henry Wellcome's Collection.

Thus at least some of the group seem to be physically fit men in their thirties and forties, prone to violence, and probably unused to guns, although four carried them on the day of the killing. The most likely reason for them being there, given Ainsworth's problems with poachers on his land, was to seek poachers out and deter them. It may be that in the mist the young Scotsman with his long stick and travelling pack looked to be carrying a shotgun or rabbits, and to be a potential poacher. The circumstances of the shooting: the creeping up without warning; the brutality of the shot to the face removing his eye; and the possible robbery from pockets, very much mirror the two newspaper accounts of Horrocks' attacks on passers-by.

Most newspapers of the time report that Horrocks was found hiding in a turf cess with a gun by his side. It was an unpleasant place to choose to shelter, and he was quickly arrested. However very soon after the arrest Peter Ainsworth arrived, no doubt alerted by his gamekeeper, and all the shooting party were quickly freed. Neither at the inquest or trial were they asked to attend or answer questions about their accounts of that day or what they were wearing, nor were their guns taken at the time and examined, as Whittle's was.

A young poacher carrying rabbits, as George Henderson may have looked in the mist carrying his pack. Illustration by Sharron Clayman.

A possible cover up?

Apart from the quick release of the arrested shooting party by Ainsworth, and Ainsworth's move to arrest Whittle the day after, there are hints in the inquest and trial of attempts to find evidence against Whittle regardless of its veracity. A thirteen-year-old boy, William Stott, who said he'd seen Whittle inside the cabin at eleven in the morning, also added that someone had offered him £100 to keep his evidence the same: 'I was told those who told the prisoner had done it would have £100'. A large life-changing sum for poor folk in those times. Although there was some limited attempt at the trial to find out who had told him so, his evidence remained vague on the matter. Joseph Halliwell, the corn dealer from Skipton, the one person who claimed to have seen Whittle running from the killing but was not believed by the jury because of his drunken state and confused account, was found and brought to the inquest and trial at some expense and trouble. It is not clear who made sure he attended, but someone of means seems to have been very keen to see Whittle found guilty.

From the site of George Henderson's murder looking across the moor and towards Bolton and Horwich. Photograph ©Tony Greenwood.

In contrast, a lack of support was associated with attempts to fund Whittle's defence at his trial. Taylor tells us in his autobiography that he worked on the case in February and March 1838, suspecting he would not be paid.[13] It was only the night before the trial in a hotel when he and Wilkins, another young lawyer, met to discuss the case that they decided to go ahead regardless of funding. Taylor had been promised payment from a group of Whittle's friends, but none had come forward. No one spoke in Whittle's defence, and it was likely that many were afraid to do so. His father tried to at the inquest but was led away in tears. However, whilst produced for the prosecution, the witnesses very often gave useful evidence about his movements which added to his defence case. Magistrates in this period were few, wealthy and powerful. They were effectively the major engines of the local judicial system. Most of the folk on the moor depended on Ainsworth or Wright, the major landowners, for their livelihood. Whittle and his father took five years after the trial to pay off their lawyers' £50 fee, but they did so.[14]

When looking at different accounts of the trial, it is interesting to note that the further the newspapers were removed from Peter Ainsworth's influence, the more positive they were about Whittle. In fact, we know that Ainsworth made the *Bolton Chronicle* apologise for saying Horrocks was found in suspicious circumstances after the killing, even though both the *Manchester Times* and *The Liverpool Mail* also said so.[15] The *Bolton Chronicle* of 24 November 1838 said they should not have reported that Roger Horrocks was found thus and that it was 'from information given to us with a satisfactory reference'. They now accepted he was there 'with four other persons in the company of a gamekeeper in the pursuit of game' and 'not the strictest imputation ought to rest upon Roger Horrocks from being found aforesaid'.

The way Whittle was described in the newspapers also varied markedly. *The Liverpool Mail* called him 'a well looking man' and described him later at trial as a 'tall and rather good-looking young man with dark eyes and hair. He stood firmly at the bar'.[16] They reported that Lambert's young niece, a maid at his inn, described Whittle as 'always a peaceable, good tempered, well behaved young man'. However, the *Bolton Chronicle* account of the inquest said he was about twenty-two years, six feet tall, and 'of morose unpleasant appearance...a known poacher', and further had formed 'an illicit connection with a young woman in the area, who he should have married a week before'.[17]

A month later the Watch Committee's first meeting in Bolton, of which Ainsworth was a member, reports that it would no longer use the *Bolton Chronicle* to place advertisements, as it 'being so scurrilous and personal a newspaper'.[18] *The Blackburn Standard* of Wednesday 21 November 1838 echoes some of the *Chronicle's* words about Whittle: 'The prisoner who is about twenty two years of age and nearly six feet in height possesses a dark morose unpleasing countenance but a strong athletic form. He has long been a lawless dissolute and reckless character and but for the forbearance of the neighbouring gentry would long ago have been incarcerated for his propensity to poaching, to which he was so much addicted that he never thought of pursuing his lawful avocations while he could obtain subsistence by the sale of his midnight spoil'.[19] It also mentioned his girlfriend. Even the wording seems suspiciously similar and prejudiced, especially its inclination to praise the 'neighbouring gentry'.

After the trial, the signs of a cover up continued. Horrocks seems particularly to have led a charmed life. After the incident involving his attack on Thomas Greenhalgh in May 1846, which involved theft and assault and which was sent to the Liverpool Assizes as highway robbery, the trial took place in August 1846. Unlike Whittle who was jailed on remand for six months before his trial, Horrocks was allowed bail, thanks to an interesting supporter, the Mayor of Bolton, Stephen Blair Esquire, a well-known Mason, and friend of Peter Ainsworth.[20] The *Bolton Chronicle* has numerous accounts of the two attending events, entertainments, and

Etching of James Whittle from *Blackburn Gazette* November 1838. Courtesy Gordon Hunt who found it in the attic of his Bamber Bridge cottage.

Peter Ainsworth (1790-1870) the owner of Smithills Hall and organiser of the shooting party. From *The Ainsworth Family of Smithills Hall*. Courtesy The Friends of Smithills Hall.

meetings in this period together. Both were later to become MPs. At Horrocks' trial in Liverpool all the prosecution witnesses decided not to give identification evidence, and he was acquitted.

We gain a few telling glimpses of James Whittle from the evidence given at the inquest and his trial, and there was also one interesting question he asked at the inquest, which was ignored and remained unanswered. The account of William, son of James Fletcher, who walked with him for a short distance that morning shows a playful friendly man enjoying his day off. The account of Matthew Lambert after the killing that afternoon shows a man concerned by the circumstances of the killing and feeling the killer deserved to be punished. At the inquest, Whittle asked one question, 'if a person were shooting on the moor without a certificate (licence), whether or not that person might shoot them?' The new shooting licence laws had just come into force in 1831, which allowed those purchasing licences to shoot game birds over a specified area.

1831 Licence to sell game caught by an authorised person. Courtesy UK Government, Open Government Licence v3.0.

Lambert had one, and his niece Mary Cross said, 'My uncle had the right of shooting over the moor'. However licences were outside the means of ordinary folk. Whittle's question suggests he thought Henderson had been shot by people without licences who were looking for poachers, but no one seems to have recognised the question's significance at the time. Or if they did, watched on by

Peter Ainsworth who asked numerous questions and almost seems to have taken over the inquest, they decided it was best to ignore it. It is one of the few hints we have that some people were aware of the significance of the shooting party in the killing but were afraid to say anything directly.

Indeed, myths and legends remain even today about Whittle. There are tales of sudden blindness, early death, and death bed confessions, but no evidence. In fact, what is available in the national records about Whittle's later life seems somewhat ordinary. In the 1841 census, no longer at Five Houses, he was with his father John and mother Alice on New Road, Halliwell. He appears to have married his girlfriend Mary Rigby as soon as he had paid off his lawyer, at St Mary's, Deane on 12 June 1843. Both were of full age and from Halliwell, he a collier.

They had already had a child together. By 1851 he had moved to 47 New Road, a few doors from his parents, with his wife and several children. However, from then he moves further from Bolton with his growing family. First to Bury in 1861 and then Rochdale in 1871 where his children took work in the mills after his wife died. His father died in 1867 and is buried at St Paul's, Halliwell. The most likely death for James is in Rochdale in 1880 aged sixty-six.

St Mary's Church, Deane, where James Whittle married Mary Rigby on 12 June 1843, is the oldest church in Bolton. Courtesy St Mary's, Deane.

AT THE ERECTION OF SCOTCHMAN'S STUMP

Last week's story of history being repeated at Winter Hill aroused the interest of a Westhoughton man, Mr. A. W. Gregory, who carried a half-plate camera to the moors 47 years ago to record the actual erection of Scotchman's Stump. In this group, taken at the time, are Mr. Fairclough (front), Tom Hutchinson and B. F. Davies (kneeling), with Mr. Hutchinson's daughter, May, on left, and H. D. Davies (standing to the left of the stump). Third from the right is Mr. Hutchinson's father-in-law, Mr. Heywood. The names of the two children to the right are unknown and the others standing are believed to be the gamekeeper and a friend, a Bolton solicitor and two men from Horwich on the extreme right.

From *Stumped* by Roy Davies. Courtesy Horwich Heritage.

Stump memorial as it is today. Photograph ©Tony Greenwood.

Despite the disapproval of powerful local landowners, ordinary Bolton people have continued to remember the death of George Henderson with their memorial on Winter Hill near where he fell. The first memorial was made of wood and erected shortly after the killing, but quickly failed to survive because of souvenir hunters and the weather. The second was of stone, but since then the memorial has consisted of a tall metal pole with a coloured plaque.[21] In 1901 William Lever (later Lord Leverhulme) asked Chorley Council for it to be removed, feeling that there 'should not be a perpetual memory of a murder'. There followed a dispute as to whether the memorial was on Chorley or Rivington land, with neither council taking responsibility, so Lever's request was denied, a rare event. In 1912 the post was part of the evidence for the ongoing right of way dispute that had led to the earlier mass trespass, as it marked the old way over the moor. Small groups continue to look after and preserve it to this day. In all this story, it is important we too do not forget the victim.

So, who killed George Henderson and why? For the reasons already given, it does not appear to be James Whittle. The most likely candidates seem to be certain members of the shooting party that Peter Ainsworth of Smithills Hall sent on to the moor that day. Some were no doubt innocent bystanders, but others included men with a record of brutality and dishonesty. It seems likely they were sent out that day not to shoot birds but to deter poachers, but it is unlikely they were sent to shoot to kill. Whittle's lawyer at the trial argued that the shooting was accidental. However, the killing was brutal and at close range. It may have been accidental; men using guns as clubs to frighten, only to have them discharge, but at the very least it was manslaughter, and the men who witnessed it or heard of it, especially anyone in a position of authority or influence, were prepared to see another man hang, rather than admit what they knew. In doing that, they also showed little care or compassion for the innocent victim.

Jack O' Nandies

*Chapter 6
by Laura Kovaleva*

Photograph
©Tony Greenwood.

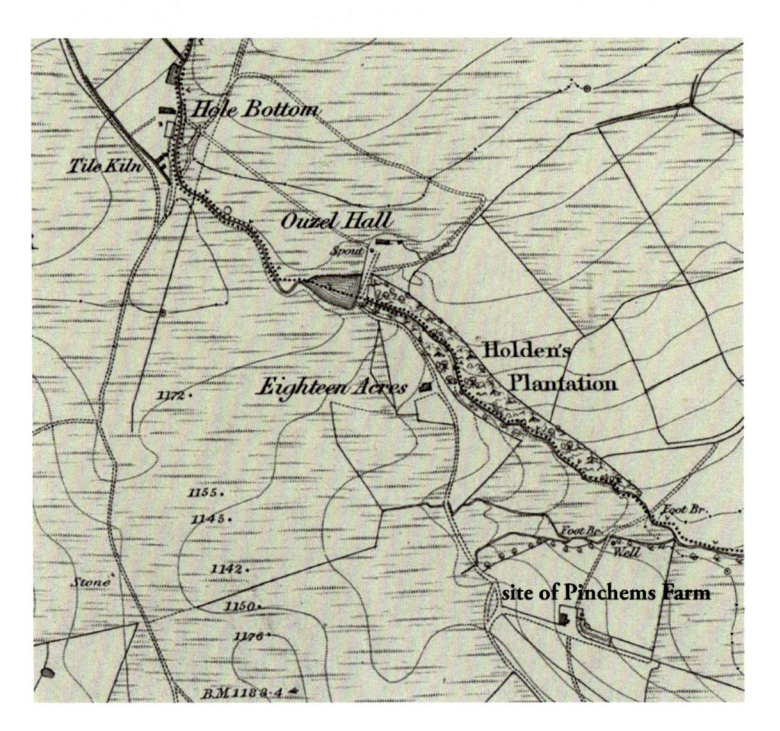

Ordnance Survey six-inch map, surveyed 1845-47. Courtesy National Library of Scotland.

Eighteen Acres Farm once stood on Burnt Edge and over the years was occupied by families of farmers and miners. In the 1840s it was home to John Heaton and his wife Alice. John was born in 1795 to a local family of yeoman farmers whose multiple members were living on various farms across Bolton. His father Nando Heaton was a farmer and weaver in the Heaton area.[1] John married his cousin Alice in 1836 and first they lived at Pinchems Farm, just next to Eighteen Acres, where John worked as a weaver before moving to Eighteen Acres itself.

Thanks to some newspaper reports of the time we can learn about John's character. In 1844 he was convicted for maltreatment of a neighbour's cow.[2] John found a Mr Eckersley's cow trespassing in one of his fields and 'beat it in a most brutal manner', breaking its hip and leg. As a result the animal had to be put to death. It is mentioned in the article that he had already been convicted for the same crime earlier. John was sentenced to three month's imprisonment.

In September of the following year John was charged again, this time for obstructing Mr Butcher, an inspector of weights and measures.[3] Butcher visited John's farm on the '5th instant' and requested him to find his scales and weights for inspection. John said that he had lent them to Thomas Schofield, his neighbour, and took Mr Butcher to the door to show him where Thomas lived. But as soon as the inspector stepped outside, John closed and bolted the door so the inspector could not re-enter the house. John was fined 20s. and costs of 11s. 6d.

His name appeared on the newspaper pages again the next year, but this time he was charged with a much more serious crime. As we already know, John was living with his wife Alice at Eighteen Acres Farm. Sadly, around 1843, Alice was struck by palsy resulting in muscle

From the *Bolton Chronicle*, 19 December 1846. Courtesy *The Bolton News*.

weakness, and she became bed ridden. The details of events tragically leading to Alice's death were described in an article published in the *Bolton Chronicle* on 19 December 1846.[4] Clearly Alice required a lot of care which John failed to provide. Once a week Alice's sister Nancy came to look after her and every time found Alice in a terrible state, she was very weak and covered in filth. Margaret Schofield, the Heaton's neighbour, sometimes visited Alice and fed her with wine, water and bread. Whenever Margaret asked John how Alice was, he said, 'She's living yet' or 'I don't know' or 'I have given her a potato or two'. After three years of suffering, Alice died. The state of her body when it was examined following her death led to a charge of manslaughter being instigated, and John was taken into custody.

Making more mischief

In spite of the terrible crime he committed, John was not charged, and he was released. Could he have bribed the court? He did not wait long to commit another offence, and in March 1847 he was charged with stealing coal from William Garbutt of Horwich.[5] John filled a sack with coal at a brick kiln but was seen by one of the carters. In self-defence he said that he did not take them – he was only going to do it! He had to pay a fine of £2 10s. 6d.

Surprisingly, just less than two years after the terrible death of his wife Alice, John remarried in September 1848. His new wife was fifty-eight-year-old Alice Greenhalgh (née Pendlebury), widow of John Greenhalgh, a blacksmith from Bob's Smithy Tavern. The tavern had been managed by the Greenhalgh family for generations and gets its name from the smithy which was located on the opposite side of the road.[6]

Eighteen Acres Farm ruins. Photograph ©Laura Kovaleva.

Bob's Smithy and Inn, 1910. Courtesy *The Bolton News*.

It is evident that John and Alice were living in Bob's Smithy after the marriage as in October 1850 John's name appeared in newspapers once again.[7] This time he was trying to sell rotten meat from diseased cows. Mr Fogg, the inspector, caught him in the Commercial Inn tap room with a basket of meat for sale. John was fined 40s. and costs. John and Alice did not have a long time together as Alice died in 1853, aged sixty-three. After that, traces of John are lost for several years.

Jack O' Nandies

The next interesting evidence about his life was discovered by chance while researching newspaper archives. It takes us to Scant Row, a terrace of nine stone cottages on Chorley Old Road not far from Bob's Smithy. The article 'Character. Inspector of Nuisances wanted at Heaton' published in the *Bolton Chronicle* on 18 February 1860 tells us about an eccentric character from Scant Row, widely known as Jack O' Nandies.[8] He has a 'confirmed taste for small pickings' and 'filled his tiny room which measures fifteen feet by nine, with useless lumber of all sorts, including old horse gears, pieces of carts, barrows, broken tools, sticks, old decayed clothes, rags, bones and offal'. Moreover, Jack bought the entire carcass of a cow, salted the whole and hung it in his room. 'The place which could be called his bed has never been cleaned or changed for years'. The stench was described as unbearable and the whole place compared with the ancient Augean stables.

Scant Row, now a terrace of nine Grade II Listed cottages on Chorley Old Road, near Bolton. Courtesy Plucas82, CC BY-SA 4.0.[9]

Surely, the above description reminds us of the already well-known character of John Heaton, whose stinginess and cruelty to animals we are familiar with. The 1861 census records confirm our assumption showing John Heaton, a widower of sixty-six, residing at 1 Scant Row. Shockingly, according to the newspaper article, despite the dirt and awful stench, there is a woman cohabiting with John. Her name remains unknown though it is really alarming to think that, knowing about his cruel and deceitful character, any woman was still willing to live with John.

The last piece of the puzzle to solve is to find out why John Heaton was widely known as Jack O' Nandies. First, Jack is a diminutive of John. Second, as we already know, John's father was called Nando Heaton. Consequently, John Heaton got the nickname of Jack O' Nandies which probably started off as Jack O' Nando's.

Over the next decade, John likely continued his life wandering about Bolton, collecting all kinds of rubbish to fill up his tiny home. He was getting older and weaker though, and by 1871 he had become an inmate at Bolton Union Workhouse.

He died there in 1871 aged seventy-six and was buried at Holy Trinity Church, Horwich. That was the end of Jack O' Nandies, one of the many Heatons, but whose notorious character would make people shudder for many years to come.

A CHARACTER.—INSPECTOR OF NUISANCES WANTED AT HEATON.—In a mean dwelling called a cottage, at Scant-row, Heaton, near Horwich-moor, there resides an eccentric person, popularly known as "Jack o' Nandies." He is now getting into years, and has a confirmed taste for small pickings-up as he goes about, which he has accumulated until his domicile almost rivals the description given of most notorious misers. About Christmas last he bought, for 25s., the entire carcase of a cow, which he took "home," and having flayed, salted the whole, and hung it up for protracted use. Last week he became owner of a putrid dead calf, which he treated in a similar manner. His place—one room only—measures fifteen feet by nine, and is seven feet from floor to ceiling. It is filled with useless lumber of all sorts, old horse gears, pieces of carts, barrows, agricultural and other broken implements and tools, sticks, old decayed clothes, rags, bones, and offal. There is what is called a bed in the place, and a most miserable berth it is; neither it nor the hovel in which it stands having been cleaned or changed for years; indeed, there is only about space enough uncovered for two persons to stand upright on. And, strange to say, a woman lives and cohabits with "Jack" amidst all this dirt and discomfort, and filth and foulness, vileness, and want of ventilation. To one unaccustomed to the odour, the stench of the place, we are told, is unbearable; and yet there are no powers in operation to clear and cleanse this caricature of a home for human beings, which is in reality somewhat like the ancient Augean stable.

From the *Bolton Chronicle*, 18 February 1860.
Courtesy *The Bolton News*.

Bolton Union Workhouse.
Courtesy *The Bolton News*.

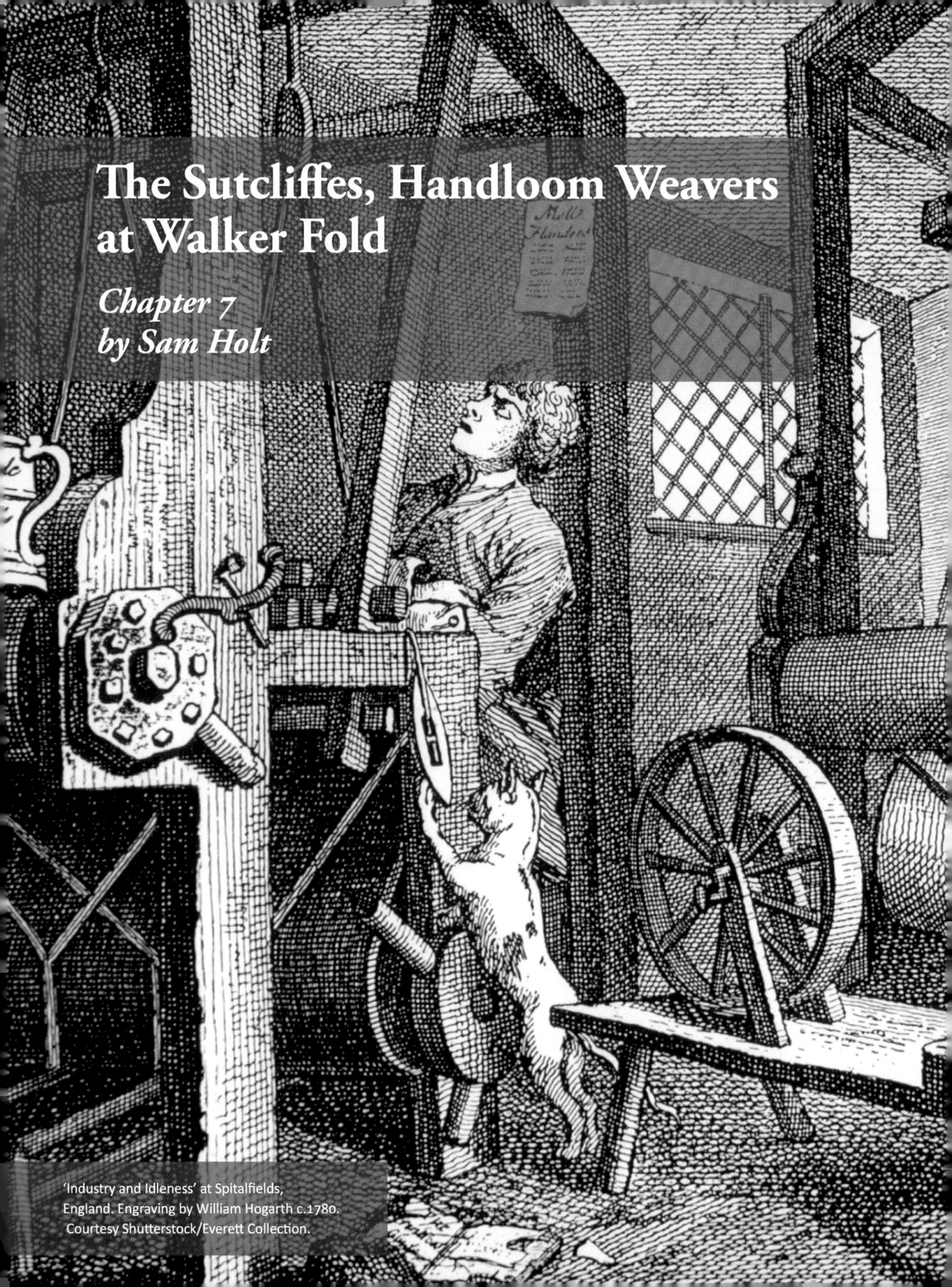

The Sutcliffes, Handloom Weavers at Walker Fold

*Chapter 7
by Sam Holt*

'Industry and Idleness' at Spitalfields, England. Engraving by William Hogarth c.1780. Courtesy Shutterstock/Everett Collection.

The Industrial Revolution of the late eighteenth and early nineteenth centuries had a profound effect on a number of trades, and cotton was amongst the first to become industrialised with the use of power-driven machinery.[1] Perhaps the most affected by the mechanisation of the cotton trade were the handloom weavers who wove spun cloth at home. Over time, weavers became unable to compete with the productivity of mechanised weaving in factories and saw their wages plummet, eventually making it impossible for those dependent on the trade to earn a living. The transition of cotton weaving from a primarily domestic and cottage-based industry to a factory system represented the development of a new urbanised society which is often depicted as 'the cruel displacement of the hardy domestic textile worker by the dark satanic mill'.[2] The adoption of power loom weaving and the replacement of the hardy, rustic handloom weaver with the urban mill hand was gradual but inevitable, and it had a dramatic effect on the pattern of life and work for the weaver and his family.

Weavers at Walker Fold

The Sutcliffes are an example of the effects of industrialisation on weavers. They were a family of weaver-farmers living at Walker Fold from the late 1830s, who by 1851 were concentrating solely on farming. In 1841 there were a total of eleven separate households at Walker Fold, many of which were likely split dwellings, not unusual in the early nineteenth century. The adjoining cottages numbers seven and eight, which became Grade II listed buildings in 1966, are thought to originally have been a single dwelling and may have been separated as a consequence of these kinds of living conditions. The exact address of the Sutcliffe family is not given on the 1841 Census but this cottage is most likely where they resided as it was outfitted for handloom weavers with its specifically designed windows.

Cottages at Walker Fold in winter c.1944. Original watercolour painting by Karen Holt.

OLD HAND LOOM.

'Old Hand Loom' postcard. Richard Haworth & Co., Ltd, Cotton Spinners, Manufacturers & Doublers; Tatton Mills, Ordsall, Manchester. From the collection of Sam Holt.

As a rural cotton-weaving household this is typical of a mixed-use fold where weaving was combined with the running of a small farm, in this case a dairy farm. Smallholders were quite commonplace at the time and perhaps would have kept a few animals on a patch of land. The average work day of a farmer-weaver family would have consisted of farm work for a portion of the day, such as milking morning and night then spinning or weaving for the rest of the day. This would vary depending on the season with weavers likely to have been pressed into fieldwork during the harvest.[3]

Advancements and inventions

Ground-breaking advances were made throughout the eighteenth century that would come to influence the weaving process, making it possible for weavers to produce more cloth in a shorter period of time. Traditionally, women in the family would have been the spinners or spinsters, while a single man or older boy would control the loom. This would change with the invention of John Kay's Flying Shuttle in 1733, which allowed the freeing up of the weaver's hands as they no longer had to throw the shuttle across the loom with one hand and catch it with the other. The shuttle could now be fired back and forth across the loom by the weaver using paddles operated by pulling a string, while the foot pedal mechanism was pressed to create space for the shuttle to fly through between the warp threads.

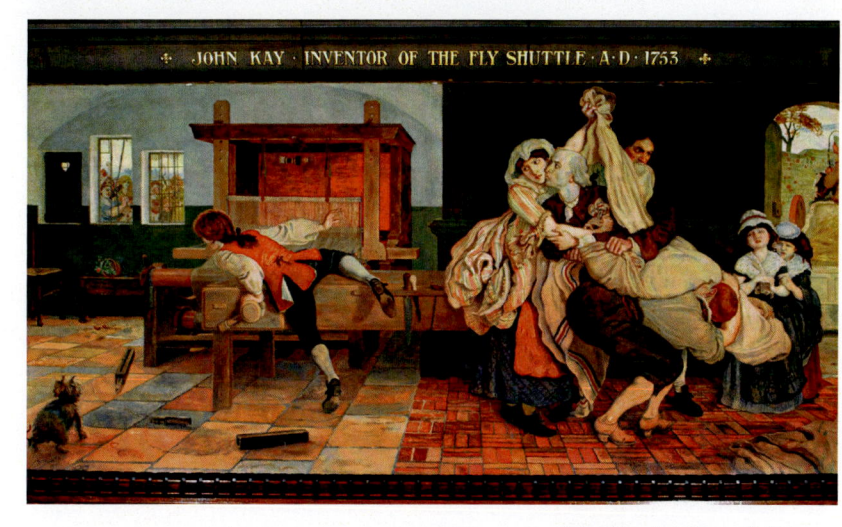

This greatly increased the pace of the weaving process and meant that it was no longer possible for spinners to keep up; one weaver alone could now potentially produce an output that required sixteen spinners to produce enough yarn.[4] It also meant that a single person could weave wider fabric which had previously required the work of two pairs of hands. As a result there was resistance to the shuttle's invention from both spinners and weavers. Ford Madox Brown's mural of the flying shuttle's inventor depicts Kay being smuggled out of his house in a bundle of cloth before rioters can break in through the windows and destroy his invention.[5]

'John Kay, Inventor of the Fly Shuttle A.D. 1753' by Ford Madox Brown, a mural at Manchester Town Hall. Courtesy Manchester City Council.

The entire weaving process would involve the whole family. Whilst weaving itself would be carried out by a single person, others would help by setting up the warp, for instance. It is likely that the Sutcliffes spread the workload between each member of the family as the task of weaving for long hours was quite gruelling, with it not being uncommon for weavers to work late into the night to be on time.

Later in the eighteenth century James Hargreaves' Spinning Jenny and Samuel Crompton's Spinning Mule allowed for the spinning of multiple threads at once, which would provide weavers with a constant supply of yarn and led to a significant boom in trade due to the increase in production.

'Spinning Mule', 1779. Courtesy Bolton Council.

'Spinning Jenny', Hargeaves' multi spindle spinning frame, 1767. Line drawing or engraving. Courtesy Shutterstock/ Morphart Creation.

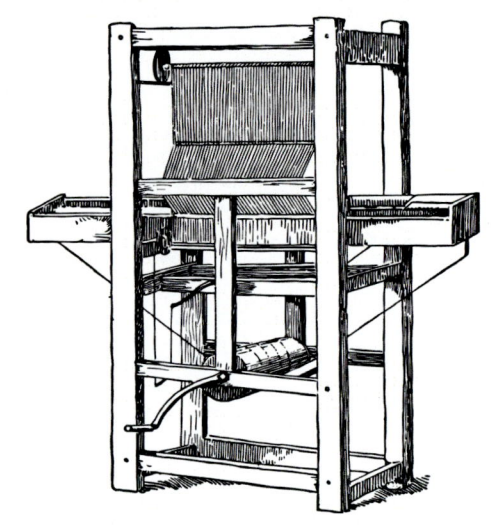

Cartwright's power loom, 1786, which eased the process of weaving fabric. Courtesy Shutterstock/ Morphart Creation.

Power loom weaving in a cotton mill in Lancashire, England c.1835. Engraving with modern watercolour. Courtesy Shutterstock/ Everett Collection.

The rise of the power loom

But it would not be long before the entire handloom weaving industry became victim to mechanisation when the weaving and spinning of cloth by hand was replaced by power looms. Originally invented and patented by Edmund Cartwright in the 1780s, the power loom could be operated by those unskilled in handloom weaving and was first powered by watermill, then steam engine.[6]

The adoption of such technology in some parts of Lancashire was belated compared to southern Lancashire where the handloom tradition was supposedly less strong. By 1835, only 12,000 out of 90,000 total power looms were in towns such as Preston, Blackburn, Burnley and Colne.[7] Bolton had 1500 looms and there was an inevitable and rapid increase of cotton mills with their number in Lancashire overall rising from three hundred in 1819 to almost a thousand by 1841.[8] Soon the power loom would make the demand for hand-spun cotton practically non-existent and the once booming trade would eventually be brought to its knees.

The decline of the handloom

The advent of cotton spinning in mills meant factory workers could produce greater quantities of cloth at low cost compared to their handloom counterparts, and this had a catastrophic effect on the earnings of weavers. Piece-rates plummeted from a comfortable minimum earning of 21s. a week in 1802 to 8s. 9d. by 1817 and eventually a measly 6s. 3d. in 1851.[9] By the 1840s the Sutcliffes were no doubt experiencing the effects of being squeezed out of the cloth market due to the nearby expansion of Dean Mills in the 1830s. At least those with farm holds like the Sutcliffes had other ways to supplement their income, others were not so fortunate.

'Old Mills, Barrow Bridge'. 1914 postcard, R. Close & Sons, Photographers, Horwich. From the collection of Sam Holt.

Weavers in the now growing urban areas suffered a dramatic change in their quality of life, often entire families were forced to survive on a solitary meal each day of oatmeal and water.[10] Left pauperised and demoralised by prolonged unemployment from the 1820s onwards, many were forced to depend on charitable foundations to sustain themselves and their families. Such desperate conditions led to industrial action and radicalism in weaver circles. Taking into account that many weavers had to work fourteen-hour days for little pay, one could see why many decided to change profession as the price of handwork dropped.[11]

The weaving way of life

In the early 1800s, a substantial proportion of those in Lancashire had been dependent on handloom weaving to earn a living, but the decline of their trade did far more than affect them economically, it was also a threat to their way of life.

There was a general reluctance by handloom weavers to enter factories for varying reasons, being far different from the domestic trade to which they were so accustomed.[12] Factories themselves often sought to employ unskilled workers, usually young women and children. Those from weaving families took up factory work where it was available and this may have been considered by some of the younger Sutcliffe siblings.

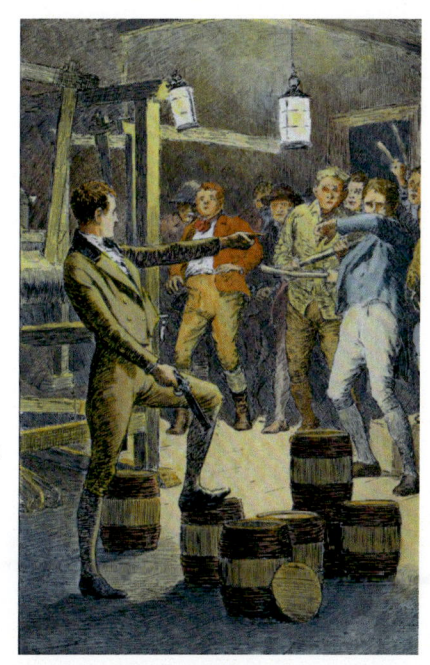

Luddites were an organisation formed to fight back against the industrialisation of weaving and other occupations. They took their name from a legendary leader, Ned Ludd of Leicestershire. The engraving shows a factory owner defending his factory against Luddites intent on destroying his mechanised looms between 1811-1816. Engraving with modern watercolour. Courtesy Shutterstock/Everett Collection.

Machines making cotton thread by performing mechanical versions of carding, drawing and roving in a mill in Lancashire, England c.1835. Engraving with modern watercolour. Courtesy Shutterstock/Everett Collection.

However, the domestic weaver had not been 'transformed overnight into a millhand' and many were either unable or unwilling to adapt to factory operations.[13] The lifestyle led by many weavers was very much in contrast to that of a mill worker who was restricted by the authority of their foreman. There was a certain freedom that came with being a domestic weaver, 'he could commence work where he liked, and leave off when he liked', which for many bred an independence of character that was incompatible with a factory setting.[14]

The life of a weaver would have been one surrounded by family, working together, living together and socialising together, and the decline of the handloom risked splitting up the household. Indeed, many have been eager to point out the underlying moral consequences of industrialisation on handloom weavers, particularly regarding rupturing the family unit.[15] One need only look to the Indian subcontinent to see the importance of weaving traditions for weaver communities and their families, traditions kept alive today although not without their struggles.

Weaver ladies in an Indian village with spinning wheel in the background at Kutch, India. Courtesy Shutterstock/mahig.

While industrialisation gave prosperity to many through increased wages and living conditions, it took away from the weavers the only way of life they had known for generations. The Sutcliffes seem to have been able to preserve this way of life in one form or another by becoming farmers, allowing them to stay together as a family unit. They were no doubt fortunate to be able to continue a discipline in which they had experience and that was compatible with their work attitude and way of life.

The Handloom Weaver's Song

The years weave in, and the years weave out,
And time like a shuttle flies,
And weaves the web of day and night
Across the eternal skies.

And flowers and light are woven in
The pattern of many a day,
For a happy some; while others weep
That the cloth is dull and grey.

Oh, weave the days and weave the nights! –
The shadow and the shine;
The sun that hopes and the stars that dream,
Through foul times and through fine.

Oh, weave the days and weave the nights!
And show the silver moon,
And the rustling trees and the fairy grove,
And the lass and the love-lorn loon.

Oh, weave the days and weave the nights
And the gold of the bridal ring;
And the silver grey of the aged head;
And the birds in the nest that sing.

The years weave in and the years weave out,
And time like a shuttle flies,
And some find faith, and some find doubt,
Few truth, and many, lies.

And the warp of the long, long years unrolls
And is crossed by the weft of the days,
And is making the cloth of finished souls,
With a pattern for blame or praise.

Oh, weave the days and weave the nights!
Weave on in joy or pain,
Whether our work be "fancy goods"
Or only common "plain."

Let the red sun rise and the white moon wane,
But work the Master's will,
Till warp and weft are together wrought
And the mystic machine is still.[16]

Allen Clarke, 1891

The Sutcliffes at Walker Fold

Eldest sibling James was a farmer of twenty-seven acres by 1851, although according to the electoral register of 1850 it was fourteen.[17] Living with him are some of his siblings who were once weavers, including two brothers working on the farm as agricultural labourers and a sister who was a dairy worker. While certainly not an easy life, the life of a farmer may have been much preferable to what the common urban weaver faced.

While the Sutcliffes may not have suffered as greatly as other weavers due to mechanisation in the weaving trade, they were not without their own misfortune. The 1840s and 50s saw several deaths in the family, the first being the youngest of the siblings, Thomas, who died in 1848 at the age of twenty-seven. He had married Mary Ann Longworth in 1844, a neighbour at Walker Fold, and together they had a son a year before his death. This was soon followed by another death in the family, as in 1849 sister Betty died aged thirty-two.

Holy Trinity Church, Horwich, cherry blossoms in spring. Original watercolour painting by Karen Holt.

Over the next few years the fortunes of the family would not change for the better as four more of the siblings died. First eldest sister Ellen, having married a Welsh surgeon in 1847 and relocated to Newcastle-under-Lyme, died in 1852. Brother Joseph died the same year. Tragedy compounded tragedy as sister Rachel and household head James both died within months of one another in 1854. All barring Ellen were buried at Holy Trinity Churchyard in Horwich.

In the space of six years, six of the siblings who were weavers at Walker Fold had passed away, their fate somewhat mirroring that of the handloom weavers. For the most part the Sutcliffes were spared the inevitable destruction of their way of life that many faced at this time. However, the once close-knit family of siblings was torn apart regardless as now there was only one living sibling, Ellis Sutcliffe. He would continue to live at Walker Fold as a farmer until his death in 1873 when, finally, the family of handloom weavers once so successful, ended with as much surety as the profession itself.

'The Breton Weaver'.
Paul Serusier, 1888.
Public domain.

The last of the weavers

From 1840 onwards the cotton handloom weaver was a rare sight but there were still those who continued the trade well into the late 1800s and even into the twentieth century, although they were small in number. The last holdouts were then very aged and consigned to operating in remote villages in obscurity.[18]

James Swinglehurst or 'J.S.', a young Boltonian and native of Barrow Bridge, who sadly died of consumption in his twenties, in his book *Summer Evenings with Old Weavers,* which was most likely written in the 1870s, gave an enthralling account detailing the perspective of these old men.[19] In it, the narrator attends customary meetings of weavers in a town that he refers to as 'Smokely', a pseudonym he uses for Bolton, where they tell him of the realities of being a weaver. Almost reminiscent of an ancient Greek symposium, the men discuss a variety of topics ranging from Chartism and their political philosophy to the smoking of tobacco. The author manages to capture the character of these old weavers in a poignant fashion as they regale him with tales of their youth, quote Shakespeare and joke of past courtships.

Chartism was a working-class political movement that emerged in the 1830s and rapidly spread across the UK. It was championed by many weavers and erupted over concerns regarding living standards for the working-class and their lack of political emancipation. In 1838 a six-point People's Charter was published that demanded: the vote for all working men over twenty-one; secret ballots; annual elections; payment of MPs; constituencies of equal size; and the removal of the property qualification for MPs. Five of these demands were met between 1858 and 1918. However, the movement was fizzling out by the time the first demand was addressed.

The Six Points
OF THE
PEOPLE'S CHARTER.

1. A VOTE for every man twenty-one years of age, of sound mind, and not undergoing punishment for crime.
2. THE BALLOT.—To protect the elector in the exercise of his vote.
3. NO PROPERTY QUALIFICATION for Members of Parliament —thus enabling the constituencies to return the man of their choice, be he rich or poor.
4. PAYMENT OF MEMBERS, thus enabling an honest tradesman, working man, or other person, to serve a constituency, when taken from his business to attend to the interests of the country.
5. EQUAL CONSTITUENCIES, securing the same amount of representation for the same number of electors, instead of allowing small constituencies to swamp the votes of large ones.
6. ANNUAL PARLIAMENTS, thus presenting the most effectual check to bribery and intimidation, since though a constituency might be bought once in seven years (even with the ballot), no purse could buy a constituency (under a system of universal suffrage) in each ensuing twelvemonth; and since members, when elected for a year only, would not be able to defy and betray their constituents as now.

'The Six Points of the People's Charter'. Broadside, 1838. Public domain.

These men were most likely the last of their ilk; there was an inevitability to their demise that is wonderfully expressed by Swinglehurst:

> *'Perhaps the handicraft will die out altogether by the time these lingerers have disappeared from the scene of their labours. Even over this row of houses, where the din of the shuttle can still be heard, a factory four or five stories high throws its darkening shadow'.*[20]

Ephraim 'Owd' Eccles pictured in 1909, he was the last handloom weaver in Darwen. Courtesy Blackburn with Darwen Library & Information Service.

Slack Hall and Newfield

Chapter 8
by Dotty Snelson

Some of the poor pasture on Smithills Estate farms. Photograph ©Tony Greenwood.

At first glance Slack Hall and Newfield would appear to be two quite different farm properties. Newfield is an ancient dwelling, probably seventeenth century, on Matchmoor Lane; Slack Hall is a later building, late eighteenth or early nineteenth century, on Burnt Edge. Both are still standing although much altered. The stories of the people inhabiting these farms from the time of the construction of Slack Hall mirror what was happening all over Britain and life here was a microcosm of life in the rest of the country. Life on the surrounding moors would have been vastly different to today when they are a magnet for walkers and nature lovers. Back then they would have been a hive of activity with people working in mines and brick works, as well as on the many farms. There would have been pedlars crossing the moors selling their wares at farmhouses, beerhouses and outside places of work.

People continued to eke out a living on the land but others were moving from agriculture to industry, to work in the burgeoning mills and factories in the hope of earning more money. Meanwhile the gentry such as the Ainsworths up at the Hall would be carrying on with their country pursuits just as they had always done, and their gamekeepers would be waging a constant battle against poachers desperate to feed their families, and who often lived in poverty.

It is possible that the farms were not always tenanted but both farms fulfilled vital roles on Smithills Estate. Newfield as an ancient upland farm and Slack Hall possibly used to serve Newfield Colliery and Fire-Brick Works (also know as Burnt Edge Colliery). Certainly, the stables there were used to keep the horses that pulled carts transporting coal from the collieries. The colliery and brick works would have employed local labour and newspapers had many adverts displaying the items which could be purchased, along with a price list. The *Bolton Chronicle* of 11 August 1860 for instance advertised 'flower pots for 1s. 6d. per dozen and pig troughs for 3s. and upwards'.[1] The occupants of Slack Hall and Newfield included people who were mobile and moved around and also those who stayed local, living all their lives within sight of Smithills Moor. Everyone would have worked long hours under harsh circumstances for little financial reward.

'Newfield Colliery and Fire-Brick Works'. *Bolton Chronicle*, 11 August 1850. Courtesy *The Bolton News*.

The Heaton family

The Heatons are to be found at several farms and locations in the area over the years. In the early 1860s Edmund Heaton was a wealthy middle-aged bachelor who had inherited his wealth from his father. He bought an estate of small farms in Bolton including Slack Hall and Newfield.[2] He lived at Newfield in the 1820s and the other farms were let out. When he died in 1842, the value of his personal estate and effects was around £600. This cannot have included all the land he once owned.

The land on Smithills Estate was largely poor pasture, suitable only for sheep and hardy cows, and the living from these farms would have been meagre. The tenants would usually have had other occupations in order to make ends meet. Edmund's nephew William Heaton had thirteen children in all and, not surprisingly with such a brood to support, struggled financially. His uncle helped him out and allowed him to live at Slack Hall where he kept sheep and cattle, as well as working as a handloom weaver. He baptised his children at New Chapel, Horwich, an independent church attended by his uncle Edmund. They were still at Slack Hall in 1829 but by the late 1830s had moved to Tar Hall at Hole Bottom where all the male members of the family were coal miners, even ten-year-old Eli.

Some of the poor pasture across the Estate farmland. Photograph ©Tony Greenwood.

By 1841 Edmund was renting out Slack Hall to James and Alice Kirkman who lived there with their son Joseph. The parents were weavers and Joseph a wheelwright, and were not dependent on the farm for their living. Edmund himself continued to live at Newfield with his housekeeper Mary Hearst. In 1841 he was said simply to be of independent means and when he died a year later he left both farms to Joseph Kirkman in his will. There must therefore have been a strong connection between himself and the Kirkman family. He also left an annuity in his will to his fifty-one-year-old housekeeper Mary who had served him loyally. Edmund is buried in the graveyard at New Chapel where he had been such a prominent member of the congregation.

One branch of the prolific Heaton family was known as the Ravenhurst branch of whom Jeremy, or Jeremiah, was patriarch. In 1881 his three unmarried children, Mary Heaton, sixty-four, her brother Edmund, sixty, and sister Esther, fifty, were farming twenty acres at Newfield, and lived there with their lodger, gamekeeper George Peachey, previously of the Sydmonton Court Estate in Hampshire. The Heatons had moved to Newfield from Pinchems Farm, near Eighteen Acres Farm where they had lived with a Robert Marsden. Mary obviously held the tenancy as when she died in 1884 it expired and Edmund was rendered homeless. He died in Bolton Workhouse in 1891. Esther's whereabouts after Mary's death are unknown. And this is the last we hear of any Heatons living on these difficult upland farms.

New Chapel, Horwich
Photograph
©Karen Holroyd.

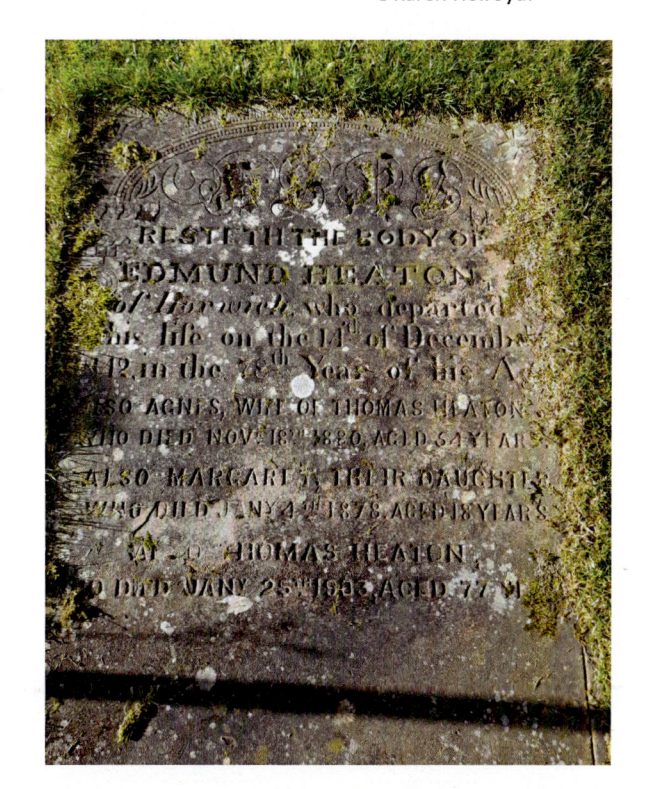

Edmund's grave where he is buried with other family members. Photograph ©Karen Holroyd.

The Culshaws of Newfield

A Roger Walch of Newfield died in 1858.[3] He had been a fire-brick maker, probably at the local works. By 1861 the Culshaw family occupied the farm. Carter Thurston Culshaw was born in Rufford where his father farmed seventy acres. He was baptised and married at St Mary's Church, Rufford and worked as a farm labourer. He married Elizabeth Ditchfield whose family were also farm labourers. They were both thirty-six and had three children. They also had a lodger, Frederick Shaw, again a carter, and a native of Salford. The opening of Horwich Locomotive Works later in the century brought great transport links to the area but at this time Thurston and Frederick probably worked together moving goods and materials by horse and cart from the mines and brick works on the moors.

The *Bolton Chronicle* of October 1858 contained an advert asking for people to tender for the construction of a new cart road from Newfield Colliery to Walker Fold (being the property of Peter Ainsworth Esquire), a distance of some eight hundred yards.[4] Ainsworth had allowed the road to be cut through his land for the use of the Colliery and Brick Works. The road was to be composed of pitching and broken stone, and sufficiently wide for one horse and cart to go by at a time. It was also to have two or three shunts or bypasses equally divided along the length and sufficient drains and water courses to carry the water clean away. It is possible that Thurston and Frederick would have helped in the construction by bringing the stone to the site. Later the new cart road would hopefully benefit them, making their lives easier when taking materials away from the colliery and brick works and onwards to whoever was buying them.

'Statutory Notice to Creditors and Others'.
Bolton Chronicle,
15 December 1860.
Courtesy *The Bolton News*.

'To Be Let'.
Bolton Chronicle,
2 October 1858. Courtesy *The Bolton News*.

The Culshaws would spend only a brief time at Newfield and by 1871 had moved to Union Buildings, Bolton. They had several more children in the interval, and Thurston was now an ostler and Elizabeth a charwoman. Two of their children were working, one as a factory operative and another in a foundry. It would appear that Thurston retained a deep love of Rufford as when he died in 1890 he was buried at St Mary's despite living in Bolton for all his later years. By 1891 Elizabeth had also died but their children and their spouses were settled in Bolton, working in nearby factories and mills.

Their life on the moors was short but indicative of many at the time. People who had to move and adapt as times were changing quickly. The great Victorian period of industrialisation was polarised in the north of England with Manchester known as Cottonopolis. Bolton was also part of this industrial expansion with its mills, factories, and mines. Work could be found easily here, although conditions were possibly not much less harsh than on the moors.

Part of the stone cart road, now known as Burnt Edge Tramway. Photograph ©Tony Greenwood.

Ostler working in a stable with a maid watching. From *The Family Friend*, published by S W Partridge & Co., London, 1874. Courtesy iStock/Whitemay.

The Oakley family of Slack Hall

James Oakley, a widower of forty-one, his forty-four-year-old wife Mary, and James' son William aged ten from a previous marriage, were living at Slack Hall in 1891. James and Mary were farmers and young William a labourer. Mary had spent her working life in the factories, first as a cloth hooker in a cotton mill, pulling cloth from a roll onto hooks so it could be folded for packing, then later as a calico finisher at a bleach works, starching or mangling the finished cloth after bleaching.

James hailed from Ivinghoe, Buckinghamshire, the inspiration for Walter Scott's *Ivanhoe.* He was the youngest of seven children and his father William was a farm labourer. The area was predominantly a farming community and all seven children worked as straw plaiters (literally plaiting straw which was to be used in the making of hats and bonnets).

'Plaiting School'. *Cassells Family Magazine,* 1882. Public domain.

Interestingly, William's death in December 1860 was the subject of an article in the *Bucks Herald.*[5] He died of hydrothorax, a disease in which fluid settles in the chest's pleural cavity. It detailed how he had been turned down for outdoor relief because he had refused 'when "the house" had been offered to him'. The house being the workhouse. The article highlighted the insufficiency of medical relief for the poor and painted a picture of a family working hard but unable to improve their lives. William had first become ill several months before his death yet still worked in the fields until harvest, beyond which time he could no longer manage.

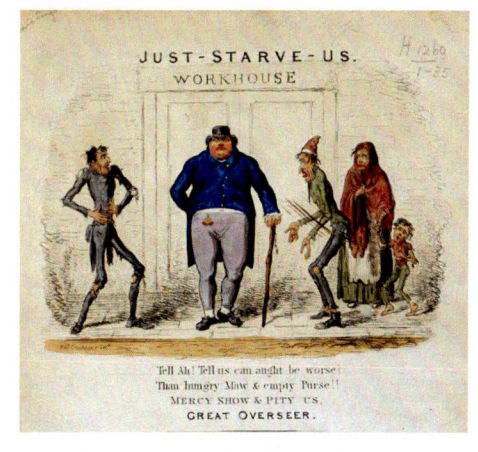

'Just starve us', comic song, words by W H Freeman, music by Auber, adapted by T C Lewis. Courtesy British Library Collection, public domain.

The Poor Law Amendment Act 1834, commonly known as the New Poor Law, sought to bring an end to all 'out relief': welfare payments made to those who preferred to continue living outside the workhouse. Following this legislation Poor Law Unions were set up and hundreds of new workhouses built across England to house those unable to fend for themselves. Harsh conditions were deliberately implemented to act as a deterrent, and it was only the most desperate who accepted the 'in relief' provided, although for some time after the Act some Unions were slow to build workhouses and 'out relief' continued. At first this tended to be elderly people or those with disabilities. By the end of the nineteenth century conditions had improved, although they were still very harsh with families separated and unable to see one another. In the twentieth century many workhouses became hospitals, but they never lost their fearful reputations with older people who remembered their past use.

'New Poor Law'. Broadside from 1834. Public domain.

James Oakley first appeared in Bolton in 1881, by which time he was already a widower. He then married local girl Sophia Ashton at St George's Church and they lived in Holland Street off Blackburn Road with their son William. James was a fireman in a cotton mill, employed to stoke the boiler furnaces which powered the steam engines and thus the loom machinery.

Perhaps he made the move from south to north to find work in the factories and mills leaving behind the more precarious agricultural life. Sophia died in 1883 and he married Mary the following year. Mary's family hailed from Horwich and by 1901 the Oakleys had left Slack Hall and were living at 43 Mason Street, Horwich. Perhaps they were lured by the opening of Horwich Locomotive Works in 1886 which brought local employment opportunities. At its peak it employed almost five thousand people. By 1901 both James and William were working there as machinists. In 1911 James and Mary were still at Mason Street. However Mary died in 1912 and James in 1914. James left a sum of £890 3s. 6d., and probate was granted to son William, now a journeyman machinist.

Again, the Oakley's time on the moors was short, and they illustrate the movement from agriculture to industry eloquently. James moved from a predominantly farming area to Bolton to work in the cotton mills, had a brief sojourn in farming at Slack Hall, and then moved back into industry at the newly opened Locomotive Works where he and his son found decent employment and better remuneration for their hard work.

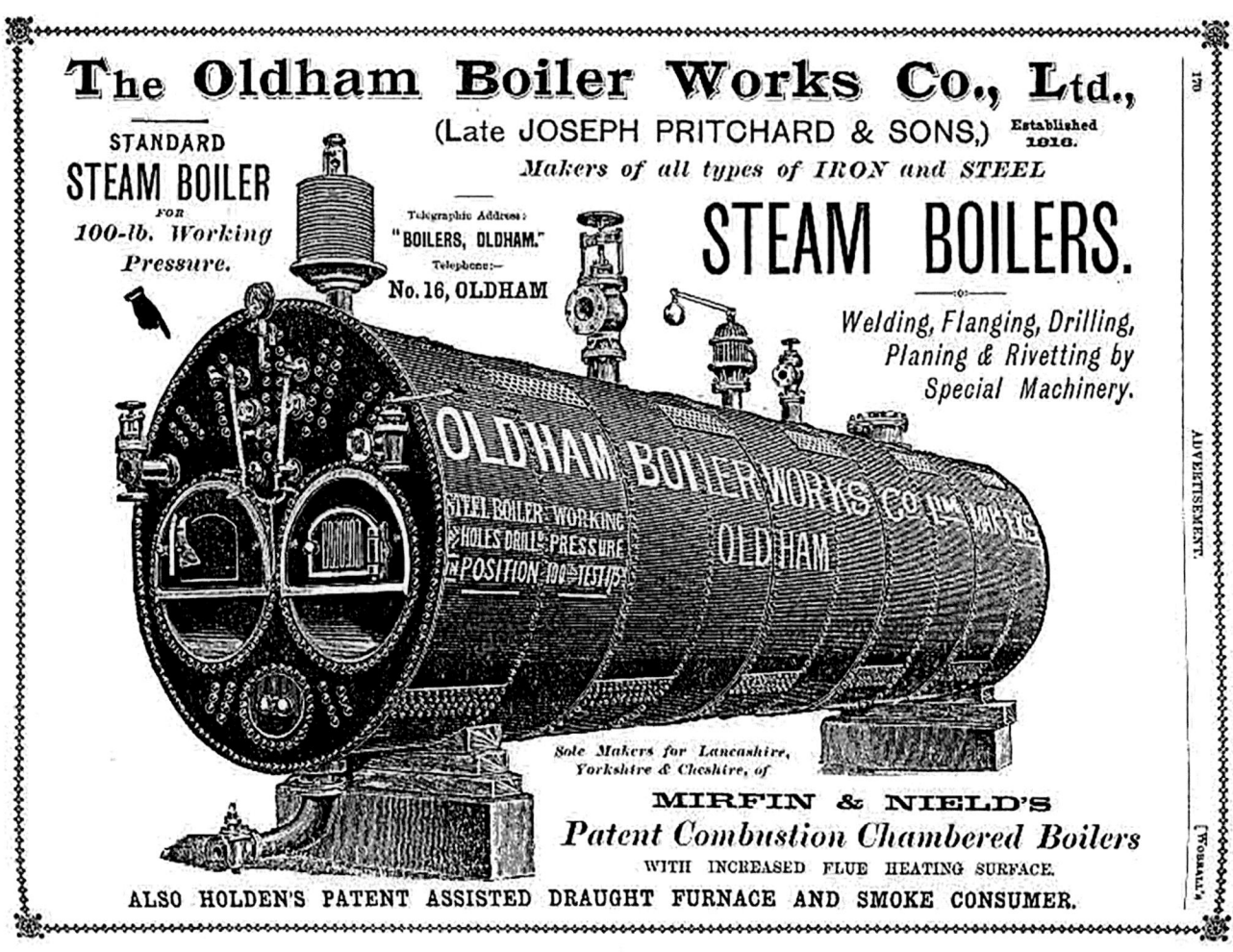

Advertisement for a Lancashire boiler, common in mills of the day, and fuelled by two furnaces at the front. *Worrall's Magazine,* 1891. Public domain.

Goldfinch, aka *Carduelis carduelis.* Photograph ©Francis C Franklin, CC BY-SA 3.0.[6]

Conclusion

If Thurston Culshaw were to return to Newfield, or James Oakley to Slack Hall, they would probably fail to recognise them as the poor upland farms where they once lived. Today they are both much modernised with little trace of the farming activities prevalent in their day. Other farms on the estate have disappeared into the grass and heather and are long forgotten. Indeed, the whole moorland area is a different place. Gone is the industry, the little shanties that supported it, some of the cottages and farms, and the buzz of constant activity. Now it is a place to enjoy for leisure rather than to toil for work. It is a place for walkers, photographers, wildlife enthusiasts, history lovers, and anyone who loves the great outdoors. Then it was the scene of people labouring long and hard for the benefit of their masters, with little reward for themselves or opportunity to enjoy any leisure time.

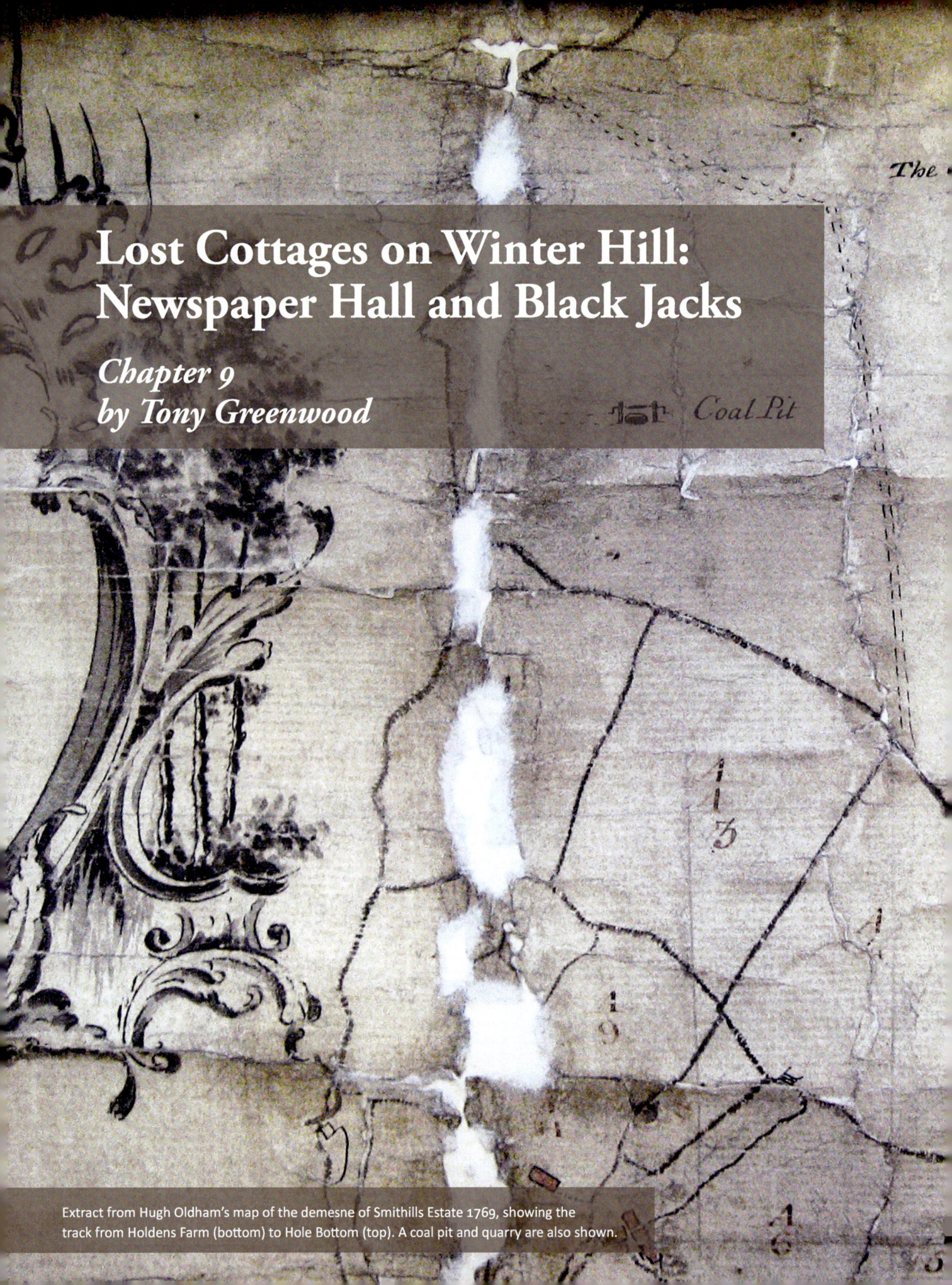

Lost Cottages on Winter Hill: Newspaper Hall and Black Jacks

*Chapter 9
by Tony Greenwood*

Extract from Hugh Oldham's map of the demesne of Smithills Estate 1769, showing the track from Holdens Farm (bottom) to Hole Bottom (top). A coal pit and quarry are also shown.

Bolton folk tell the story of Newspaper Hall and Black Jacks, cottages high up on the Winter Hill moors. Owd Reynolds, a handloom weaver, would open his house to passers-by for ale and gingerbread. Miners would gather there and he would read the news to them, other customers and his neighbours. But Newspaper Hall is not mentioned in any census or estate papers, nor on any map. Black Jacks was next to the abandoned Holden's Colliery. It is on a map, also shown as Cottage i' th' Moor, where travellers would also call for ale and gingerbread. But where was Newspaper Hall, and who were Owd Reynolds and his friend Black Jack?

Stories of these lonely places became well known at the time of the Mass Trespass in 1896 and the subsequent trial on 9 March 1897. Working folk attended court as witnesses to defend the six organisers who were prosecuted for trespass and evidence was gathered to try to convince the judge that the tracks over the moors had been rights of way for centuries. Sadly, although many of the witnesses had used the routes for many years, they could not prove that Coal Pit Road had not been commissioned by Richard Ainsworth in 1812 when he was developing his mines.[1]

Witnesses are Summonsed. Court Papers for Chancery Case Between Richard Henry Ainsworth and Defendants, 18 March 1897. From the collection of Paul Salveson. Thanks to Paul who also discovered the story of the 1896 mass trespass, and subsequent trial.

The Trial of the Trespassers, 1897

During 1896 Colonel Richard Henry Ainsworth had erected a gate across Coal Pit Road and No Trespass signs over the moors. He also blocked paths to farms and local beauty spots. The first mass trespass happened on 6 September 1896 when over ten thousand people marched through the closed off road, over the top of Winter Hill to Belmont on the other side. Despite police intervention marches continued and Ainsworth issued writs to six organisers to prevent further incursions. The case came to court six months later.

Some of the older witnesses who attended court were nicknamed Moorites. They were born or had lived on the moors. Their witness testimonies are a wonderful recorded history of their lives. They had traversed the old tracks over Smithills Moor, walking or riding from their homes to work and back. Or they visited friends and relatives on the other side of the moors, following the miners' tracks. Shopping would be done in the villages of Horwich and Belmont.

The people of Bolton keenly followed this trial, they crowded to public meetings, wrote long letters to the newspapers, mostly against the action Ainsworth was taking, and followed the correspondence and trial. Sensationalist pamphlets were published, put together by Solomon Partington, explaining his research and anecdotal evidence, although this was often wrong.[2] From these reports, plus maps used at the trespass trial and the 1838 trial of the murder of George Henderson, along with family information from census and civil records, the stories of the colourful characters that lived there can be put together.[3] Two moorland cottages in particular are referred to in the court proceedings: Newspaper Hall and Black Jacks. And these are the stories of the people who built, lived, and worked on the moors.

Remains of Newspaper Hall. Photograph ©Tony Greenwood.

Newspaper Hall: The Reynolds Family

One of the first witnesses at the trial was John Reynolds of Mount Street, Bolton. He said he had been born at Newspaper Hall in 1845 and lived there for twelve-and-a-half years, so knew the moors and tracks well. His father William Reynolds was a handloom weaver who built Newspaper Hall in 1843. William was known as Owd Reynolds, a popular character with a good line in banter and plenty of tales.[4] He had seven looms in his home on the moor, a substantial number at a time when handloom weaving was in decline. Although his son did not say, it was a strange move for Owd Reynolds, building a remote cottage at his own expense and investing in a declining trade. Money would have been tight, prices for cloth fell as the large factories in town started making it more cheaply. He would have struggled to make a living to keep his large family of at least nine children, so would take part in the illicit trade of selling beer. John Reynolds said that his father would sell gingerbread and 'gave away' the ale. Newspaper Hall was more than an alehouse then, it was an unlicenced hush shop.[5]

Hush Ale

After the Beerhouse Act 1830 was passed remote beerhouses such as those on Smithills Moor became refuges for mine, quarry, or brick work workers, helping them get away from their tiny, unhygienic, and crowded homes. They became important meeting places to catch up with friends, play rowdy games and share news, stories, and songs. Food was often served and lodging provided for travellers or local workers. But some landlords did not want to pay the licence, thinking they could avoid the Magistrate's summons by selling food and giving away beer. These were 'hush shops'. Edwin Waugh, a contemporary local writer, described them as 'generally sly spots, where sly fuddlers, who like ale for its own sake, can steal in when things are quiet, and get a belly-full at something less than the licensed price, or carry off a bottle-full into the fields after the gloaming has come on'. They were places 'where those whose psalm of life consisted of scraps of old drinking-songs, trolled out in a low chuckling tone:

"O good ale, thou art my darling,
I love thee night, I love thee morning
I love thee new, I love thee old;
I love thee warm, I love thee cold
Oh! good Ale!"[6]

Inside a beerhouse: 'An old chimney corner in Chadderton Fold' by J Houghton Hague. From Edwin Waugh, *Sketches of Lancashire Life*.

Of course, many of the other farms and cottages on the moors also sold ale brewed in the kitchen. Some were licenced, such as Garbutt's Beerhouse which was not far away at Five Houses, or the Brown Cow at Twitchells. Others perhaps just sold ale as a sideline. Newspaper Hall would also be selling gingerbread and ale on Sundays when it was forbidden, for those stopping off for tea as they walked up the few tracks not patrolled by watchmen. Perhaps, trying to improve the reputation of the hall, it also became known as Reynolds Tea House.

Landowners were of the opinion that alcohol was an evil to be avoided. New workers' villages such as Barrow Bridge were dry as the Ainsworths refused permission for beerhouses on their land and tried hard to suppress the sale of hush ale.

Handloom weaving, along with his hush shop and tea house, was not enough to stop Owd Reynolds being evicted from his home and business. According to John Reynolds his father 'were sheriffed off' their land and home (a quaint and laconic way of phrasing it) because 'Quaker Tom had struck a score of Squire Wright's voters off the list'. Being sheriffed off was an eviction by a bailiff, an officer of the sheriff, or a land steward acting on behalf of the landowner. Quaker Tom was another of William Reynolds' nicknames, somewhat ironic in view of his regular breaking of the law of the land.

After young John Reynolds left Newspaper Hall he led a very chequered life dogged by misfortune. At one time he was lessee of Bolton Baths, paying £110 a year rent for them, but that business failed.[7] He took the opportunity of publicity generated by the mass trespass to become a local celebrity. He excitedly joined in the campaign to keep the paths open and told his stories to the pamphlet writers as well as to the judge. Afterwards he would take groups onto the moors to show them where he was born.[8] His guided parties could not gain access along Coal Pit Road or Burnt Edge as the tracks were still closed. They had to go over the edge of the Ainsworth's estate from Moor Road onto the common land above Burnt Edge and over Adam Hill. On reaching Hole Bottom, he would point out the way across Smithills Moor to his birthplace at Newspaper Hall, the site of Ouzel Hall, while telling stories of his father.

Ouzel Hall shown on Ordnance Survey six-inch map, surveyed 1892. Courtesy National Library of Scotland.

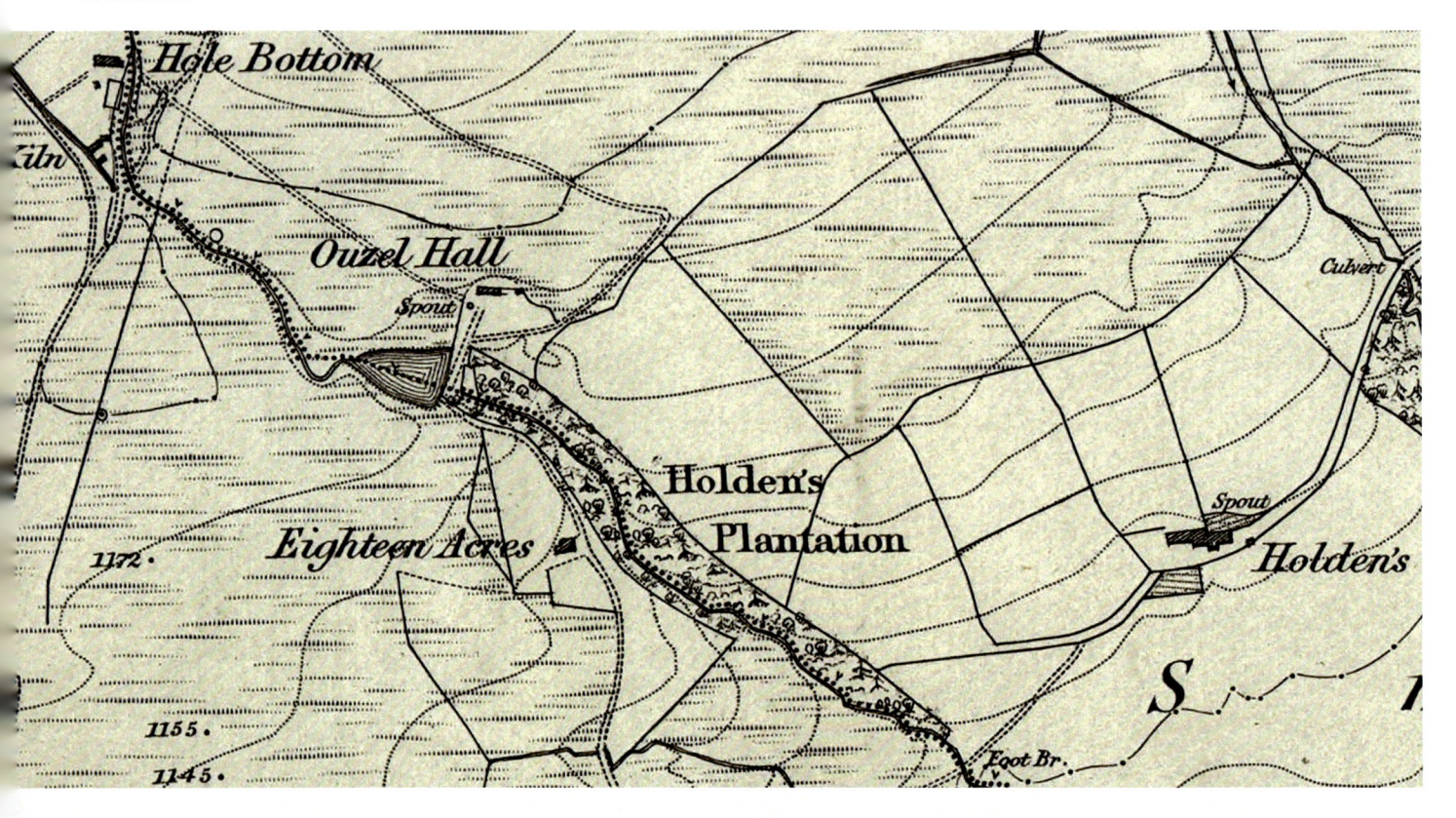

He said the hall 'had a public road skirting around it and a road to Two Lads over Wildersmoor, both now lost to the public'. So his birthplace was called both Newspaper Hall and Ouzel Hall. This is confusing. On the census in 1851 William Reynolds and his family lived at Slate Delph Brow, next door to Ouzel Hall Cottage. By 1861 Ouzel Nest was a farm of twelve acres next door to Slate Delph Brow where Richard Dickinson lived. Slate Delph Brow is an unusual name for a cottage. A delph is a stone quarry, and slate suggests it made roofing tiles from the millstone. So the hollow we now know it was built in was a stone quarry.

Back at the trial, two sisters of John Reynolds talked about their lives. Nancy Gaskell and Mary Jane Simm explained they had also lived at Newspaper Hall. Gaskell said she lived there from 1832 when she was seven and left when she was twenty-one. She said the disputed road went straight past the house and onto Black Jacks, then onto Horwich Road. This is also confusing as the disputed road was actually Coal Pit Road and did not go past Newspaper Hall at all, although a branch from the road at Black Jacks did link Holden's Colliery to Hole Bottom and Holdens Farm. The sisters told the story of how their house was built. Local farmer Thomas Pye had started to build the hall. Their father had cut the stone out of Fox's Delph for Pye, but he then whelped on the arrangement and gave up after the foundations had been laid. So Owd Reynolds had to finish it himself. Nancy explained that it was called Newspaper Hall because in times when newspapers were expensive, the Moorites assembled at the Hall to hear the news read out. The *Bolton Evening News* at that time only cost a halfpenny, so it was more likely that most of them were unable to read. Nancy recalled that events of the Crimean War in the 1850s were of particular interest.

Another Reynolds sister, Susannah, had died when they lived on the moor. Nancy thought she was ten but was actually nine when she passed away in 1857. She described Susannah's funeral procession down to Horwich. The horse-drawn hearse that would have come up Winter Hill Road (now Mast Road) could only get so close, and the family was allowed to cross the brook (probably Dean Brook) and the coffin taken across by hand to the waiting cart.[9] In an aside to the court, these two sisters mentioned a ghost at Gilligant's Farm, which was across the open moorland from the hall, but said it had not been heard of or seen by any person for some time past.[10]

Roe deer at the site of Ouzel Hall with new moorland planting. Photograph ©Tony Greenwood.

A later witness Joseph Walsh, Ainsworth's land agent who had succeeded his father as such in 1856, said he also knew the moors well. He knew of Reynolds, even Ainsworth knew Owd Reynolds, but claimed he did not recall Reynolds' place being a resort where people went for hot water, tea, and beer.

Richard Dickinson

After John Reynolds and his sisters had given evidence Richard Dickinson, a coal miner from Horwich, came to give his account of living on the moors. He had lived at Garbutt's, Five Houses and Hole Bottom before succeeding Reynolds as tenant of Newspaper Hall. He said he had known Coal Pit Road since he was eighteen in 1840 when he moved onto the moor. Looking to other sources, we now find that after the Reynolds family were evicted in 1859, Richard Dickinson moved into Slate Delph Brow with his wife Isabella and daughter Rosetta, a much smaller family now in the large hall. This reference to Slate Delph helps us locate Newspaper Hall, as on the census it is next door to Ouzel Hall. Joseph Walsh recalled that 'the Reynold house' was occupied by Dickinson until 1864 and after that was gradually pulled down.

The Heatons

Next to give evidence was Thomas Heaton, by then seventy-two, and his elder brother Joseph, still a farmer at Platt Hill Farm, Rumworth, now age seventy-five. Thomas told the court he had been born near Hole Bottom and then lived at Hole Bottom for eleven years until he was fifteen in 1840. Records show the brothers were born at Slack Hall, their great uncle Edmund Heaton's property, so there may be confusion here. He called his home at Hole Bottom Ouzel Hall.

In 1841 coal miner fifty-six-year-old William Heaton, Thomas and Joseph's father, lived at Tar (or Toor) Hall at Hole Bottom.[11] So it seems the Ouzel Hall mentioned by Thomas was actually Tar Hall. According to Thomas his father, also known as Owd Heaton, was forcibly turned out so he went and got a chain horse and pulled the whole house down. Thomas said his father was so angry that he laid stones in the road, stopping it up, which resulted in him being involved in a lawsuit in Liverpool about the matter. Sometime later they moved into the next township at Halliwell where he worked for William Garbutt in the mines along the top of the hill.

So William Heaton seems to have built Tar Hall sometime before 1838, in the quarry next to Hole Bottom surrounded by mines and pits. Most of the pits were not marked on the maps but clear on LiDAR maps, so must have been developed early on. At the trial Joseph Walsh said that there were coal workings going on the moor at that time and referred to coal workings at Holdens Farm going back to 1808. It could be that William Heaton was a squatter there. Miners that moved to new areas were allowed to build their own houses, the tradition being that if you had a chimney lit by the end of the day, you could stay.

Location of Ouzel Hall. Ordnance Survey six-inch map, surveyed 1845-47, overlayed on LiDAR map. Ouzel Hall was in the corner of the wall between the 2 and W. Courtesy National Library of Scotland.

Light Detection and Ranging (LiDAR) is an airborne mapping technique, which uses a scanning laser to measure the distance very accurately between the aircraft and the ground. It allows highly detailed representations of relief or terrain models to be generated, often at spatial resolutions of between twenty-five centimetres and two metres.

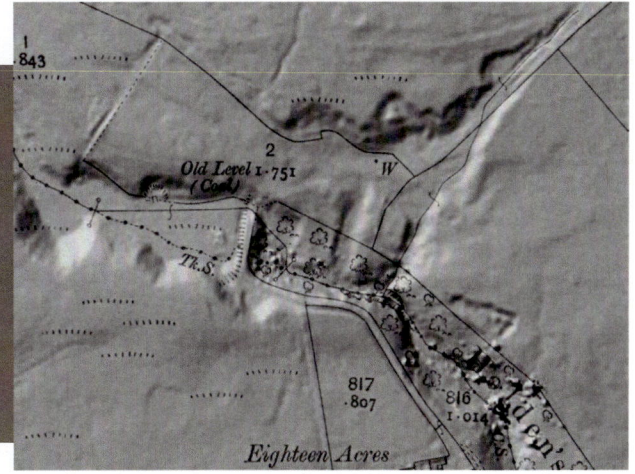

Owd William Heaton had been a handloom weaver but living at Tar Hall he was carrier with his horse and cart. He would take finished goods and coal to Belmont and Horwich, sometimes returning with stones from the delphs just the other side of Winter Hill Gate next to the large tunnel into Ainsworth mines. On the day of the 1838 murder, he had stopped at Five Houses and chatted with suspect James Whittle, and Heaton's house is shown on the sketch map made for the trial. It is located where Ouzel Hall is shown on the Ordnance Survey map just five years later. Today however there is no trace of Newspaper Hall, other than the remains of a field wall around the old farmyard.

Site of Ouzel Hall/ Newspaper Hall. Photograph ©Tony Greenwood.

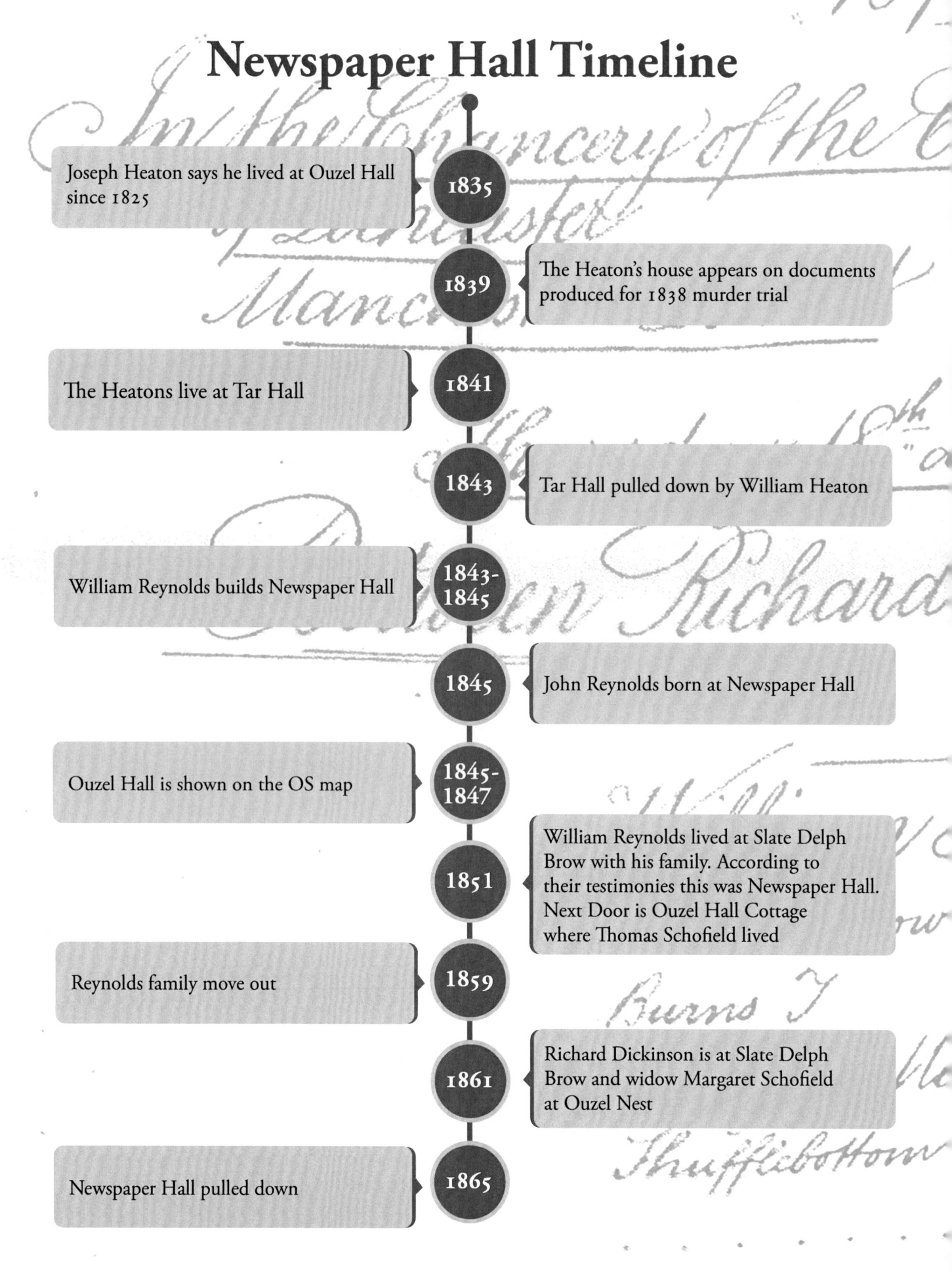

Newspaper Hall Timeline

- **1835** — Joseph Heaton says he lived at Ouzel Hall since 1825
- **1839** — The Heaton's house appears on documents produced for 1838 murder trial
- **1841** — The Heatons live at Tar Hall
- **1843** — Tar Hall pulled down by William Heaton
- **1843–1845** — William Reynolds builds Newspaper Hall
- **1845** — John Reynolds born at Newspaper Hall
- **1845–1847** — Ouzel Hall is shown on the OS map
- **1851** — William Reynolds lived at Slate Delph Brow with his family. According to their testimonies this was Newspaper Hall. Next Door is Ouzel Hall Cottage where Thomas Schofield lived
- **1859** — Reynolds family move out
- **1861** — Richard Dickinson is at Slate Delph Brow and widow Margaret Schofield at Ouzel Nest
- **1865** — Newspaper Hall pulled down

Footway D: the miners' track from Newspaper Hall to Black Jacks

Across the high pasture above Holdens Farm is an embankment track between Hole Bottom and Coal Pit Road which was built in the early 1800s to take coal and clay from Ainsworth's Holden's Colliery to Garbutt's Winter Hill Brick and Tile Works. On the first Ordnance Survey map of the moor in the late 1840s it is clearly marked, but surprisingly disappears from the next edition in 1892. National government surveyors were probably there around the time of the mass trespass and Colonel Ainsworth likely had it removed from the map despite the ongoing survey, along with the higher end of Coal Pit Road.

Footway D marked on 1897 court documents.

At the trespass trial in 1897, an annotated copy of the early map was used with this track shown as Footway D, going from Cottage i' th' Moor to Winter Hill Road at Hole Bottom. Independent surveyor F W Thompson traced the hard metalled road up from the disputed gate and from Reynolds' to the wall at Dean Ditch past Black Jacks. This track had been used for many years according to many witnesses, they believed it was a public right of way connecting their homes and workplaces. William Heaton and his family living in Newspaper Hall in the 1830s used this track as a way of getting to Belmont and Bolton via Black Jacks. Later, Black Jack and his family would cross the open moor to visit Owd Reynolds and travel down to the small village of Horwich. Travellers crossing the moor would use it to get from Holdens Farm to Belmont Road. Sometimes people from Bolton would use this track to get to the fair at Rivington at Easter.

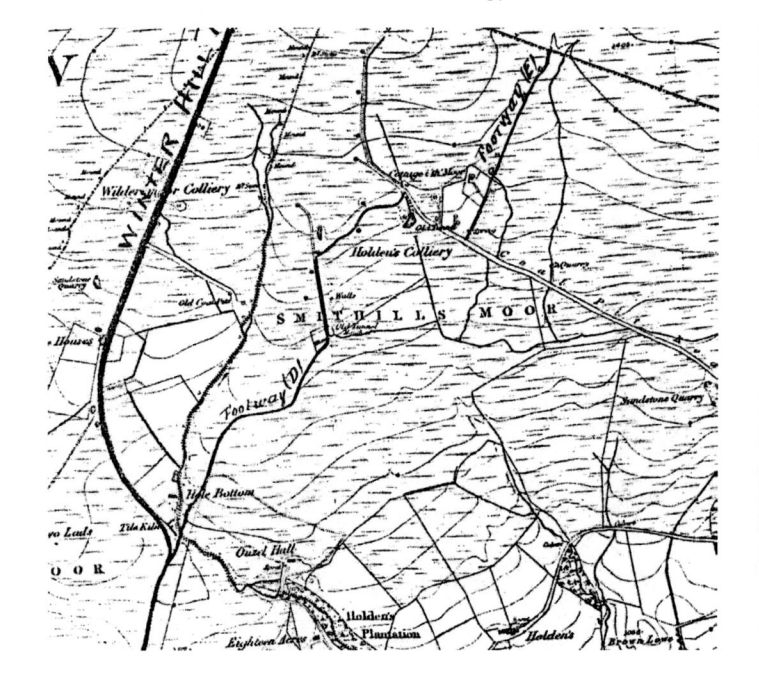

This track was there before the Ainsworth's coal roads. A map exists of the estate in 1769 showing a track from Holdens Farm to Hole Bottom past an old coal pit.[12] This was the same track shown in the first Ordnance Survey map, joining Ouzel Hall to Hole Bottom. The track is still there today, although it is difficult to find, and eventually becomes lost in the peat and heather.

Allen Clarke in his book *Moorland and Memories,* recalls a walk through Holdens past Ouzel Hall and Five Houses. 'From the top of Brian Hey (Smithills Dean Road) you keep straight on, up the lane called Coalpit Road, through Holdens Farmyard, to the moor road – near the tile works – where the track on the left leads to Horwich or back to Bolton, to the hill called Burnt Edge, and the one to the right to Winter Hill and Belmont…Here you are in the very solitude of heather and whin and birds, including grouse—you are on Winter Hill. At some part of the road you pass the remains of some old cottages – one of them was once an inn, 70 or 80 years ago, in the Chartist Days…whose meetings were prohibited by law, used to assemble secretly in one of those cottages'.[13]

Cottage i' th' Moor or Black Jacks

Remains of Black Jacks Cottage. Photograph ©Tony Greenwood.

Just a pile of stones, tumbled walls, and bits of old plumbing hidden in a fold on the heather are all that remains of Cottage i' th' Moor. Above Coal Pit Road, most people will walk up the track and not be aware the ruined cottage is there.

Across the other side of the Smithills valley from Newspaper Hall, the upper end of Coal Pit Road went up above Gilligant's Farm, giving access to the pits on the high pasture moors. Many small pits can be seen either side of the track, some of which were in use back to Tudor times. But at the beginning of the nineteenth century Richard Ainsworth wanted more coal to fuel his bleach works and drafty cold hall. So in 1812 he opened up more pits and built a road to them.

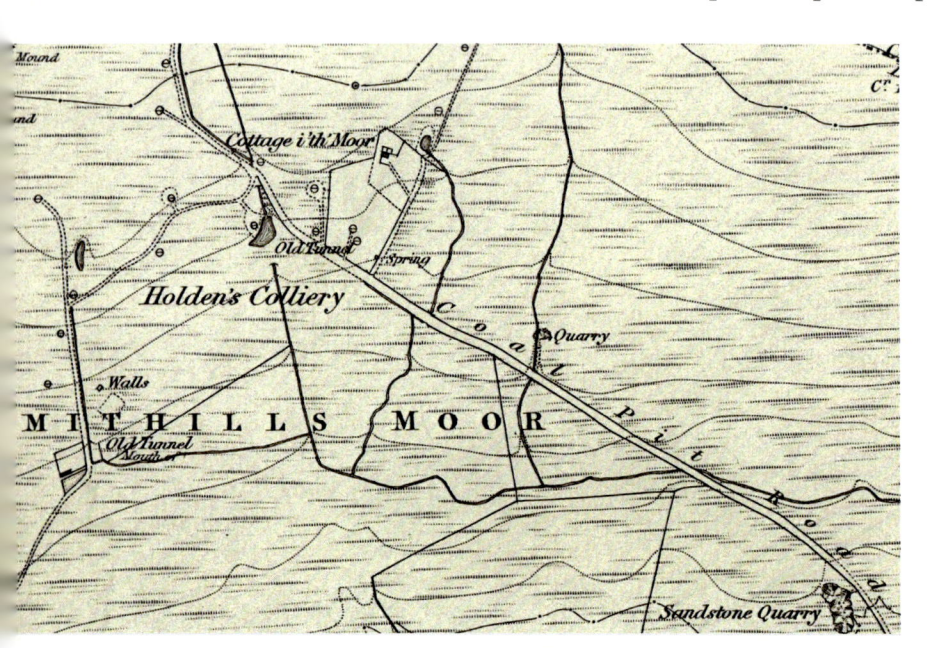

Owd Morris seems to have lost farmland in the process, but he was an opportunist. He built a row of eight stone cottages a hundred yards from the colliery buildings. Unlike William Garbutt's brick built Five Houses, Morris' houses were built from stone, broken from a small delph nearby. This was a lodging place for coal miners, some sharing rooms, others living with their families.

Cottage i' th' Moor on Ordnance Survey six-inch map, surveyed 1845-47. Courtesy National Library of Scotland.

At its busiest in the 1820s and 1830s, some fifty or so miner families lived there and worked in the colliery below. The whole family would work the pits, the small children and women crawling along the narrow tunnels. One house would be the farmhouse for the few acres left of the farm. Witnesses at the trial of the trespassers in 1897 talked about this cottage, known to them as Black Jacks.

Luke Morris was the son of Owd Morris, and a butcher in Manchester. He said his father had built the cottage on the site of the eight old cottages. Owd Morris was a stone-waller as well as a farmer and had been employed by the Ainsworths to build the wall above the cottage at Dean Ditch. His testimony was not a help to the trespassers as he admitted that people did not go or come from Belmont as, despite what the defence claimed, there was no road over the wall. However, he confirmed there was a path to their home from Hole Bottom and remembered the keepers on the moors abusing those crossing the moors, including those who lived there and were going about their family business.

Mary Anne Hamer, who then lived in Blackpool, was the daughter of John Hamer, known as Black Jack. She went to live at the house on the moors around 1841 when she was seven, shortly after it was built, living there until 1850. Mary Anne said she had never seen anyone but the shepherds, the shooters, or those who lived on the moors cross the boundary wall by means of the stones. Those that used the road up to the pits usually went to Reynolds' or to their house, although one or two went on to Two Lads. According to John Reynolds, Black Jacks was built out of the debris of the eight houses when they were razed to the ground in 1840 or 1841.

Stone and clay pipe found in the remains of Black Jacks. Photograph ©Tony Greenwood.

Thomas Whitehead, born 1836, and his brother Alexander Whitehead, born 1840, used to live at Roscow's Tenement. They would walk up from their farm next to Coal Pit Road and over to Belmont past Black Jacks. This was likely to be along the upper parts of the road and not over the Black Jacks stone wall. They also spoke of others who would walk up there, mentioning an old Scotsman,

Alexander Sproat, a commercial traveller who would call at Black Jacks and other houses on the moors selling his wares. They had seen people using Black Jacks path after both Black Jacks and Newspaper Hall had been pulled down, although claimed they never knew anyone being stopped.

According to land agent Joseph Walsh, Black Jacks was pulled down in degrees to repair other places. Henry Peachey the gamekeeper remembered people going to the cottage then on to Reynolds. He also remembered people going to Black Jacks after the Harmers had left. An Andrew Berry, shepherd and occasional watcher during the 1860s, had never seen anyone going over the boundary wall to Black Jacks except Walsh and Black Jack himself. The other shepherds at the trial mentioned that this part of the moor was swamp, which it still is to this day.

One of the characters of the moors was Black Jack's nephew W R Gordon-Stewart (previously Enoch Toothill before an inspired name change) of Tong Moor, who used to visit and said his uncle left the moors in 1856. Local stories suggest it was another cottage used as a hush shop, and that Black Jack sold gingerbread like his friend Owd Reynolds, providing a free ale to wash it down.

By 1871 the cottage was uninhabited. By the time of the mass trespass it was in ruins. Today these barely survive, as most were lost during the 2018 fires. So this is the story of Black Jacks Cottage.

Finds after the 2018 fire, Holdens Pasture on Footpath D. Ink bottle, parts of good quality china and clay pipe fragments. Photograph ©Derek Cartright.

Black Jacks Timeline

- **1812** — Morris' Cottage built to house miners at the top of Coal Pit Road
- **1814** — Morris' Cottage in Smithills Estate Rentals
- **1839** — James Morris' house shown on map used at murder trial
- **1841** — Eight Houses mentioned in census returns
- **1841** — Eight Houses razed to the ground and Black Jacks built out of the debris
- **1841** — Mary Anne Hamer, daughter of John Hamer, moves to Black Jacks
- **1845-1847** — Shown as Cottage i' th' Moor on the new OS Map
- **1850s** — Black Jacks is a hush shop
- **1861** — Richard Walch and his wife Maria live there
- **1871** — Uninhabited
- **1880s** — Pulled down by degrees to repair other places

The Freeman Sisters, a Story of Victorian Laundresses

*Chapter 10
by Laura Kovaleva*

Ordnance Survey six-inch map, surveyed 1892. Courtesy National Library of Scotland.

Life at Dean Gate Farm Cottage in 1851

If you take a stroll along Smithills Dean Road you will go past an old stone farmhouse: Dean Gate Farm. The datestone above the front door reads P A 1842 which stands for Peter Ainsworth, who made some building improvements that year. There is a small cottage next to the farm and our story will take us to this place as it was in old Victorian England in 1851.

If you had walked there at that time you would have found yourself immersed in the smell of soap, starch, and wet laundry. You would have heard the bubbling and gurgling sounds of washing water, and the noise of a mangle being used for wringing out wet clothing, bedding, and other washday items. You would have also heard women's voices chatting and laughing. The older voice belongs to Maria Freeman née Beswick, who turned seventy-three last year. She was born in Liverpool but later moved to Bolton where, in 1795, she married house painter Richard Freeman, sixteen years older than her. They had lived a long life together until Richard's death in 1832 and had eleven children: three boys and eight girls.

The younger voices you can hear belong to two sisters, Jane, thirty-two and Sarah, fifty-two, who help their mother in the laundry business. They have never married or had children but are happy to look after their nephew, Benjamin, the son of their sister Mary, born out of wedlock nine years ago. The other two family members residing at the cottage are eighteen-year-old Jane and twenty-two-year-old Richard, the children of Maria's son Walter and his wife Margaret, both of whom sadly passed away in 1834.

Dean Gate Farm. Photograph ©Yelena Overchenko.

Dean Gate Farm Cottage. Photograph ©Tony Greenwood.

Family business

Before moving to the farm cottage, Maria and her daughters lived in Little Bolton and later on Halliwell Road, where they worked as washerwomen. It was quite common for laundry to be a family business. The work could be fitted into the home routine and allowed women to look after their children. From a young age children, especially daughters, had to help their mothers and according to writer P E Malcolmson, 'older children laboured at the washtub, mangle, and ironing board, while younger children sorted and packaged bundles and helped to carry the laundry to their mother's customers'.[1]

Laundresses were often described as tough and resourceful, and as stated by one witness before the Royal Commission on Labour in 1894, they are 'the most independent people on the face of the earth'.[2] They would need some entrepreneurial skills and sometimes had to be assertive debt collectors as not everyone was willing to pay for washing on time.

Laundresses also had to be tough to deal with thieves trying to steal their laundry, as it was often left to dry on a field hedge or in the garden and was an easy target. Local newspapers report a number of incidents of laundry being stolen. For instance, in November 1838 the *Bolton Chronicle* wrote about two shirts and a towel stolen from Maria Freeman by seventeen-year-old Joseph Darwen.[3] Joseph was watching Maria's washing hung in her garden on Halliwell Road and when nobody was around he ran away with the shirts. Unluckily for the thief someone saw it and pursued him, calling out, 'Stop thief'. Darwen, in fear of detection, also called out, 'Stop thief'. It did not help him and he was caught and brought to justice. In addition, it was discovered that Darwen, who was a sweep, had some stolen tools hidden at his mother's house.[4] He was sentenced to three months' imprisonment, the last seven days of which he spent in solitary confinement.

'On a Washing Day' by O G Rejlander, 1854-56. Courtesy Zeno.org.

'A Breezy Day', Charles Courtney Curran. Courtesy Pennsylvania Academy of the Fine Arts.

Maria Freeman died in 1853 and was buried at St George's Church, Bolton. Her daughters carried on the laundry business at Dean Gate Farm Cottage. In 1871 three sisters, Jane, fifty-two, Sarah, seventy-two and Martha, fifty-five, were recorded as laundresses. It must not have been easy for them to continue with all the laborious tasks involved in the laundry process of that time. Jane and Martha stayed at the cottage until at least 1891, still working as laundresses.

How to wash the clothes in the Victorian way

The laundry weekly cycle usually started on Monday and took at least four days to complete if the weather was not too bad. The work started at dawn and continued until late evening. According to a book on the history of laundresses, 'the early part of the week was occupied with the collection, sorting, marking, soaking, washing, mangling, blueing, and starching of laundry, while the latter part of the week was devoted to ironing, airing, folding, packing, and, finally, delivery of the snowy linen'.[5]

Most parts of the laundry process were done in the house causing major disruptions to domestic life: 'Imagine what it is like in wet or wintry weather to have the narrow passage filled with a double line of wet clothes, and the one living room completely blocked up with them'.[6]

Victorian Laundry Tools. Photograph ©Laura Kovaleva. Courtesy Horwich Heritage.

Water had to be heated in a copper, a large metal vessel set in brickwork, and heated by a fire lit underneath. It was then transferred to a washing tub together with the washing itself and some soap. Laundresses plunged a washing dolly up and down, twisting it from side to side so the water was agitated as much as possible. This process that modern washing machines do for us required a lot of strength and energy.[7]

Washing recipe from *The Workwomen's Guide* of 1840
To make linen white that has turned yellow: heat a gallon of milk with one pound of scraped soap till dissolved, 'put the linen in, and let it boil sometime, then take it out, put it into a lather of hot water, and wash it properly out'.[8]

Photograph ©Yelena Overchenko.

It is quite possible that the Freeman sisters used Sunlight Soap, the world's first packaged and branded soap, invented by Bolton chemist William Hough Watson and introduced by the Lever Brothers in 1885.

Sunlight Soap advertisement, *Illustrated London News,* 1907. From the collection of Tony Greenwood.

The new age of laundry

In 1861 Sarah and Jane Freeman had their fifteen-year-old niece Maria Freeman, the daughter of sister Rebecca, living with them at Dean Gate Farm Cottage. Maria was probably called after her grandmother and she continued the family tradition by becoming a laundress. She married Richard Haddock and in 1891 they lived at 3 Holmes Cottage both working in a laundry business. Interestingly, Richard was recorded as a laundryman. As laundry was a family business, men sometimes took on heavier tasks, such as turning a mangle, carrying water, or pounding clothes with a washing dolly.[9]

Maria and Richard's son Thomas followed in his parents' footsteps and opened a laundry. According to the *Post Office Bolton Directory 1902-1904* , North End Steam Laundry was located at 41 Ulleswater Street, off Blackburn Road. Thomas lived next door at 39 Ulleswater Street.[10] At the turn of the century laundries were

Wringer and mangle advertisement. Collection of Nineteenth Century American Trade Cards. Courtesy Boston Public Library.

changing from being a domestic industry, 'organised upon the economic principle of one woman one wash-tub' to a 'modern machine business with sub-division of labour and the use of a labour-saving machinery'.[11] However, quite often a small laundry could be found at the back of a row of houses, which were adapted for this purpose. The back yards were roofed and packed with machinery, driven by an engine installed at one end of the row. It is quite possible that Thomas' laundry was an example of such a house-factory laundry.

It would have been interesting to know what the older Maria Freeman, who worked all her life as a laundress, might have said to her great-grandson. Surely Thomas was proud to carry on the family tradition and he would have heard a lot of stories from his mother telling him about his grandmother's hard work, resilience, and readiness to support her family.

Nowadays the laundry process requires minimal effort and hardly anyone would think about all the hardships the Victorian laundresses went through in their daily life. Still, from time to time, while taking the laundry out of the washing machine and hanging it outside to dry on the washing line, it is good to remember the Freeman sisters from Dean Gate Farm Cottage and their industrious, hardworking lives.

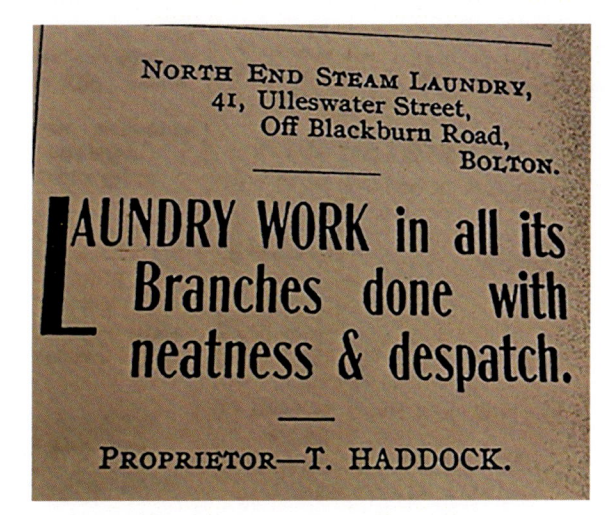

North End Steam Laundry advertisement, *Post Office Bolton Directory 1902-04*. Photograph ©Laura Kovaleva. Courtesy Bolton Council.

Leaving the Estate Far Behind

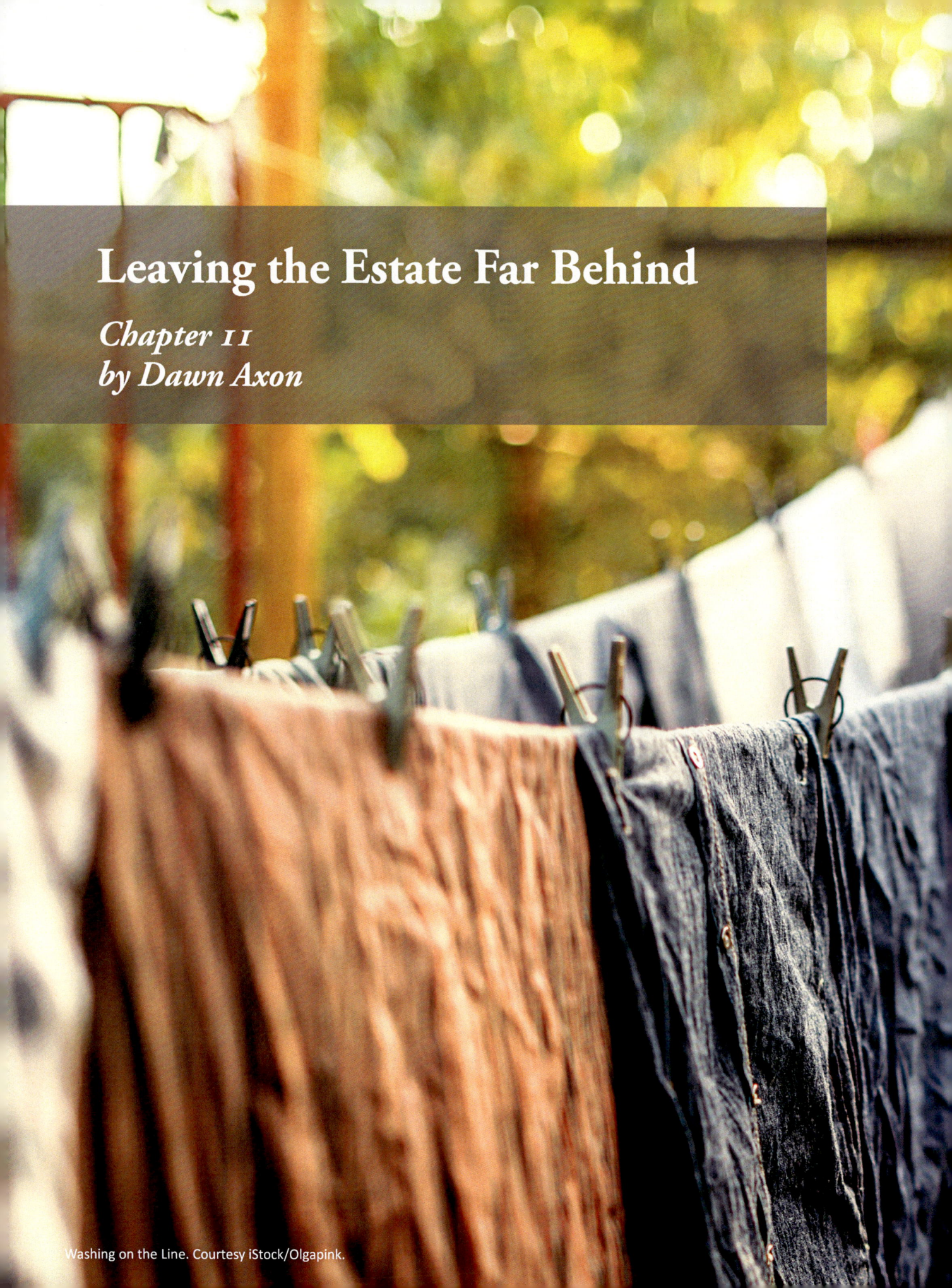

Chapter 11
by Dawn Axon

Washing on the Line. Courtesy iStock/Olgapink.

15 January 1855. Another damp and misty Monday morning in the cottage overlooking Smithills Moor and every bone in Mary's body ached as she dragged herself out of bed. She wearily contemplated life's usual problems. How was she to feed her family on the little money she had available? How was she to get the washing dry with this interminable drizzle? 'Surely', she muttered to herself, 'there must be more to life than this?'

Her husband was afflicted by bouts of melancholy and often wanted to give up but since the introduction of the New Poor Law in 1834 and the abolishment of 'out relief' they both thought that the only option available to them would be to enter the dreaded workhouse where they would be separated from each other and their children. That is however, maybe, until they spotted an advertisement promising a life 'free from the gripping curse of poverty'.[1]

Some Boltonians were early pioneers. In April 1840 Thomas Bramwell, a shoemaker of Bolton, received a letter from a friend who had travelled to New South Wales, Australia. He reported to Thomas that he soon got work at 7s. a day in the building trade and could save more than he could do at home. However, many there were 'ungodly and drinking prevails to an alarming extent'.[2] Despite this, he still maintained that 'friends would be a great deal better here than at home'.

It is not hard to imagine that a new life far away from Bolton would have seemed a very attractive proposition for many of our families on the estate, and the 1850 British Emigration Act paved the way for the setting up of Emigration Societies which ran similarly to Friendly Societies. Those who wanted to emigrate would have their passage paid for on the condition they would repay

Washing implements.
Photograph ©Dawn Axon.

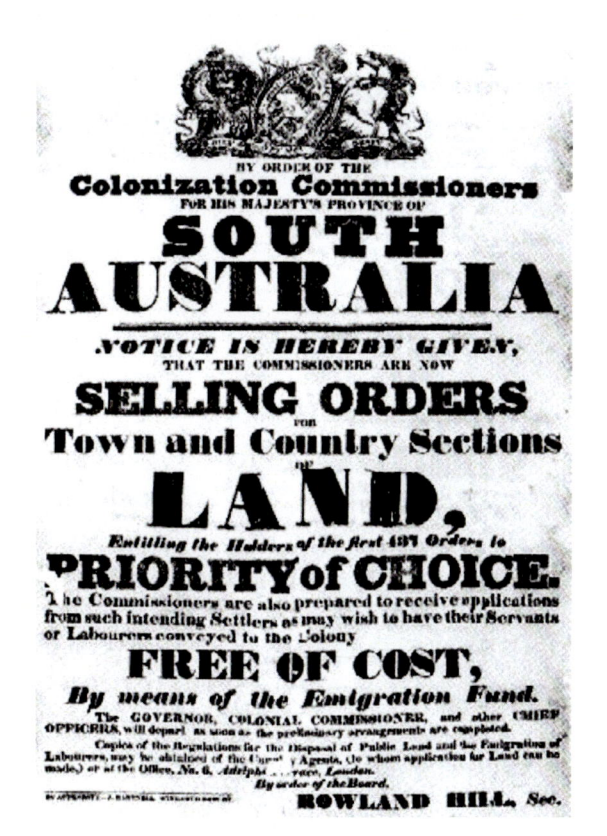

'Land For Sale'.
Courtesy National Library of Australia.

Gold diggers hut of canvas and bark in the Australian gold fields in the 1850s. The Australian population of 437,655 doubled in the 1850s stimulated by the gold rush. Courtesy Shutterstock/Everett Collection.

it when they were settled. Unfortunately, due to prevailing conditions many had no way to pay it back so just disappeared or saved enough to travel home.

Thomas Bramwell heard from another friend, Enoch Davis, who told him that a lot of his shipmates who travelled out to be miners did not stay in Australia. There had been strikes due to poor pay and hard work and an increase in the price of provisions. By 1850 Enoch had to start paying back his passage and travelled to Sydney for work where a new railway was to be built. By 1852 Australia was in the grips of the gold rush, and he too was in search of gold. He appears to have been unsuccessful and by 1854 he wrote that he was married and settled back in mining but still complaining of the price of provisions.[3]

John Dunmore Lang, originally from Glasgow, was a Minister of the Scots Church in Sydney. He realised the system did not work but, still being approached by many from his homeland wanting to emigrate, supervised the creation of the Moreton Bay Immigration and Land Company. The Company purchased huge swathes of land at the government's minimum suggested value of £1 per acre.

'Industrious families from the mother country' would then apply to emigrate through their local Emigration Society. Under the scheme set up in 1854 a family of five who could raise sixty pounds would be entitled to their passage and ownership of forty acres. Families only able to raise half this amount could lease the land with the Company holding it as security until the balance was paid. The object was to create settlements of 'industrious, virtuous and Christian populations'. A minister and school master were to be engaged by the Company for each settlement with free passage.

Reverend John Dunmore Lang. Courtesy National Library of Australia.

This would have sounded like heaven on earth to some of the families on Smithills Estate. Mary, daughter of laundress Maria Freeman, was living at Dean Gate Farm Cottage when she married John Elliott in 1854. They chose to emigrate with their baby in 1855.[4] John was described as a carpenter, aged forty-two, Mary was forty-one and baby Louisa less than a year. The Legislative Council published detailed immigration records and that year it specified that 11,871 people had arrived from Great Britain, some 240 from Lancashire.[5] Most were agricultural labourers and 'many who claimed to be able to read could do so only in the most imperfect and unsatisfactory manner'. For those not able to avail themselves of a scheme such as the Moreton Bay Immigration and Land Company's the average passage was sixteen pounds, way out of reach for the tenants of the Estate's farms and cottages.

'Practical Hints for Emigrants'. Courtesy Board of Trustees of NMGM (Merseyside Maritime Museum).

In 1855, the average length of the voyage to Australia was ninety-eight-and-a-half days. Steam technology was still too inefficient to make the long voyage, so ships used a combination of steam and sail. Storms were common and this could make conditions uncomfortable, particularly for those in steerage. They would dread the shout 'batten the hatches' as this would mean being confined below deck, often with little ventilation or light. These cramped conditions led to very poor hygiene levels and disease was rife. For many emigrants who would rarely have left their hometown before it must have been quite terrifying.

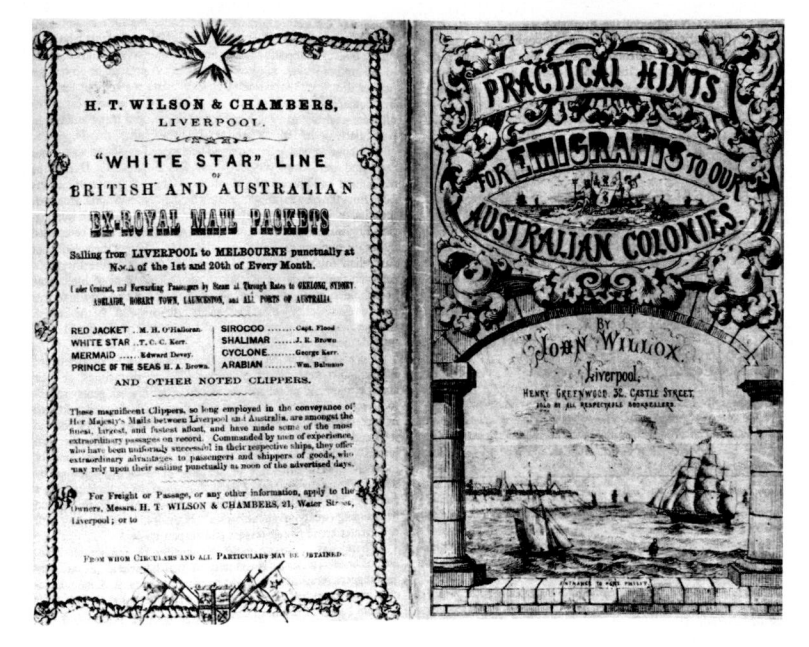

> Our water barrels were rolling from side to side and our cans, teapots and cooking utensils were adding to the confusion by bouncing one after the other down the area between the bunks. Some of the young ladies [were] screaming and some tried to climb up the hatchways screaming to the officers to let them out.
> – Anne Grafton migrated from England in 1858.[6]

Ally Heathcote travelled from Northumberland to Australia in 1874 with her parents and two siblings, detailing the whole voyage in a diary. It is one of many which describe the sorrow at leaving family members behind, the events of the voyage, and the excitement of arriving in a far-off land. She sent the diary to her aunt and uncle with the hope that it may inform others and even hoped for it to be published.

Diary of Ally Heathcote. Courtesy Museums Victoria.

EMIGRANTS AT DINNER.

Married Couples Accommodation in Steerage, artist unknown. Courtesy State Library of Victoria.

Many young men travelled out alone, applying for their sweethearts or sisters to join them when they got there. The Legislative Council's report also detailed that many young ladies were put on ships for Adelaide when they had purchased tickets for Melbourne to join relatives. They were told it was 'quite easy to get from one to the other'. The *Adelaide Observer* urged an urgent enquiry be made in the UK into the 'wholesale case of kidnapping'.[7] Imagine the poor girls' terror at arriving in a foreign land alone and realising they were over four hundred miles from where they were supposed to be.

Voyages therefore were not without risk. In 1855, 161 children were born at sea and 138 persons died (of which 105 were children).[8] Straw bedding, often infested with cockroaches and lice, became soaked in harsh weather and epidemics of influenza, cholera and tuberculosis were common. Infection was spread at alarming rates due to the confined spaces below deck and the inevitability of sea sickness.

'[It is] enough to pitch my insides out. It's all up to me. I am not able to stir. The doctor can give me no relief, but at that I am not surprised. He is very young, never been to sea and is just as ill as all the other people.'
– William Merrifield travelled to Australia on the *Lincolnshire* in 1858.[9]

The Elliotts set sail for South Australia on 30 January 1855, on the *Europa* from Birkenhead. They arrived at Port Adelaide on 12 May after an eventful voyage. There were complaints of a short issue of water but this was investigated by the Immigration Board and dismissed. This could have been caused by the ship having to make an intermediary docking at the Cape of Good Hope due to a serious mutiny by members of the ship's crew.[10] The ship's log also notes that the 'young women by this ship were most unsuitable' but did not clarify what this referred to!

> **Account of a Serious Mutiny at Sea from the South Australian Register, Monday 14 May 1855 courtesy of *The Ships List***
>
> 'On board the government emigrant ship *Europa*, which arrived on Saturday last, the 12th instant, from Birkenhead, a serious mutiny occurred. The following particulars of which are extracted from the official log book, which was politely handed to our outside shipping reporter: "The origin of the mutiny arose through one of the apprentices who, having misconducted himself, was confined by the captain in the storeroom until he thought proper to apologize for his misconduct. The confinement of this boy so exasperated the crew that they, in a most daring and insolent manner demanded his release, and threatened that if the captain did not immediately accede to their wishes they would take him (the boy) by force...On the 22nd March...Mr. Eastrook the chief officer went forward to issue instructions to the boatswain relative to putting the men of his watch to work, when three of the men came up armed and interfered. The chief officer, requesting them to mind their own duty and to go into the forecastle, was replied to by a blow from a slingshot in the back of the head, which brought him to the deck, the skull being laid bare by the shot, which penetrated the scalp"'.

Despite the mutiny lasting six days, the ringleaders were caught, imprisoned, and sentenced to three months hard labour building roads.[11] Arriving safely in Australia, however, were four plasterers, nine masons and bricklayers, eighteen joiners (of which John Elliott would have been one), one baker, eight sawyers, six blacksmiths, one school master and 205 male and female domestic and farm labourers. There were seven births at sea, one death from diarrhoea and eight cases of bronchitis.

Kapunda, the town where the Elliotts settled, was in a British colony established as a commercial venture by the South Australia Company, through the sale of land to free settlers at £1 per acre. It was a town which grew around a discovery of copper in 1842 and the subsequent mine became the first successful metal mine in Australia. There was a huge influx of miners, particularly from Cornwall. Lots of new houses were needed and a joiner would have been seen as a valuable tradesman. Mary and John never left Kapunda, Mary living to the great age of eighty-two. Other family members joined them, mainly those with trades such as bricklaying and stonemasonry, mostly living close by.

Miners Cottage, Kapunda. Courtesy Bruce Elder, Aussietowns.com.au.

Mary's older son Benjamin from a previous relationship and his cousin Jane were listed on the ship's manifest in 1857 and both settled in the boom town of Gawler, South Australia, about twenty miles from the other members of the family in Kapunda. Jane married a widowed stonemason, Thomas Garnett, from Shuttleworth. He had emigrated with his wife in 1858 but sadly she was to die, aged only twenty-six, of a fever. Jane and Thomas went on to have twelve children together, including a pair of twins in 1865 and finally a set of triplets in 1874, none of whom sadly survived.

Gawler around 1850. Courtesy Gawler History Team.

In 1837 the Surveyor General for the Colony of South Australia recognised the potential of the location for South Australia's first country township outside Adelaide. It was located very consciously beside a river and surrounded by rolling hills. As they had both been country dwellers in England, maybe it was this that attracted Jane and her new husband? Gawler went on to become one of the most populated early towns in South Australia and a centre for both mining and agriculture.

The Bunyip Newspaper Offices. Courtesy Bruce Elder, Aussietowns.com.au.

The Gawler Arms and *The Bunyip* newspaper offices are two examples of buildings which were constructed in the 1860's around the time that Jane and her husband settled there. Gawler Arms. Courtesy Bruce Elder, Aussietowns.com.au.

Jane's husband died in 1880, aged just forty-six. An inquest found he had died of natural causes, but it left Jane with six children to look after. Her sons became farmers, as their ancestors had been at Smithills and, like her Aunt Mary, Jane lived into her eighties. Mary's son Benjamin married Sarah Durant in 1873 and went on to have eleven children, six of whom survived into adulthood. Sarah died in 1913, and Benjamin died in Goolwa, on South Australia's coastline, in 1924.

The branches of the family became well established in Australia, though no doubt not without much hard work, and they appear to have lived lives far removed from how their life would have been had they remained on Smithills Estate; certainly, a long way from that dreary Monday morning in 1855.

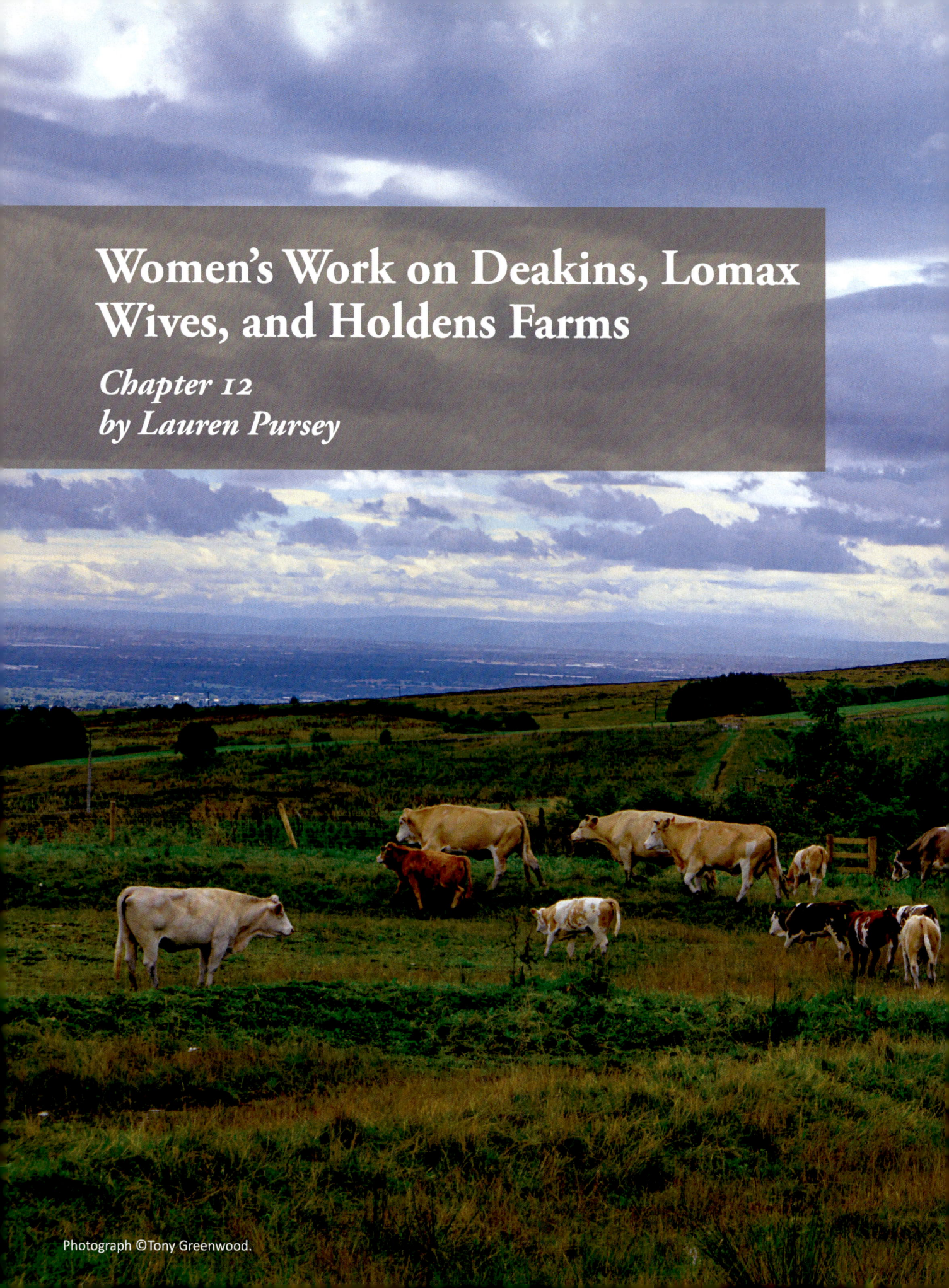

Women's Work on Deakins, Lomax Wives, and Holdens Farms

Chapter 12
by Lauren Pursey

Betty Longworth is born in 1843 to Sarah and Thomas Longworth and into a farming family. Age seven, we find Betty living on Smithills Estate at Sheep House Farm with her parents and six siblings. She occupies her days as a scholar, likely at the local school on Colliers Row.

By 1861, the family has moved to Lomax Wives Farm, and Betty has started her working life as a dairy maid. For at least the next ten years, though the family moves slightly down the road to a farm in Halliwell, she helps provide for the family farm business as a servant. Betty never marries despite the patriarchal expectations of the time and instead lives a remarkably independent life. By 1881 she is not only the head of household at Smith Fold Farm in Little Hulton, where she lives with two of her younger sisters, but is also the farmer of its twenty-one acres. Later in life, she moves away from agriculture and in 1901 is a cotton weaver living with a sister and brother-in-law.

Sheephouse Farm. Courtesy Halliwell History Society.

Betty's working life reflected the key occupations of many women from Smithills Estate. After leaving school they began work as early as ten or less, either on family farms or in the textiles industry. If these women married they often continued working and contributing to their new families' farms, although most left both domestic service and the textiles industry at this point to undertake unpaid and often overlooked work within the household.

Holdens in Winter. Photograph ©Tony Greenwood.

The aim of this chapter is to present a clearer picture of the working lives of the women on the estate, with a particular focus on agricultural work. It tackles the common notions surrounding what life was like historically for women, such as the idea that all women were dependants whose sole purpose was to marry and do needlework. This is of course an over-simplified statement and, though it does contain some truth about the patriarchal limits to women's freedom, they did not sit idle throughout history. As we will see throughout this chapter, working-class women were vital economic providers for their families through their work both in and outside the home. A sample of census entries taken between 1841 and 1911 detailing the occupations of women who lived at Deakins Farm, Lomax Wives Farm, and Holdens Farm will assist in the construction of a broad picture of women's occupations.

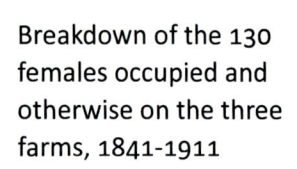

Breakdown of the 130 females occupied and otherwise on the three farms, 1841-1911

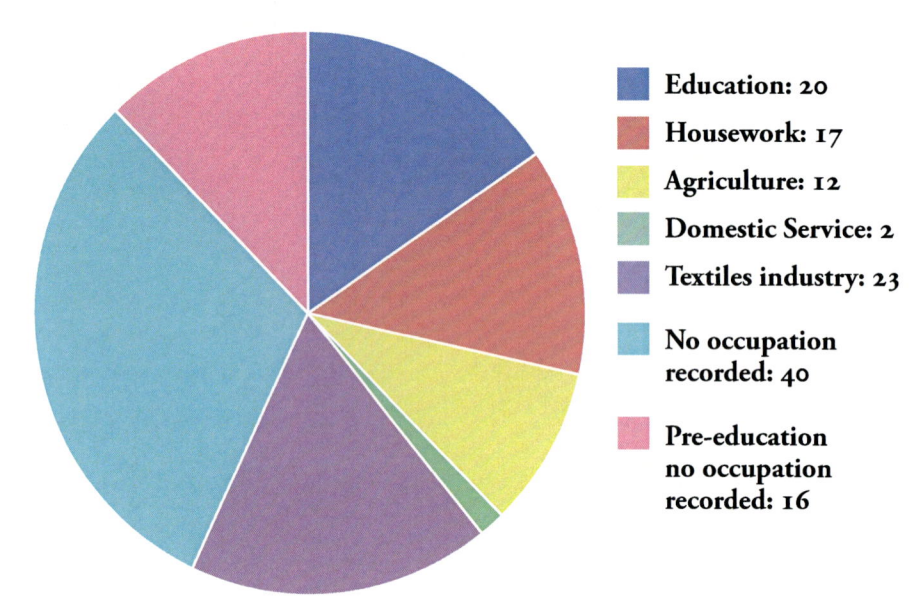

- Education: 20
- Housework: 17
- Agriculture: 12
- Domestic Service: 2
- Textiles industry: 23
- No occupation recorded: 40
- Pre-education no occupation recorded: 16

Deakins Farm consisted of a farm and cottages on the western edge of the estate, Lomax Wives Farm, a smaller holding of around ten acres to the north of Coal Pit Road, and Holdens, a large farm of fifty-seven acres found on the northwest of the estate all the way back to 1322. Across our period there were a total of one hundred and thirty females recorded on the censuses across seven classes. Each of these will be discussed in turn throughout the chapter.

Scholars

Number of female scholars within the three farm households, 1841-1911

1841	1851	1861	1871	1881	1891	1901	1911
0	6	4	1	1	5	0	3

Most girls on the estate would start school at either four or five years old and leave before their teens. For example, sisters Margaret and Mary Thornley at Deakins Farm were aged eleven and nine in 1861 and were both employed as cotton factory workers, whilst their siblings Jane and Anne aged seven and five were still in education. We see how class could factor into a woman's education as the oldest girl from our census entries to still be in education came from an upper-class family. Rachel Eatock, daughter of local yeoman farmer Robert Eatock, and sister of Timothy and Robert, was fifteen in 1851 and still a scholar, likely because there was little necessity for her to work, whereas Margaret and Mary came from a working-class family. Their father worked in a quarry and they had to help their parents provide for themselves and their three younger siblings.

Women and the textiles industry

Number of female textile workers within the three farm households, 1841-1911

1841	1851	1861	1871	1881	1891	1901	1911
3	6	6	2	2	0	4	1

The Thompson family of James and Jane Thompson and their five children lived at Deakins Farm from 1881 to 1911. Their four daughters were engaged in textiles work. With the nearby Dean Mills and Halliwell Bleach Works the estate was well situated to allow women to actively contribute to their family's income through waged work. In 1901 Anne, Alice and Fanny Thompson aged eighteen, seventeen and fourteen, were employed as grey stitchers at a calico bleach works. Their job was to join together the unbleached (grey) rolls of cloth. Through the censuses we can get a sense of the variety of jobs available in textiles: doffers removed full bobbins; doublers combined fibres for spinning; finishers cleaned up the surface of bleached cloth; thread winders wound spun cotton; cotton weavers ran the looms; and packers packaged the finished goods.

Female workers at Barnes Mill, Bolton. Courtesy *The Bolton News.*

The oldest of our women working in the textiles industry was Mary Constantine who was recorded as 'making cotton' aged twenty-seven in 1881. Mary stands out because she was married at this time, whilst it was much more common for women employed in textiles to be in their early teens to early twenties and unmarried. Though she had perhaps returned to work in order to help provide for her widowed mother, Elizabeth Sewart, who we discuss later.

The Thompson family's eldest daughter Mary was born around 1879 and grew up on Smithills Estate before becoming a self-employed dressmaker by 1901, perhaps showing some of the enterprising spirit now familiar in the women working independently on the estate. In general, dressmaking was the most common self employment business for women, and in 1911 it accounted for thirty percent of all female entrepreneurs in business, many of whom were in the fifteen to twenty-four age range.[1] By 1911 we find Mary with no occupation recorded that year and living with her husband Harry Clayton, a general labourer, and their son James on Chorley Old Road. This gap in the census may well have been down to her being a married woman where her occupational details were deemed unimportant rather than her having given up her profession.

Women and agricultural work

Number of female agricultural workers within the three farm households, 1841-1911

1841	1851	1861	1871	1881	1891	1901	1911
0	0	2	2	5	0	2	1

Mary Constantine's mother Elizabeth was born around 1824 in Breightmet. She married John Sewart, a collier, and moved in with his family at Lower Tongs Farm where in 1851, like many women at the time, she contributed to the household income by working in a local cotton mill. By 1861 the couple had moved to a cottage at Lomax Wives Farm and had four children between the ages of two and nine, having moved up in the world since John found employment as a mechanic at a bleach works. The couple then turned their hand to farming and in 1871 John was listed as a farmer of ten acres and Elizabeth as a farmer's wife busy with six children to look after. Sadly, in March 1879 John died leaving a widowed Elizabeth, aged fifty-five, as the head of household and farmer of their ten acres. It was fairly common for the wife or daughter of a farmer to take responsibility for the family farm on the death of the male head of household as the nature of farm work meant women such as Elizabeth gained a wide range of skills, connections, and experience relevant to the running of a farm and had less need to remarry.[2]

As scholar Nicola Verdon notes, one additional task assigned to farmer's wives included overseeing the brewing of ales and non-alcoholic beverages.[3] This is an activity we see evidence of on the estate with local historian W D Billington stating that the Wagstaff family, who are recorded as having lived at Deakins Farm at least between 1901 and 1911, sold home brewed ales and herbal drinks to tourists travelling through the estate.[4]

Recipes from the Diary of Thomas John Leech

Gingerette Cordial + Brandy Recipe

- 1 Penny-worth of tincture of ginger
- 1 Penny-worth of the tincture of capsicum
- Mix together
- Then take a half pound of lump sugar and dissolve it in a pint of hot water
- When cold add sufficient ginger and capsicum to suit the taste
- This may be made into ginger brandy by adding one bottle of spirits of wine to every gallon, colour with burnt sugar.[5]

Blackberry Wine Recipe

- Gather your blackberry when full ripe. Take 12 quarts and crush them with your hand
- Boil six gallons of water with 12 pounds of brown sugar for a quarter of an hour
- Scum it well then pour it on the blackberrys and let it stand all night then drain it through a hair sieve
- Put into your cask 6 pounds of malaga raisins, a little (salt or oat?) Then put the wine into the cask with 1 ounce of isinglass which must be dissolved in a little cider.
- Stir it all up together close it up and let it stand for six months and then bottle it.[6]

Cordial recipes from the diary of Thomas John Leech, 1880. From the collection of Karen Holroyd. Photograph ©Karen Holroyd.[7]

Given the agricultural nature of the estate many women were either born into or married into farming families. From our data there are twelve women across the three farms who are recorded as having farming related occupations, which seems a fairly low number given the prevalence of farming. There were a range of titles given in our census entries for women's work on farms which highlights that women of all ages and relationship to the farmer contributed. We have: four entries for farmer's wife, four for farmer's daughter, two entries of female farmers in their own right (one of whom is Elizabeth discussed above), one dairy maid (Betty who we met at the start of the chapter), and even one farmer's niece.

When many of us think about women in this time period we imagine them mostly as the 'angel in the house', confined to their homes and occupied with domestic work.[8] While this is true of some more well-off women for many working-class women this was not an attainable lifestyle. The gendered spheres, in which the home was the woman's domain and the outside world of work the man's, which we often take as typical of this period, were not realistically applicable in households where everyone, parents and children, had to work in order to survive. The historian Ellen Ross estimates that prior to World War I only about five percent of unskilled workers' households could live off the man's wages alone.[9] Returning to our discussion of women's work on the estate, we will explore how the women's sphere of work was extended, in households such as the Longworths and Sewarts, out of the farmhouse to encompass the kitchen garden, the dairy and the farmyard, as highlighted by the scholars Nicola Verdon and Ivy Pinchbeck.[10]

Dairy cart. Courtesy Beamish Museum People's Collection.

So, what sort of work would these women have carried out?

One area of the farm in which women's work was especially prominent was the dairy, which on smaller northern farms remained the woman's domain into the early twentieth century.[11] This is evidenced in our data for Deakins Farm from the 1911 Census in which Edith Wagstaff's occupation was specified as 'farmer's daughter dairy work'. The work of farmer's wives and daughters in the dairy was of the utmost importance; in addition to having an in-depth knowledge on the making of dairy products they also had to manage and train other workers and were involved in the process from the very start, often advising their husbands on which calves to purchase and then rearing the animals themselves.[12]

Their days would have been long, beginning with milking the cattle at three or four in the morning. Their work would often continue until late afternoon, the production of cheese in particular could be physically strenuous with the process requiring 'pressing, salting, turning, cleaning and wiping'.[13] Although the making of butter was a quicker job, often only taking place during the morning on a couple of days a week.[14] The production of these items was economically important for the household, as it was also the farmer's wife's job to sell them at market, the money from sales, referred to as 'pin money' being used to supplement the household and purchase essentials such as food and clothing.[15]

Out in the farmyard, it was the woman's job to manage the kitchen garden and any pigs and poultry in order to provide food for the family, with any excess again being sold to help supplement family income. In many cases women's tasks also included weeding, clearing stones from the fields, leading horses at the plough, planting crops such as peas, beans, and potatoes, digging up and cleaning vegetables. They would also play a significant role during haymaking, and pitch in to help with reaping the harvest.[16]

Advert for a farm couple, specifying the need for a woman to manage the dairy. *Blackburn Standard,* 9 June 1852. Public domain.

Traditional butter churn. Courtesy Shutterstock/Janelle Lugge.

Haymaking. Courtesy Beamish Museum People's Collection.

These women's work did not finish there as it was also expected they would keep up with domestic duties, which at their most basic included preparing food for their family and any workers, cleaning, and raising children. All of which were incredibly time consuming, especially when we consider that even basics like bread would be baked from scratch. Food for winter often needed to be prepared and preserved in advance, wood had to be collected to keep fires burning, and so the list goes on.[17] To top everything off, the women of the household, including any servants, would often spend their evenings sewing and mending garments, linens and blankets for the family.[18] At Holdens, the largest of our farms, we find in our data two domestic servants hired to help with such tasks.

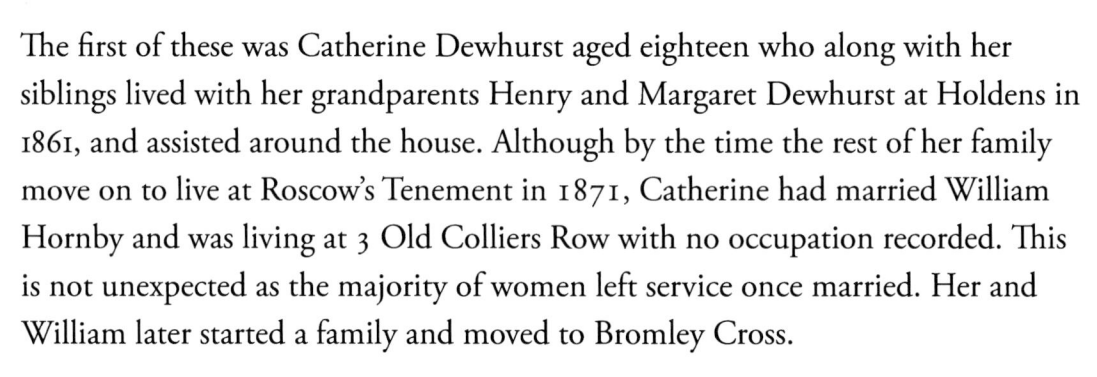

The first of these was Catherine Dewhurst aged eighteen who along with her siblings lived with her grandparents Henry and Margaret Dewhurst at Holdens in 1861, and assisted around the house. Although by the time the rest of her family move on to live at Roscow's Tenement in 1871, Catherine had married William Hornby and was living at 3 Old Colliers Row with no occupation recorded. This is not unexpected as the majority of women left service once married. Her and William later started a family and moved to Bromley Cross.

'A Month's Darning'. Watercolor by Enoch Wood Perry. Courtesy MET Museum.

Women in charge of farming households would need to know about a variety of medicines and remedies in order to ensure the health of their family and workers. *The Compleat Housewife: or Accomplished Gentlewoman's Companion*, first published in 1728, gives us an idea of what sort of remedies might have been used.[19]

Treatment 'For a Burn or Scald'
'Take laurel leaves, chop them in hogs-grease; strain it, and keep it for use'.

Treatment 'For a pain in the Stomach'
'Take a quarter of a pound of blue currants, wipe them clean, and pound them in a mortar, with an ounce of aniseeds bruised; before you put them to the currants, make this into a bolus with a little syrup of clove-gilliflowers; take every morning the quantity of a walnut, and drink rosemary tea, instead of other tea, for your breakfast; if the pain returns, repeat it'.

Moving cattle on Smithills Estate. Photograph ©Tony Greenwood.

It is worth mentioning the ambiguity surrounding job titles, which is one pitfall of the census as a source. Although here we have interpreted domestic service as indicating a paid occupation for Catherine it could also have been the case since she was living with family that her housework was unpaid. Similarly we find Eliza Dewhurst of Lomax Wives Farm recorded as a housekeeper in 1891 which we could interpret as signifying that another family employs her to run their household. However, it is also common for this to refer to a woman performing domestic housework duties at home. As Eliza was living with her husband and four young children, she was most likely the latter.[20]

Women's housework and hidden work

Number of blank occupation spaces in female entries within the three farm households, 1841-1911

1841	1851	1861	1871	1881	1891	1901	1911
16	6	8	4	4	8	7	6

Looking at our data, by far the most common entries in the occupation column are blank spaces. Out of the one hundred and thirty entries, forty have no occupation recorded. We can see why scholars suggest there is an under recording of women's work, since this is almost double the twenty-two entries for the next largest occupational category of textiles. Several reasons for this have been identified including social ideas and biases surrounding their careers and place in the home. Changes to guidance regarding recording women's work across this period, for example census enumerators were told not to record farmer's wife as an occupation after 1871, and of course the fact that much of women's work was unpaid and therefore unrecorded, all go towards hiding women's contributions.[21]

Number of female houseworkers within the three farm households, 1841-1911

1841	1851	1861	1871	1881	1891	1901	1911
0	4	6	6	0	1	0	0

Not all women's domestic labour went unrecorded, and in our data we find seventeen entries which list housework as the woman's occupation. Notably, this does not include only married women with children but younger women too, including sixteen-year-old Margaret Winstanley who lived with her older brother at Deakins Farm in 1861. Also her niece Elizabeth Winstanley who in 1871 aged six classed housework as her occupation. Entries for housework across the three farms peak in 1861 and 1871. We do however see a large decline in the recording of women's housework from 1881, with a single housework entry in 1891.

The language used in the census data can also give us an insight into social and economic elements of these women's lives. The clearest example of this in our study comes from the 1851 census listings for the occupants of Deakins Farm and its surrounding buildings, where three women express that they are occupied by housework all using different phrasing, which reflects their class and potentially also their level of education. Mary Thornley whose husband worked as a quarryman has her occupation listed as house wife. Similarly Mary Fairhurst whose husband was a farmer had 'work in house' listed as hers. In comparison to these working-class women Martha Eatock, wife of the aforementioned Robert, listed her occupation as a much grander 'angel in the house' title: 'mistress of domestic affairs'. This likely meant that she oversaw her servants carrying out the actual work.

The Farmer's Wife or Complete Country Housewife Cookbook. Alex Hogg, London, 1780s. Courtesy Wellcome Collection and Leeds University Archive.

Conclusion

It is hoped that this chapter has illustrated that although women's work was often under recorded the women of Smithills Estate worked tirelessly and skilfully to provide and care for their families. These women often started working in childhood, either on the family farm or in the textiles industry, and once married continued with domestic labour. To put it simply these women, like countless other working-class women across the country, made history in their everyday actions.

'Where There's a Will, There's Always a Way': Up the Sixty-three Steps to Twitchells Farm and the Brown Cow Beerhouse

Chapter 13
by Tony Greenwood

Sixty-three Steps, 'No Trespass' sign on path to High Shores Clough. Postcard. From the collection of Tony Greenwood.

At the top of the Sixty-three Steps a path winds through a narrow field with old woodland hanging on the steep sides of the clough. The field, shaped like a withered tongue, gradually rises through young trees to a pile of rubble overgrown with brambles, a holly tree, and weeds. This is the remains of Twitchells Farm. A place known to the people of Bolton as the old farm which sold beer to the residents of the dry Barrow Bridge, and to the colliers on their way to and from work at the mines. Now it is just a ruin where the butterflies and birds gather in the summer, and the mice and voles rustle through the undergrowth. A place to stop and think about the families and workers that lived there, their sometimes difficult lives, and the pleasure they might have had from living at such a lovely spot.

The strange shape of the land is caused by two fast flowing brooks coming from the south west edge of Smithills Estate, joining at a point next to the path at the bottom of the steps. Dean Brook and Dakins (or Deakins) Brook flow here through small wood-filled ravines known as cloughs. At this spot three townships meet: the old parish of Deane to the south; the south east edge of Horwich township in the centre; and Halliwell to the north east. A flight of steps leads up onto this triangular piece of land from the road at Barrow Bridge, formerly an old packhorse route between east Lancashire and Blackrod.

Stories of the deserted village of Barrow Bridge became popular at the turn of the twentieth century, when local author Allen Clarke brought people from all over the north of England to his mass picnics. Ten thousand visitors came in 1901 and gathered along the village street.[1] Some walked to the site of the first mills where the old packhorse route crosses the river to find this well-known flight of steps. Some would climb up to Twitchells Farm, take their picnic in the field next to the farmhouse, and be served tea by the family that lived there.

Photograph ©Tony Greenwood.

Twitchells in 1932, from the *Bolton Journal*. Courtesy Bolton Council.

Clarke recalled in his book *Moorland and Memories,* 'Twitcham Arms, an old farm with a beer licence at the top of Sixty-three steps. It was not allowed to sell on a Sunday, a little difficulty cunningly disposed of by cutting out a pane of glass and selling pints through the window, showing that where there's a will there's always a way. There was no inn in the village and any spinner in the village wanting a drink had sixty-three steps to mount- he earned his liquor didn't he'.[2] In 1860 the farm lost its licence when young widow Ellen Guest was caught by magistrates selling beer after hours. She was fined 20s. plus costs.[3] But who else lived there, what did they do and what was the story behind the farm and beerhouse?

Bolton Chronicle,
1 December 1860.
Courtesy *The Bolton News.*

HORWICH AND RIVINGTON.
BEERSELLER FINED.—At the County Police Court, Little Bolton, on Thursday, Ellen Guest, beerseller, of Horwich, was fined 20s. and costs for having the house open for the sale of beer at 11 20 p m on Saturday last. An excuse was attempted as an answer to the effect that the pot on the "hob" had tea in it, but the magistrates had not faith in the transformation of the decoction of John Barleycorn into that of John Chinaman.

Over time, this spot has had a number of names, Twitchills or even Twitchems, now we know it as Twitchells. A 'twitchel' is an old Lancashire word for a ginnel or short-cut. So this piece of land would have been a way up to the old farms further up the hill from Bolton. William Senior's 1620 map does not show Twitchells but does show Toot Hill. This old map also shows the tongue of land as recently developed farmland, probably part of Deakins Farm, a farm next to the small hill with a lovely viewpoint up to the moor. Toot means 'look out' as in the local phrase, 'What are yer tootin' at?'

Detail from Senior's 1622 map of Walker Fold - Twitchells on far right between the two brooks. Courtesy Bolton Council.

156

Going further back in time, an early history of Lancashire says that, 'in 1322–3 the herbage of the wood called Le Twecheles, (now Twitchills), could not be agisted, through the deficiency of cattle in the district, owing to the Scottish raid at midsummer, 1322'.[4] Agist was a farming practice. Livestock were taken-in for payment and fed in the woods and pastures. A tax would be raised when this was practiced in the King's forests. It was the Scots of Robert the Bruce who raided south Lancashire and were known to have been as far south as Chorley. So perhaps it was local bands of outlaws and not the Scots who raided the farms and churches after the Scots had left Lancashire. Raiding parties were sent out by the local lord of the manor to steal possessions from the fleeing people from north Lancashire.

Not a lot else is known about this area until around five hundred years later when a farm was built on the tongue of land owned by yeoman farmer Robert Eatock of Deakins Farm. He owned it from around 1830 to 1864.[6] Twitchells was a small farmhouse, with a barn and a well, pastures and meadows, and part of the woods.

Toot Hill. Photograph ©Tony Greenwood.

1844 Rating List[5]
Twitchells: Henry Guest
Owner: Robert Haytock [Eatock]
Daffodil Meadow
Tongue
Near Pasture
Far Pasture
Shrugs or Wood
Far Croft
House + Barn

Twitchells ruined farmhouse beside paths to Walker Fold and Deakins. Photograph ©Tony Greenwood.

It appears that the flat enclosed grassy fields of Twitchells used to be a croft. In Lancashire these croft fields were used for bleaching. Yarn and cloth would have been brought from the handloom weavers in their cottages at Walkers Fold and Deakins Farm and laid out in the croft. They were spread out on the grass and hedges and bleached using the strong powers of sunlight. During the late eighteenth century this process was improved by using chemicals. Raw cloth would then be given many soakings in a solution of potash and lime with buttermilk and water before being laid out in the sunshine. But by the turn of the nineteenth century the factories further down Dean Brook took over the bleaching and the crofts returned to farming.

Below our farm on the tongue the clough was developing and changing from a lonely spot to a rural mill setting. A cotton spinning and carding factory was built next to the ford across Dean Brook in the 1790s. It moved to a larger site down the clough and across the brook from Barrow Farm and was named Dean Mills. Weavers who could no longer make a living from handloom weaving would travel to the new mill for work, and the crofters would walk to the bleach factory, using the paths past Twitchells. As the mines opened up on Winter Hill in the 1820s, miners working in the moorland collieries travelled up to their work in the other direction.

Photograph
©Tony Greenwood.

In his book *Moorlands and Memories* Allen Clarke says of the area:

'Sixty-three Steps has no antiquity, but is comparatively modern. Before the mills and houses were erected, in the first half of last century (ie 19th century), the site of our village (Barrow Bridge) was a moorland slope at the entrance to bonny Halliwell glen. The road past the old mills … to Sixty-three steps was not in existence – In fact there was no Sixty-three steps. The original road from Walker Fold ran down the slope … The Steps were put up to make it easier and cleaner access to the moorland track to Walker Fold and Horwich (past Twitchells)…from which came some of the first workers at the Barrowbridge Mills.

It was a steep and slippery slope, and in rainy weather a very "slutchy" and rather dangerous ascent. –In order to come down safely the people had to sit down and slide down. There is a legend that one woman after coming down one wet morning was so thick with mud that she had to be put in the brook and washed and scraped'.[7]

Building steps up the steep muddy trail was a great way to encourage them to walk past the farm where home-made ale would be available. According to local stories, Robert Eatock built the steps to his farm at Twitchells. It became the Brown Cow, a beerhouse ready to catch all the passing trade as well as the visitors from Barrow Bridge, a temperance village at the time. The steps were likely built around the same time as Twitchells farmhouse, but are not shown on the first Ordnance Survey map (1845-47) which does show the tracks past the farmhouse, but not the steps.

Ordnance Survey six-inch map, surveyed 1845-47. Courtesy National Library of Scotland.

Official records do not often mention the beerhouse at Twitchells. As we have seen in 1844 it was just a farm, with Henry Guest the tenant farmer. He lived there with his wife Ellen, two sons and eight daughters, including Rachel who would marry Thomas Turner and farm at Harricroft and Haslams before emigrating to Canada in 1912. Henry's daughters worked as doublers in the mill, probably Dean Mills. He also had a side line with Timothy Eatock, son of landlord Robert, and brother of another Robert Eatock who later emigrated to Kansas, selling timber from the clough.[8]

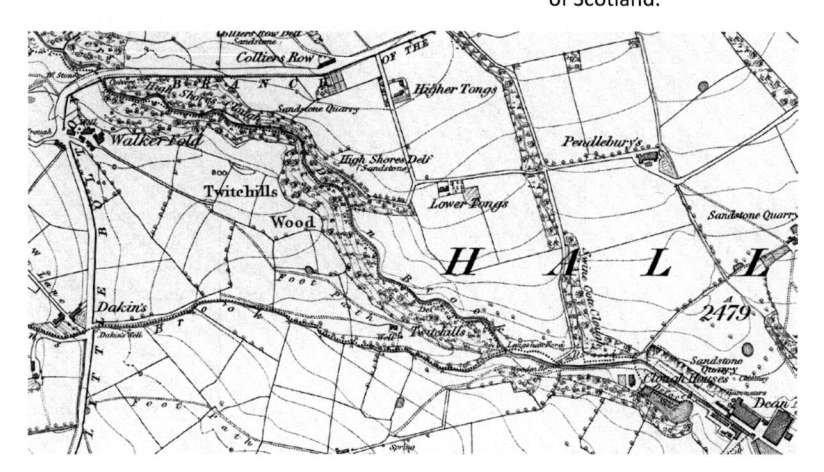

TO BE SOLD, some valuable TIMBER (in lots to suit purchasers) at DAKIN'S WOOD, Horwich, near the Dean Mills, comprising 170 Oaks, 57 Ash, and 38 Birch Trees.—For further particulars apply to Mr. T. EATOCK, of Rivington Lodge, Horwich; or to HENRY GUEST, the tenant, on the premises.

Bolton Chronicle, 24 March 1860. Courtesy The Bolton News.

Henry Guest died in November 1860 age only fifty-eight and his widow Ellen continued to run the beerhouse along with the small nine-acre farm. It was a week or so after Henry's death that Ellen was caught by the magistrates serving beer late into the night. I would like to think they were having a wake for Henry. A few years later, the beerhouse quietly closed. Twitchells was advertised for sale in the *Bolton Chronicle* in 1865 without mention of it. It was the first lot of twelve in the sale of Robert Eatock's estate.[9]

Ellen Guest left Twitchells and three Fairhurst families moved in together. Head of the house was John Fairhurst, a farm labourer, perhaps at Deakins Farm where he had lived as a boy. Deakins had been a handloom cottage where his father James worked his looms. Mary Fairhurst, John's wife, worked as a cotton operative leaving her two young children in the care of Aunt Ann. Ann being the wife of Ralph Fairhurst, John's brother. Mary and John had two children by 1871, Jane and Mary, born at Colliers Row. Ralph worked at the bleach works as a cotton cloth finisher, whilst Ann looked after the house and the young children. Also living in the farmhouse is John and Ralph's youngest brother, Wright. Wright worked with John on the farms and Charlotte, Wright's young wife and youngest sister to Mary and Ann, joined the others walking down to the cotton mill every day.

Mary, Ann, and Charlotte Fairhurst were Greenhalgh sisters from Colliers Row. They also came from a family of handloom weavers. So, the three Fairhurst brothers married three Greenhalgh sisters and they all lived together at Twitchells. Head of household John Fairhurst died in 1871 aged thirty-eight and so the rest of the Fairhursts moved out, going their own ways. Both Ralph and Wright had long lives in Bolton with large families.

Although Twitchells and Deakins are freehold farms, they became part of the Ainsworth's Smithills Estate, maybe the family bought the underlying freehold in 1865. After inheriting in 1870 Colonel Richard Henry Ainsworth would call there on his rides around his estate, taking his horse up to Bob's Smithy for shoeing, which at that time was run by another member of the Greenhalgh family. The estate gamekeeper Joseph Towler moved into Twitchells after the Fairhursts left.

Ordnance Survey six-inch map, surveyed 1892. Courtesy National Library of Scotland.

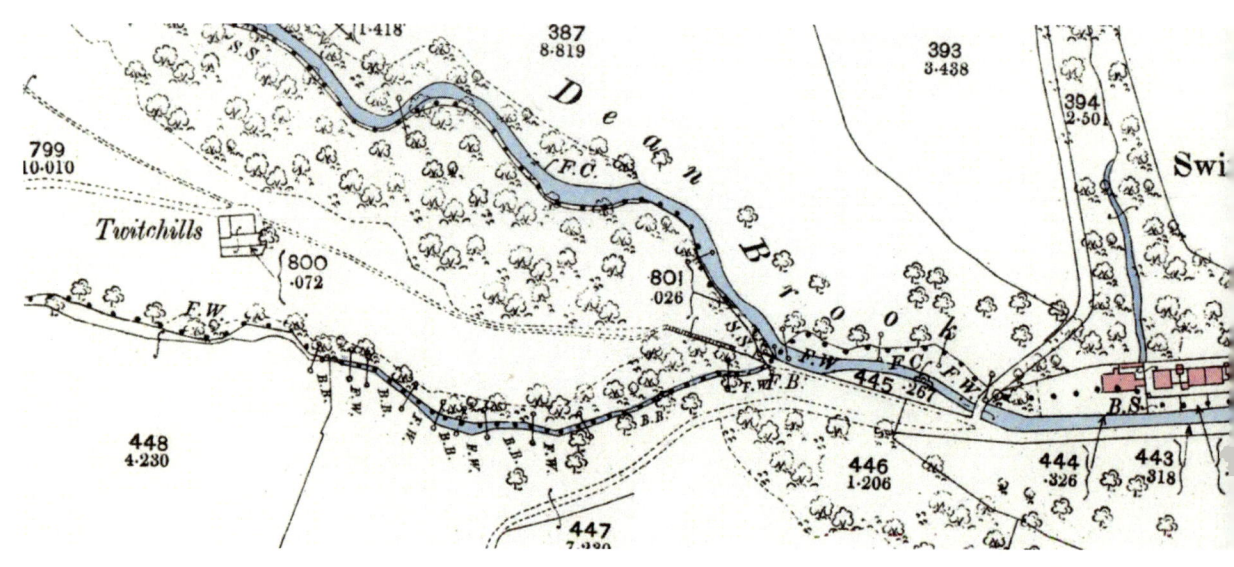

Joseph and his wife Mary lived there in 1881 with their five young children. Alice, the eldest daughter, worked at the bleach-works, Alexander, their fourteen-year-old son was a gardener, possibly at Smithills Hall.

After this, Twitchells farmland was incorporated into the land of other farms, and the house became a cottage for local people to live in whilst working on the farms at Walker Fold and Deakins, or the mills and bleach works. Richard Fielding, a fifty-eight-year-old farm labourer, lived at the cottage in 1891 with his wife Ellen from Yorkshire, before John Holdsworth moved in with his wife Elizabeth and their family in the early 1900s. John was a Quaker and gamekeeper to Colonel Ainsworth.[10] He worked as a bleacher at a calico works so his gamekeeper job was likely to be as a watcher for trespassers on the estate and a beater when shooting parties were on the moors. Elizabeth Holdsworth was well known for her cooking and baking and the Colonel often went to the cottage for meals.[11] There was room in the cottage to take in boarders who worked at the bleach works and cotton mills. It could also accommodate packmen as they travelled through the village with their ponies.

Sadly, John Holdsworth died at Twitchells in 1904 from bronchitis and cardiac failure when he was forty-two. Just four days after his eighteenth-month-old daughter had also died of bronchitis. Elizabeth was left a widow with three young children and two boarders. She was still there in 1911 with daughters Catherine and Ruth ages sixteen and ten and son James thirteen. Catherine worked at the bleach works as a cloth finisher and so walked down the steps to the works with James who also worked there along with boarder Thomas France. Ruth was still at school. All the children had attended Colliers Row School, joining the children from Barrow Bridge who would walk past their house every morning. Thomas became stepfather to the three children when he married his landlady Elizabeth in 1912 and they went on to have two more children of their own.

Elizabeth and Thomas still lived there in the 1920s with their five children. In June the front of the house was a mass of climbing roses, but water came from a nearby well and there was no electricity, so their lives were somewhat spartan. Elizabeth supplied tea to those who visited the cottage, 'at the top of the steps the whole area surrounding the farmhouse was speckled with families sitting on the grass and Elizabeth supplying jugs of hot water and tea

'Visitors from Allen Clarke's Barrow Bridge Giant Picnic', 1901. Postcard. From the collection of Tony Greenwood.

"63 STEPS" RESTORED

The "63 steps" at Barrow Bridge are now restored. The steps have been firmly cemented into place by Bolton Corporation employees, and it is probable that a handrail will be erected. Of the original steps, 14 were missing, and have been replaced by new ones to make a flight 126 feet long.

Horwich Journal and Guardian, December 1939. Courtesy Horwich Heritage Centre.

to all and sundry for a small remuneration'.[12] A frequent visitor to Bob's Smithy via Twitchells complained that the path from the top of Sixty-three Steps was out of bounds during the Colonel's time, although he could have been referring to the path next to Dean Brook. A sign was erected in 1896 to keep trespassers out before all the problems at the mass trespass that year.

The steps seem to have been refurbished during Elizabeth's tenure, and old postcards from the time the visitors started coming to Barrow Bridge show the steps in good order. But wear and tear would have its own effect and occasional flooding would wear away the steep slope either side. By 1939, the steps were worn down again and repaired by Bolton Corporation who also replaced the rotten handrails with metal. The farmhouse was still on maps around 1938 but

Small Skipper

Small Copper

Small Tortoiseshell

Butterflies found today at Twitchells

Speckled Wood	Green-veined White
Meadow Brown	Gatekeeper
Small Skipper	Orange-tip
Ringlet	Peacock
Small Copper	Small White
Red Admiral	Large Skipper
Small Tortoiseshell	Wall
Comma	Small Heath
Holly Blue	Brimstone
Painted Lady	Large White

Speckled Wood

had gone by 1948. There was no one living there by 1939, so it could have been abandoned in the 1930s and demolished in the later 1950s.

Nowadays Twitchells is a lovely, lonely country meadow, with wildflowers, butterflies, and lots of singing birds. If you are walking through the fields, reflect on the colliers, the mill workers, and travellers passing along the paths to work or home. Some would stop at the beerhouse after work for a late night ale. Then after all the factories closed visitors took strolls through the quiet village to enjoy a picnic and visit the tea shop at the old rose covered cottage at the top of the Sixty-three Steps.

Photographs
©Tony Greenwood.

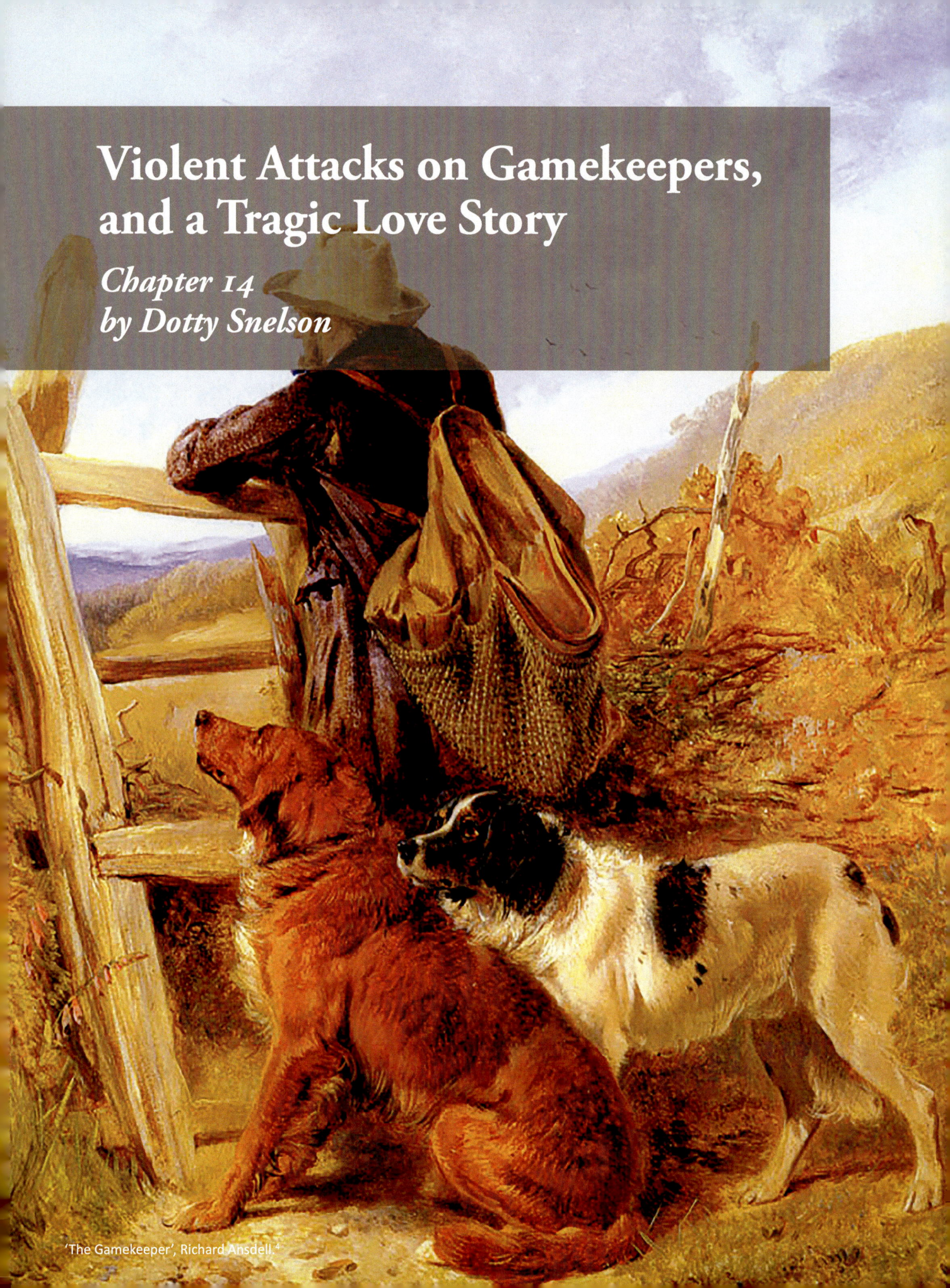

Violent Attacks on Gamekeepers, and a Tragic Love Story

*Chapter 14
by Dotty Snelson*

'The Gamekeeper', Richard Ansdell.

Hunting has long been a passion of the wealthy, and the moors of Smithills Estate presented the occupiers of Smithills Hall with fertile hunting and shooting ground. The heyday of the gamekeeper was from the mid nineteenth century to World War I, although there are examples of gamekeepers working on the moor before this. After the war many large estates were sold off or broken up due to death duties and a lack of available staff. To keep the moor viable gamekeepers could be valuable assets to their masters, but what was it like as a gamekeeper on the moor?

Henry Jennison Peachey

Sometimes inexplicably known as Fred, Henry Jennison Peachey was born in Suffolk in 1837, one of at least five siblings born to John Peachey, a farmer. By 1861, he had travelled up north and was a gamekeeper boarding at a house in Buckshaw Village near Cuerden. He married Ann Pert from London in 1870 and they took up residence in Sharples, probably due to his getting a job as a gamekeeper on Smithills Estate. Newspaper articles of the day often reported on affrays between poachers and gamekeepers and Henry featured large in some quite bloody incidents.

Shooting Party from Smithills Hall, including Nigel Combe Ainsworth. The chap on the far left may well have been a gamekeeper but not Henry Jennison Peachey who died in 1908. *Bolton Chronicle,* 15 August 1930. Courtesy *The Bolton News.*

An article appeared in the *Edinburgh Evening News* of 1882 detailing a 'poaching outrage' in Bolton.[1] By this time Henry was living at 3 Harricroft Cottages and the vicious encounter saw him come across poachers netting rabbits early one morning. Henry captured one poacher, who proceeded to wrestle Henry's stout walking stick from him and beat him with it. Another poacher returned and beat Henry around the head with a stone until he collapsed. His fellow keepers found him with terrible head wounds, poor Henry had come decidedly the worst off in this encounter. The one poacher actually caught in connection with this incident had come all the way from West Leigh, some ten miles distant. What is interesting is that what we would consider a local domestic incident nowadays should be reported in depth in a newspaper as far away as Edinburgh.

Harricroft Farm with Harricroft Farm Cottages to the left. Courtesy Halliwell Local History Society.

In another newspaper story he had to shoot a mad dog in Heaton. The dog had been worrying sheep on the Ainsworth estate. Yet more poachers were after conies (rabbits) at Dean Gate Farm, and Henry sent his own ferret down a rabbit hole to flush out the poacher's ferret. The said ferret was produced as evidence at the trial, and the poacher asked for it back. He was refused and fined 20s. He told Henry in court that, 'he was not such a grand gentleman' because he would not give the ferret back to him.[2]

'A Mad Dog Shot at Heaton'. *Bolton Chronicle*, 14 January, 1871. Courtesy *The Bolton News*.

A MAD DOG SHOT AT HEATON.—For several days past the inhabitants of Heaton have experienced some uneasiness on account of a dog, evidently mad, roaming about the neighbourhood. Acting under the advice of P.C. Fitton, Henry Peachey, gamekeeper to R. H. Ainsworth, Esq., who had a sheep bitten about a week ago, and which subsequently went mad, shot the dog on Monday.

In a locally reported instance, Henry Peachey and two under keepers saw poachers laying nets. When searched nothing was found but Peachey took possession of their greyhound. The poachers managed to snatch back the dog. They had four greyhounds in total but told Peachey and his companion John Sewart that they were merely walking them. Sewart challenged one of them named Coop, who kicked him and struck him on the head, as did another. Coop was fined 30s. and the rest 20s. plus costs. They were prosecuted for a breach of the Gaming Act.[3] Gamekeeping was obviously not for the faint hearted! During the mass trespass of Winter Hill in 1896 a keeper, possibly Henry, tried to stop the walkers accessing a path and was thrown into a brook. All in a long day's work for the much-maligned gamekeeper.

'The Gamekeeper', Richard Ansdell.[4]

Munsche's treatise on game keeping had said that employers treated the keepers as servants.[5] This notwithstanding, Henry J Peachey was one of only two retainers to ride in a funeral carriage in the procession at Peter Ainsworth's lavish funeral in January 1870. Nearly forty years later Henry was living in Westminster Road, off Blackburn Road, when he died at the age of seventy-one in 1908. He left to his wife his effects, which totalled £1982, not an inconsiderable sum. He was buried at St Paul's Church, Astley Bridge, but due to many of the older gravestones having fallen over his grave is impossible to locate.

What was it like to be a gamekeeper in the nineteenth century?

A gamekeeper needed a knowledge of wildlife and the ways of the countryside. Gamekeeping often ran in families with fathers instructing their sons from an early age. The fathers would remain in their post if their health allowed because they often lived in tied cottages.

They would often hand-rear pheasants for the shoot, break in hunting dogs, see off poachers, and keep estates clear of vermin by setting traps for rats and other nuisance animals. From the early 1900s the gamekeeper role developed when the 'battue' method of hunting was introduced. With this method estate workers acted as beaters, driving birds towards the guns and thus increasing the size of the 'bags' of game. A gamekeeper's knowledge meant the difference between a good day's shoot and a bad one. The gamekeeper was also responsible for enforcing the highly unpopular laws for the preservation of game. He could search labourer's cottages for snares, nets, and illicit game. It was he who would haul poachers before the Justices of the Peace for trial and punishment. He managed an area of countryside, to ensure that there was enough game for shooting, stalking, or angling, and acted as guide for these pursuits. Even though he could receive a cottage on the estate to live in, as well as his salary, it was a time-consuming and often taxing job.

Munsche depicts the gamekeeper as hated by the poor and treated not much better in other quarters, that is by his employer. According to Munsche a gamekeeper combined ignorance and authority, all too often making him brutal and arrogant. It was probably unfair to categorise them all in this way. No doubt there were decent ones, trying to keep a balance between enforcing unpopular laws, keeping on the right side of their employer, and keeping on friendly terms with the locals.

'Hunting Dog and Pheasants'. John Smith, 1680s. Mezzotint. Courtesy Yale Center for British Art.

'A chat with the keeper', Henry Peach Robinson, 1882. Courtesy iStock/duncan1890.

Nevertheless, the job could be dangerous at times. There are numerous accounts of altercations between poachers and gamekeepers. There was little provision for the poor in those days, no food banks or welfare benefits so hard-pressed poachers often had to defy the law in order to feed their families. The gamekeeper was equally determined that they would not get away with it. Between 1880 and 1896 thirty serious incidents were reported, resulting in the death of either poachers or gamekeepers.[6] In 1891 on the prestigious Chatsworth estate, a group of poachers armed with stones and cudgels got into a fight with estate workers.[7] Several workers were severely injured, including one poor man whose head injuries were so severe that he lost his senses and ended up in an asylum.

'The Gamekeepers Attacking the Poachers', George Cruikshank, early eighteenth century. Courtesy Yale Center for British Art, Yale University Art Gallery Collection, B1998.14.101.

Preparation for the hunting of birds provided employment for several on the moor. Alexander Arthur Beamish was said to have lived at Holdens Farm where he kept a pheasantry. After he left Holdens continued to be a pheasantry until shooting on the moors ended. For many years, prior to his move to Smithills, Beamish had been Head Gamekeeper for the late Colonel Peter Ormrod of Wyresdale Park, Scorton. Maybe in later life he decided to put his knowledge to effective use and breed birds himself for hunting on the estate.

Joseph Walsh of Park Cottage was Agent for the Ainsworths and would have been involved in managing gamekeepers as part of his job overseeing Smithills Estate business. He worked with his father for around five years before succeeding him in 1856. He was an important figure, even being the executor of Peter Ainsworth's will in 1870, and the books which the agents kept, detailing their work, go back to the early 1800s. Peter Ainsworth liked hunting but not shooting and had employed keepers since inheriting Smithills Estate from his father Richard in 1833. He also hired extra men as watchers to deter trespassers.[8]

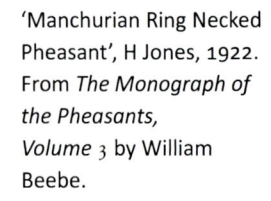

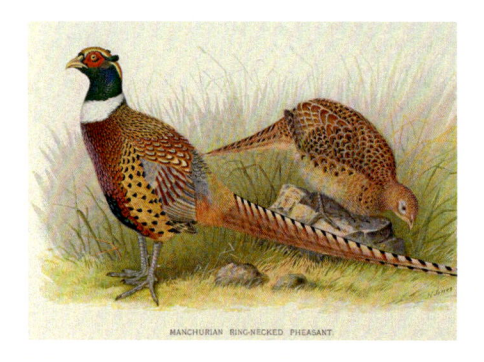

'Manchurian Ring Necked Pheasant', H Jones, 1922. From *The Monograph of the Pheasants, Volume 3* by William Beebe.

The *Leeds Times* of 1873 reported on the conduct of David Curwen, gamekeeper to Colonel Richard Henry Ainsworth.[9] The headline to the article read 'Outrageous Conduct of a Gamekeeper'. Curwen encountered a coal miner from Scot Lane,

Blackrod, one Edward Roberts, crossing a field along with his three dogs. Roberts said he was going to the farm of a Mr King to help get rid of his rats. Roberts threw up a pigeon and at that point Curwen shot the most valuable dog. A bullet grazed Roberts' foot causing bleeding. Curwen then wrestled Roberts to the ground and pulled from his pockets a ferret, two purse nets and two sovereigns; the proof he required that Roberts had been poaching. Many families lived in abject poverty, and the temptation of a tasty rabbit for the stew pot, would overcome the fear of punishment. Curwen then attempted to throttle Roberts! When the case came to court, the assault was considered unjustifiable and aggravated, and Curwen was fined £3 plus costs. It was reported that this charge would not disqualify him from carrying on as a gamekeeper.

I recently came across a grainy photo on social media of a man holding a shotgun. It was John Watson-O'Hara who died in 1924. He had lived at Green Nook, Smithills with his family of ten children and had been a gamekeeper covering a large area of Smithills, Horwich and Belmont. He and all those before him show that gamekeeping had been a substantial part of rural life in this area for centuries.

George Peachey's Story

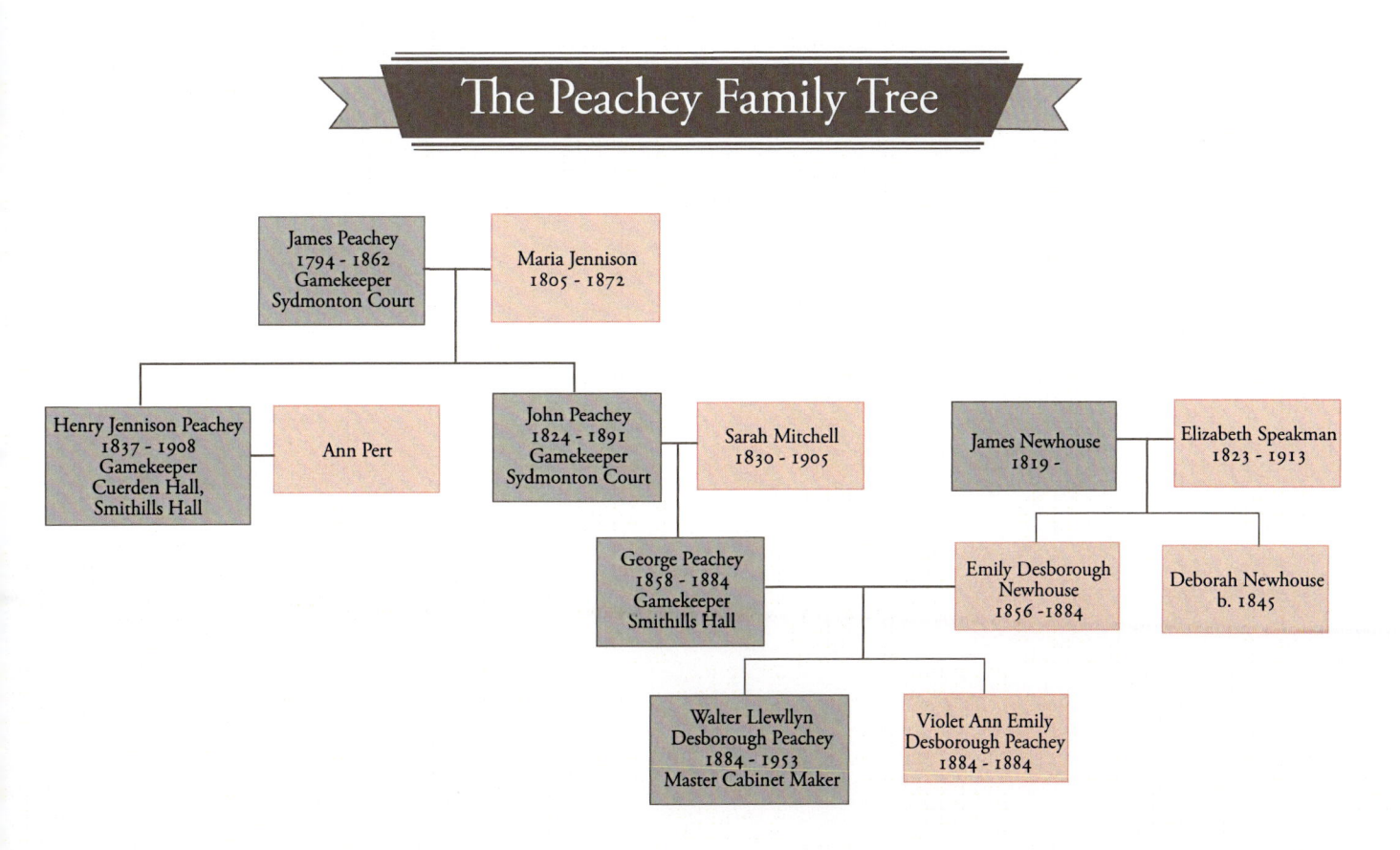

The Peachey Family Tree

- James Peachey 1794 - 1862, Gamekeeper Sydmonton Court — Maria Jennison 1805 - 1872
  - Henry Jennison Peachey 1837 - 1908, Gamekeeper Cuerden Hall, Smithills Hall — Ann Pert
  - John Peachey 1824 - 1891, Gamekeeper Sydmonton Court — Sarah Mitchell 1830 - 1905
    - George Peachey 1858 - 1884, Gamekeeper Smithills Hall — Emily Desborough Newhouse 1856 -1884
      - Walter Llewllyn Desborough Peachey 1884 - 1953, Master Cabinet Maker
      - Violet Ann Emily Desborough Peachey 1884 - 1884
- James Newhouse 1819 - — Elizabeth Speakman 1823 - 1913
  - Emily Desborough Newhouse 1856 -1884
  - Deborah Newhouse b. 1845

'The Gamekeeper', William Henry Hunt, 1834. Courtesy Yale Center for British Art, Paul Mellon Collection, B2001.2.939.

Nephew of Henry, George Peachey's story began in late 1856 in rural Hampshire where his father John was a gamekeeper on the vast Sydmonton Court estate, which had been home to the Kingsmill family from Tudor times. A Lady Alice Kingsmill married Bishop Pilkington of Rivington, the founder of Rivington Grammar School, during the reign of Elizabeth I. Elizabeth frowned on married priests, so they had to keep the marriage quiet. This is an early instance of a link between Sydmonton and the Bolton and Horwich areas. George's family lived in Pound House Cottage, a tied cottage on the estate. He would have learned about game keeping from his father, no doubt from an early age. When his father's brother Henry Jennison Peachey moved north and became a gamekeeper on the Smithills Estate this perhaps inspired George to also head north.

In 1881 we find George Peachey at the age of twenty-four living with the Heaton family at Newfield Farm. He is carrying on the gamekeeping tradition and working as a gamekeeper on Smithills Estate like his uncle Henry. It was against a background of profound change that a young George arrived to continue his family's tradition of gamekeeping. He was probably nervous yet excited, having travelled some distance to start his new life in the north of England. Sydmonton Court was a vast estate of some five thousand acres, and Smithills would seem small in comparison. He lodged with Mary Heaton who was farming eighteen acres with her sister and brother. The next two years were to be ones of seismic change for George and of tragedy too.

'Welcome to the Land of Freedom'. Frank Leslie for *Illustrated Newspaper*, 2 July 1887. Courtesy of Library of Congress.

George's gamekeeping career at Smithills, unlike that of his uncle Henry, was brief. Not long after the 1881 Census he emigrated to America. I have tried to trace his actual journey but with no success. However, there is no doubt that he arrived in America, as on 23 October 1882 in Fayette, Iowa, he married Emily Newhouse of Bolton. He may have met and courted Emily in Bolton and they decided to emigrate for a better life with more opportunities. Alternatively, they could have met on board ship and fallen in love. They may even have only met when they arrived in America, thrown together by chance.

However it happened, they were not alone in emigrating to America or Canada at that time. Many people were doing the same thing, as attested to by newspaper adverts and articles of the time. Again, what the significance of Iowa was, we can only guess. Did they have relatives there who had emigrated earlier? Fayette was once a Native American village, and no legal white settlers were there in 1840. They could not register and buy land until 1850, and the 1850 to 1873 years were the pre-railroad days when commerce would have depended on horse and cart or oxen power. The boom years were from 1874 with the coming of the railroad. From 1880, the railroad went both north and south, opening up opportunities for trade. Iowa also played a prominent part of the 'Underground Railroad', helping enslaved people who had escaped from their plantations to finally reach freedom.

Pictures of Fayette at that time show something of a 'one horse town' as depicted in many of the western movies of the 1940s and 50s. That is no reflection on the Fayette of today, which is a thriving city with a university. However, at the time that George and Emily were there it would have seemed very far removed from the Bolton they had left behind.

Experiences of emigration

George and Emily were not alone in wanting to find a better life abroad. Newspapers of the day were full of adverts and articles relating to emigration. Instead of a long voyage under sail, the new steam ships meant a speedier crossing and cheaper fares. Shipping lines such as Cunard and White Star were growing fast. Times were hard, particularly in the Highlands of Scotland and Ireland, so emigration was happening on a grand scale. Land might have been cheaper, but sometimes the experience failed to live up to their expectations.

Fifteen fugitive slaves arriving in Philadelphia along the banks of the Schuylkill River in July 1856. Engraving from William Still's history *Underground Railway* 1872 with modern watercolour. Courtesy Shutterstock/Everett Collection.

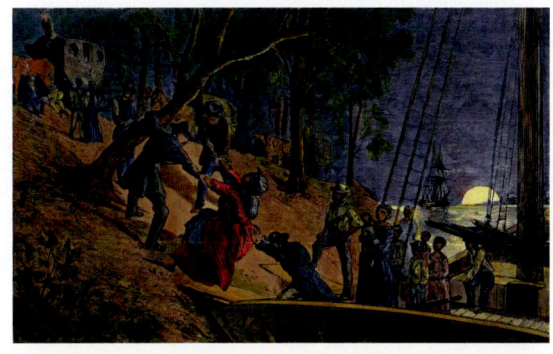

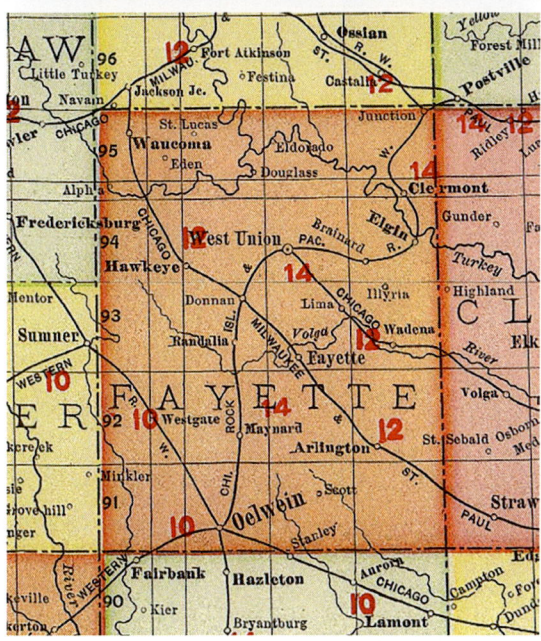

Detail from Rand McNally map of Iowa, 1903. Public Domain.

'Emigrants Guide to America', *Bolton Chronicle*, 24 June 1854. Courtesy *The Bolton News*.

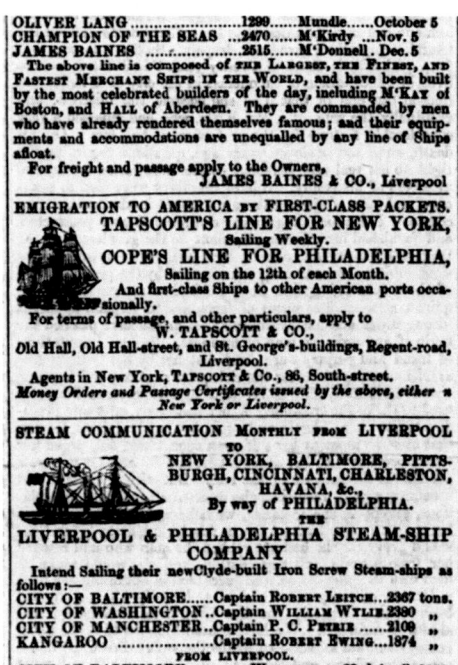

'Emigration to America', *Bolton Chronicle,* 19 April 1856. Courtesy *The Bolton News.*

Even in the early years of the nineteenth century people were leaving for better lives abroad. A reader's letter in the *Sussex Advertiser* of 1828 hinted that with so many industrious, tax-paying people immigrating to the New World, taxes might have to rise for those remaining.[10] By the 1850s newspapers were warning of terrible conditions aboard so-called 'Plague Ships'. In 1853 the *Bolton Chronicle* expressed concern when on one such ship cholera had broken out and ninety-six passengers, almost all of them steerage, had died.[11] First- and second-class passengers were mainly immune, due to their superior quarters. In steerage, conditions were said to be miserable and impoverished, with only fourteen square feet of space per passenger.

By the 1880s when George and Emily left for America news reports were more optimistic. The *Bolton Evening News* detailed the prospects for those wishing to emigrate and the type of people various areas were looking for. A report of 1882 told how six steamers loaded with six thousand would-be settlers had set off for America, and amongst them were fifty brewers from Preston.[12] They had sufficient capital to enable them to start brewing English ale in Philadelphia, and they were obviously an enterprising bunch with a plan, and with money. Those with sufficient funds behind them to ride out any initial problems probably stood the best chance of success.

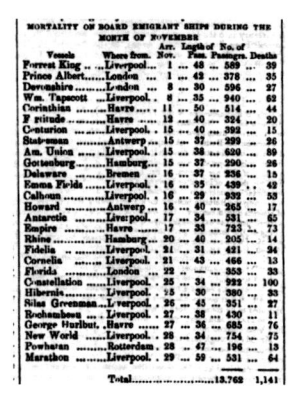

'Mortality on Board Emigrant Ships', *Bolton Chronicle,* 24 December 1843. Courtesy *The Bolton News.*

But it was not all positive. Some newspaper articles painted a bleak picture of the reality for some when they arrived in this Brave New World. You needed to be hardy and resourceful to make a go of it in a new country. This would have been what George and Emily, and thousands of others, would have faced once there. It is easy to see why disillusionment and homesickness could have set in.

From the *Carlisle Patriot:* A man from Chard emigrated along with his family in 1817.[13] They were unable to find a home to sleep in, and the man had to split wood for four shillings a day. This was not enough to feed his family. He recommended staying in England unless you had plenty of money. 'The inhabitants of Boston curse the English in the street'. He had been a farmer in Somerset but now had to go one thousand miles inland in search of work.

From the *Cork Examiner*, 1864: A man induced to emigrate by a friend, who painted a rosy picture of what he would find once there.[14] The man was very disillusioned. He reported business to be humbug and farming equally so. One might get a small house in the woods at a low rent, but you had to cut timber and clear the ground. As you travel the country all you see is uncultivated and uncut land. You may get a large amount of land cheap but have to labour alone, as there is nobody to help. You are miles from any decent creature. Better off at home on £50 than on £200 in America. His friend's place was dire, and miles from anywhere. He had talked of farming sheep, but the lambs at home were bigger than his sheep. It was all falsehood. Everywhere people were vying for work, with a hundred applicants for every post.
'You who have, for the time being, comfort and enjoyment, are far better off at home.'

What of George and Emily?

Whatever the circumstances of their meeting or their reasons for going to America, surprisingly they were back in Bolton just two years later. By June 1884 they were living with Emily's family, the Newhouses. There could be several reasons why they returned to Bolton. Homesickness, disillusionment, lack of money, or the fact that Emily was pregnant with twins. Whatever the circumstances they returned to live at 45 Tyndall Street where Emily's elder sister, Deborah, and her mother were making a living from trading in woollens and hosiery. The Newhouse family hailed from Farnworth, where Emily's father had once managed a cotton mill. When he died the family moved to Bolton. George started to work in the Newhouse family business as a commercial traveller, selling their goods around the district, a departure from his gamekeeping background.

Sadly, Emily died aged twenty-six whilst giving birth to their twins, a girl, Violet, and a boy, Walter. George was broken-hearted and never recovered from her tragic death. He remained at her side and would not move until she was finally laid to rest. He was inconsolable and often spoke of wishing to join Emily in death. Only eleven weeks later, he committed suicide.

A young pedlar carrying his wares. Illustration by Sharron Clayman.

An inquest held two days after this tragic event detailed how, at 2.30pm on Monday 23 June 1884, the witness (his sister-in-law Deborah Newhouse) asked the deceased to take a winding wheel to the blacksmith.[15] (This illustrates that Deborah and her mother were weaving the goods themselves on the premises.) She thought that he had gone out with the wheel. About three, she went upstairs to fetch some worsted for a customer. She saw a hank of wool hanging on the door but could not open the door. She thought he might be lying down and called his name but no answer. She returned to the customer. Later her mother arrived home and they noticed George's coat hanging on the door and knew he had not gone out. They tried the upstairs door, then cut the wool and heard a heavy thump on the other side of the door. The door still could not be opened.

'Sad Suicide in Halliwell', *Bolton Chronicle*, 25 June 1884. Courtesy *The Bolton News*.

A neighbour, Mr Thornley, climbed a ladder to the window to get in. He said he could see a man sitting behind the door and he was afraid to go in. Deborah entered (obviously braver than the neighbour!) and George was leaning against the door with the wool around his neck, his body still warm. The doctor was there within five minutes and pronounced him dead. The coroner said that at five feet eleven the deceased could not have hung himself from the door; he must have died from strangulation. The inquest recorded that there was a strong bond of love between the deceased and his dead wife and he could not bear to live without Emily. A verdict of suicide whilst in a state of insanity was returned. He was stated to be financially secure, so money was not a deciding factor. It was the fact that he was heartbroken and unable to live without Emily by his side. He was twenty-seven when he died, although at the inquest this was stated as twenty-six.

Sadly, that was not the only tragedy to befall the little family. Only weeks later, baby Violet died too. Her death certificate gives the cause of death as a wasting disease and the poor baby would have been emaciated by the time she died. It must have been difficult for Emily's unmarried sister and elderly mother to care for two newborn babies, whilst trying to make a living running their own business. Perhaps they would have had to either hire a wet nurse from amongst girls in the workhouse who had either lost their babies or had them taken away, or use 'pap bottles' to feed the babies.

Alternative feeding methods for babies had been in existence since ancient times and by the early nineteenth century various forms of pap bottles, boats and teats were in use. Unfortunately they were incredibly difficult to keep clean and this resulted in a build-up of bacteria which, combined with poor milk sterilisation and storage, resulted in a third of artificially-fed babies dying before they reached their first birthday.[16] Although more effective vessels began to be manufactured mid-century, it was not until 1896 and the development of an open-ended bottle that artificial feeding became a safe and popular choice.

Pap boat in silver, spout at one end, at the other end a pierced nipple spout and the top half covered. Courtesy Wellcome Trust, CC BY-SA 4.0.

Violet was possibly the weaker of the twins from the outset. All three, George, Emily, and Violet were buried at St Anne's Church, Turton, in unmarked graves. George's inquest verdict of temporary insanity would allow him, despite his suicide, to be buried on the outer fringes of hallowed ground.

Happily the surviving twin Walter thrived, cared for by Deborah and her mother. They later moved to Eskrick Street and continued in business there. At sixteen, Walter was apprenticed to a cabinetmaker and prospered in that trade. By 1924 he had his own premises in Bath Street where, according to the trade directory of the time, he was a Master Cabinet Maker. He later married and had a daughter, Elizabeth.

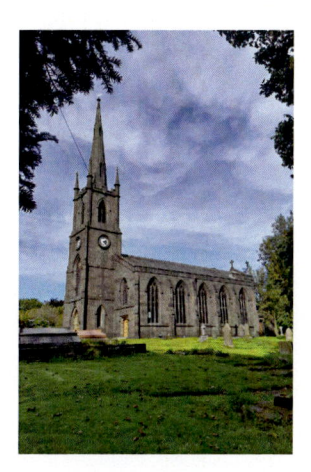

George and Emily's short lives were lived against a backdrop of profound change. People were moving into towns to work in the factories and mills, creating overcrowding and slum dwellings. Slaughterhouses, middens, and all manner of noxious businesses stood alongside crowded cottages and doss houses. In Bolton, places with pretty names like Spring Gardens and Velvet Walks were in reality ratinfested hovels. Work was hard and hours long, in both mills and factories. Conditions on the moors, in the mines and brick factories, were no better. Little wonder then that life expectancy was poor.

St Anne's Church, Turton. Photograph ©Karen Holroyd.

Despite the harsh times, George and Emily's strong bond of love shines through. The fact that Walter went on to thrive and become prosperous shows that a degree of social mobility had begun. By dint of hard work, you could now prosper and rise above your humble origins. George and Emily would surely have been proud of what Walter achieved.

Horwich Casanova

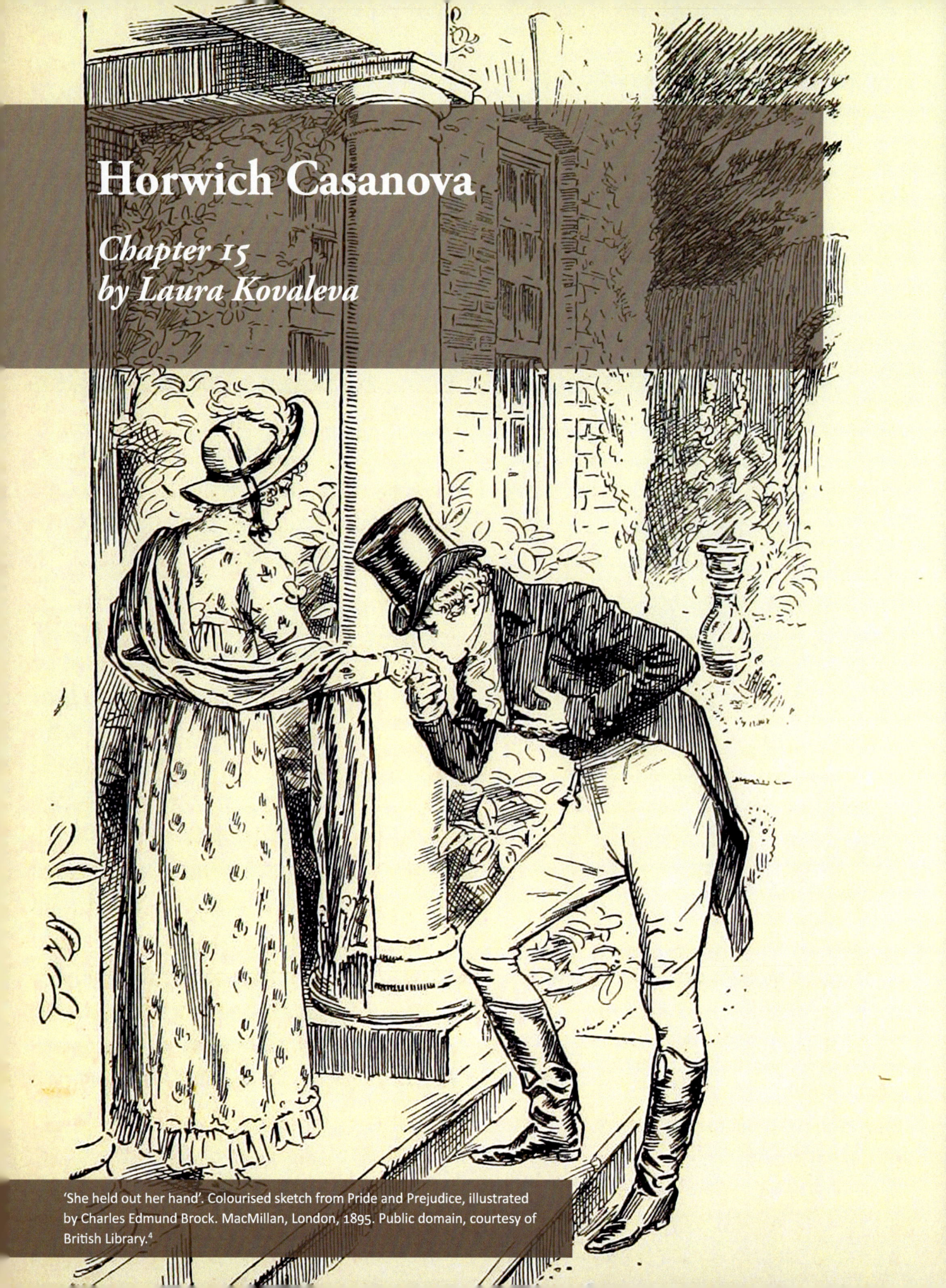

*Chapter 15
by Laura Kovaleva*

'She held out her hand'. Colourised sketch from Pride and Prejudice, illustrated by Charles Edmund Brock. MacMillan, London, 1895. Public domain, courtesy of British Library.[4]

'A Picnic to Whittle Springs and its result'

This was the title of an article in the *Preston Chronicle* from 10 August 1872 which surely stirred up a range of emotions in readers. The same story was published in many other newspapers around the country, and it reported a breach of promise case of Pendlebury v. Eatock heard at the Manchester Assizes two days earlier.

The plaintiff Eleanor Pendlebury, 'a very respectably-dressed young woman, of some personal attractions', said that she was twenty-seven years of age and resided with her father Abraham Pendlebury in Horwich.[1] She assisted her father who was a tailor and draper, and often visited different ladies in the course of her business. Eleanor had met Robert Eatock in 1870 when on a picnic party in Whittle Springs, Whittle-le-Woods, near Chorley. On multiple occasions he also escorted Eleanor from the houses where she went on business. After some time, Robert proposed and by the end of 1870 she accepted him as a suitor.

Robert Eatock was from a decent family of local farmers residing at Rivington Hall Farm. He told Eleanor that he had a good deal of money invested in shares and had a working capital of £1200. He was a well-off young man. Everything seemed to be going well until on one occasion Robert expressed his doubts about Eleanor's chastity as she visited lots of houses, and he even tried to 'take liberties with her' which made her incredibly angry and hurt her feelings.[2] Later on, Eleanor sent him a letter:

> 'Now, I wish to tell you that I am not a flirt, nor one that will go with any man but wish to be honourable with you, as I thought you were with me. If you had told me that I was not a suitable person for you, and that you wish to part with me, it would not have hurt my feelings one-half so much as it has done, you telling me that I had not my honour and my virtue…and though my circumstances are not in as good position as yours, yet I have my hands to work with, and I am not afraid. As far as my virtue goes, I consider myself worthy of a king'.[3]

Whittle Springs advert from the *Bolton Chronicle*, 31 May 1856. Courtesy *The Bolton News*.

Rivington Hall Farm. From the collection of Laura Kovaleva.

Eventually, Robert apologised and continued escorting Eleanor home. In October 1871 Eleanor found herself in the family way and they started discussing their marriage arrangements. However, it seemed that Robert's intentions were not so sincere as his visits became less frequent and soon Eleanor found out that Robert was spending time in the company of a Miss Tinsley. Eleanor sent him numerous letters but received no reply. In one of her letters she wrote:

> *'Why do you keep back from me?...Think of what you have both said and done these eighteen months. Think of the state you have brought me into...I have now left my home; lost the love of my brother and sister. I am here not fit for work, nor have I got money to keep me, depending on my brother-in-law for food'.*[5]

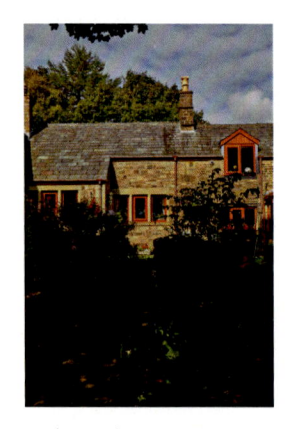

After receiving no answer, Eleanor wrote another letter in total despair saying that Robert 'brought her and her family to the worst disgrace' he possibly could.[6] Despite Eleanor's pleading, on 1 February 1872 Robert Eatock married Ann Tinsley. Two-and-a-half months later Eleanor gave birth to a boy, Frederick. At the court hearing Robert Eatock denied he had promised to marry Eleanor but admitted the seduction. The hearing concluded with the verdict for the plaintiff for £450, a good sum that would have given her and Frederick a cushion in life. Eleanor's father also received £59 as recompense for losing the services of his daughter in his business whilst she was pregnant. After meeting the two main characters of our story, let us have a closer look at their lives.

Little Deakins Farm. Photograph ©Yelena Overchenko.

Little Deakins Farm Datestone. Photograph ©Yelena Overchenko.

Robert Eatock

Robert was born in 1849 to a family of Horwich yeoman farmers. Robert's father, Robert Eatock Senior was born in 1789, and between 1836-1851 he resided with his wife Martha and their children at Deakins Farm. He also owned Twitchells. Robert's brother Timothy Eatock was in the timber business there with tenant Henry Guest. His sister Rachel was born at Deakins in 1836 and was a scholar in 1851.

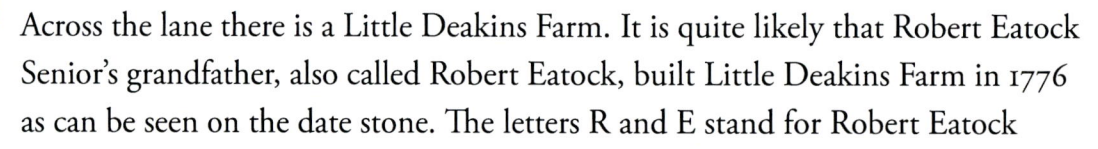

Across the lane there is a Little Deakins Farm. It is quite likely that Robert Eatock Senior's grandfather, also called Robert Eatock, built Little Deakins Farm in 1776 as can be seen on the date stone. The letters R and E stand for Robert Eatock while the remaining symbol is a bit of a mystery. Usually a wife's initial was carved on date stones next to her spouse's. The construction of Little Deakins Farm was completed in 1776, the year Robert's wife, Martha Heaton, died. The possible theory is that it might represent a menorah, a multi-branched candelabra, which is a symbol of the afterlife, often found on graves of women in Jewish tradition. We do not know if the Eatock family had any Jewish connections, but it could be possible that Robert borrowed a symbol that he had seen elsewhere.

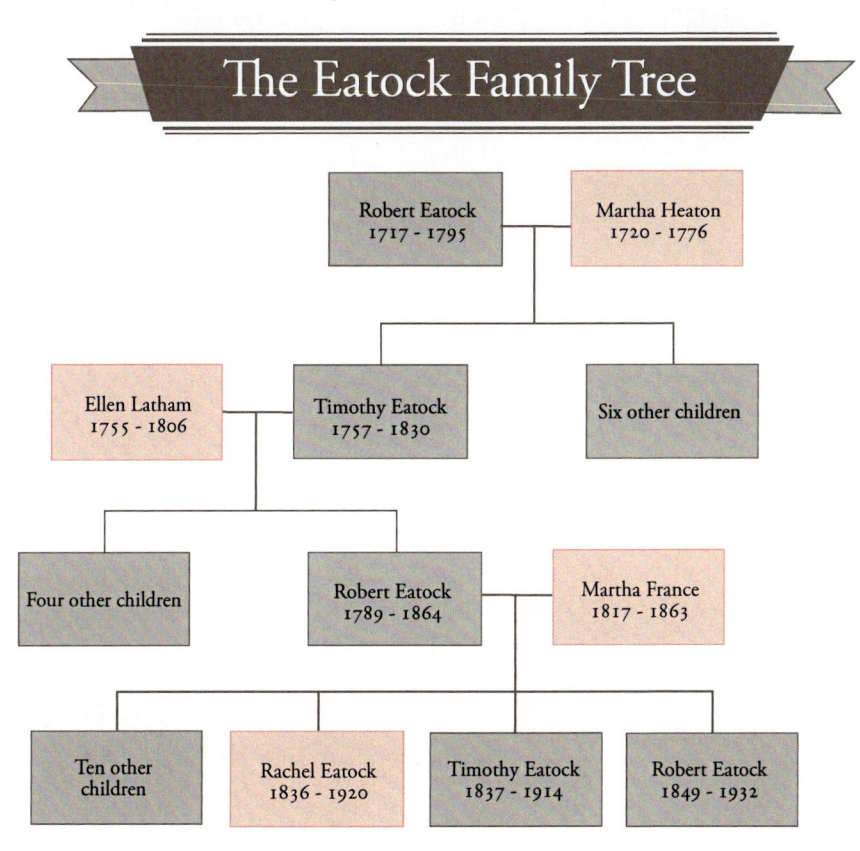

The Eatock Family Tree

- Robert Eatock 1717 - 1795 — Martha Heaton 1720 - 1776
  - Ellen Latham 1755 - 1806 — Timothy Eatock 1757 - 1830
  - Six other children
    - Four other children
    - Robert Eatock 1789 - 1864 — Martha France 1817 - 1863
      - Ten other children
      - Rachel Eatock 1836 - 1920
      - Timothy Eatock 1837 - 1914
      - Robert Eatock 1849 - 1932

Robert Eatock Senior was forty-eight when he married his Martha, twenty-year-old Martha France, in 1837. After giving birth to thirteen children, Martha died in 1863 and is buried at Horwich Trinity Church. Robert outlived his wife by just one year and passed away in 1864, leaving £12,000 which was divided between his children. Four months after his father's death, fifteen-year-old Robert joined the Merchant Navy as an apprentice. He spent four years on board the *Scimitar* in the employment of Findlay, Campbell and Company of Liverpool and London, sailing to the East Indies.

Scimitar, operational between 1863 and 1889. From the State Library of Victoria, Malcolm Brodie shipping collection.

Scimitar was built by Martin Samuelson of Hull and was launched in July 1864. It was 'a full-ship rig sailing ship…with painted dummy gun ports', intended to put off pirates.[7] During his time on board Robert made multiple return voyages between London and Mumbai (Bombay) and by the end of his service he was 'an able seaman before the mast'.[8]

After returning home around 1869, Robert started farming a sixty-six-acre farm which he stocked with cows. In addition, he owned a smaller farm, let by him to Ellis Crompton for £36 a year. These facts can tell us about Robert's spirit of enterprise which will become more evident later in the story. Now let us leave Robert for a while and have a look at the fate of Eleanor and her child.

Eleanor Pendlebury

Eleanor was left heartbroken but, as she mentioned in her letter to Robert, she was not afraid of work. So, after giving birth to Frederick she may well have returned to dressmaking, although her settlement would have allowed her some choice in this.

When Frederick turned eight in 1880, Eleanor left him with her parents as she decided to start a new married life. Her new husband's name was Anthony Carr, a beer seller at the Wagon and Horses on Manchester Road. Sadly, happy married life did not last long for Eleanor. Anthony died one year later in September 1881, the same month their new-born son Anthony was baptised. Bad luck continued to follow her and her son Anthony died the next year. Eleanor took charge of her husband's business after his death, and the pub's license was transferred to her name. He also left a sum of £964 in his will which allowed Eleanor to not worry about money for some time.

Dressmaking was one of the few ways women could earn money through self-employment. Illustration by Sharron Clayman.

Married Women's Property Act 1882

The law in England strongly emphasised a woman's subordination to her husband. This meant that any property or wealth she was in possession of before marriage became her husband's. Although unmarried women did not have the same restrictions, since men were more likely to inherit land and property many women remained at the whims of their fathers and brothers. Whilst an 1870 act had given women some rights, it was not until 1882 that married women were able to take full charge of their own financial affairs and decide for themselves what they did with their assets.

In 1881, eight-year-old Frederick was living in his grandfather's house at 19 Church Street, Horwich. By 1890 Frederick had decided to try his fortune and emigrated to Chicago where five years later he married Mary Scholes. They went on to have four children. Unfortunately, traces of Eleanor's life after 1881 are lost in time and cannot be tracked. We can only hope that she managed to find her happiness at last.

Robert gets into trouble

The same year Eleanor got married, Robert got into big trouble, as in February 1880 his wife Ann petitioned for divorce. It seems that our Casanova could not change his old ways and, as reported in Ann's petition, 'in the days of March 1879 and some other days committed an incestuous adultery' with her seventeen-year-old niece Mary Tyrer.[9] When a couple married, in the eyes of the church they became one, and so Ann's niece was deemed also to be Robert's blood relative, hence incest. Robert denied all allegations and demanded that the petition be rejected.

However, by the time of this petition, Mary had already given birth to Robert's daughter, Martha, in January 1880. Census records from 1881 tell us about Mary who is recorded as an assistant of a stationer and a widow. She is living in her parents' house in Wigan with fifteen-month-old Martha. The divorce petition did not have any outcome as Robert decided to flee and in October 1880 he boarded a ship sailing from Liverpool to New York.[10] Interestingly, according to the crew list, he was accompanied by Mrs Robert Eatock.

South Water Street, Chicago, 1893. Courtesy Library of Congress.

Divorce and Matrimonial Causes Act 1857

The first divorce in England was granted in 1670. From then until the 1850s, separate Acts of Parliament were required for each divorce, and whilst this was not an issue in the seventeenth century by the 1850s divorces were taking up much valuable parliamentary time. In the Act, divorce became a civil matter to be dealt with by London courts. Cases increased dramatically and women became over a third of petitioners. As previously, adultery remained the only allowable reason for divorce. However, whilst a man could divorce his wife on grounds of adultery alone, a woman was required to provide further aggravating factors, including cruelty, incest, desertion, bigamy, sodomy, and bestiality. This remained the case until the law changed again in 1923.

Life in the New World

Five years after his escape, Robert was living in Reno, Kansas. His wife's name is recorded as Annie, born in England, and it was possibly his wife, Ann née Tinsley. However, it seems a bit odd that after petitioning for a divorce she decided to continue living with her husband in a strange country.

From the local newspapers of that time we can find out what kind of life Robert and Annie had. Robert bought a ranch west of Reno and a local journalist visited, describing Robert's home as being 'situated in a beautiful grove, among orchards of peach, pear and apple. Some of the apple trees are heavily freighted with good winter apples'.[11] Robert took him on a tour and showed him kennels of dogs. The dogs were pedigrees and one of them, Lord Neversettle, was worth over £1000 and belonged to Mr H C Lowe of Hutchinson. Two females, Patera and White Lips shared nine pups, two of which were going to be sent to England and were worth £500 each.

Kansas State Fair, Hutchinson, 1900s. Courtesy Kansas Historical Society.

Cattle Branding. From the *Caldwell Advance*, 20 September, 1883.

Mr Eatock seems to be immensely proud of his achievements as he tells the journalist that he has, '4,000 bushels of corn; his peach crop was immense and his apples, of which he will have about 50 or 75 bushels, are excellent'. In another newspaper, a pear from Eatock's orchard is described as 'a great juicy fat fellow, and with a flavour as fine as silk'.[12]

Alas, this luxurious wealthy life did not last forever because fate played a trick on Robert. He started a cattle business but something went wrong resulting in him losing his fortune. It seems that Robert then had to search for another source of income, and he remembered the passion of his youth – the sea! In the 1900 US Census Robert is recorded as a marine captain living in Astoria, Oregon, a city on the Columbia River near the Pacific Ocean. A few years later, in 1907, he is 'a second-class pilot in charge of a passenger steamer *Peerless*' in the district of Juneau, Alaska.[13]

Are you wondering what happened to his wife Ann? A report from the *Hutchinson News,* Kansas from 23 July 1920 can shed some light on her fate. It says that, 'Mrs Anna Eatock, who thirty years ago was living in luxury in Reno County, the wife of the wealthy stockman of this county, died today a pauper, at the county poor farm, penniless, helpless, and alone'. Ann was seventy-nine years old and had no children. Robert Eatock outlived Ann by twelve years and died at the age of eighty-three in February 1932 at Port Townsend, Jefferson, Washington. He probably went out to sea until the very end.

Port Townsend, Washington, 1890. Courtesy University of Washington Digital Library.

We have approached the ending of our story and it is time to say goodbye to our characters. Though they lived more than a century ago, with just a bit of imagination I can see them as real people in front of me, with their ambitions and misfortunes, dreams, and longings. I hope you can see them too.

Old and New Colliers Row, and Colliers Row School

Chapter 16
by Phil Orth

Pupils of Smithills Dean School

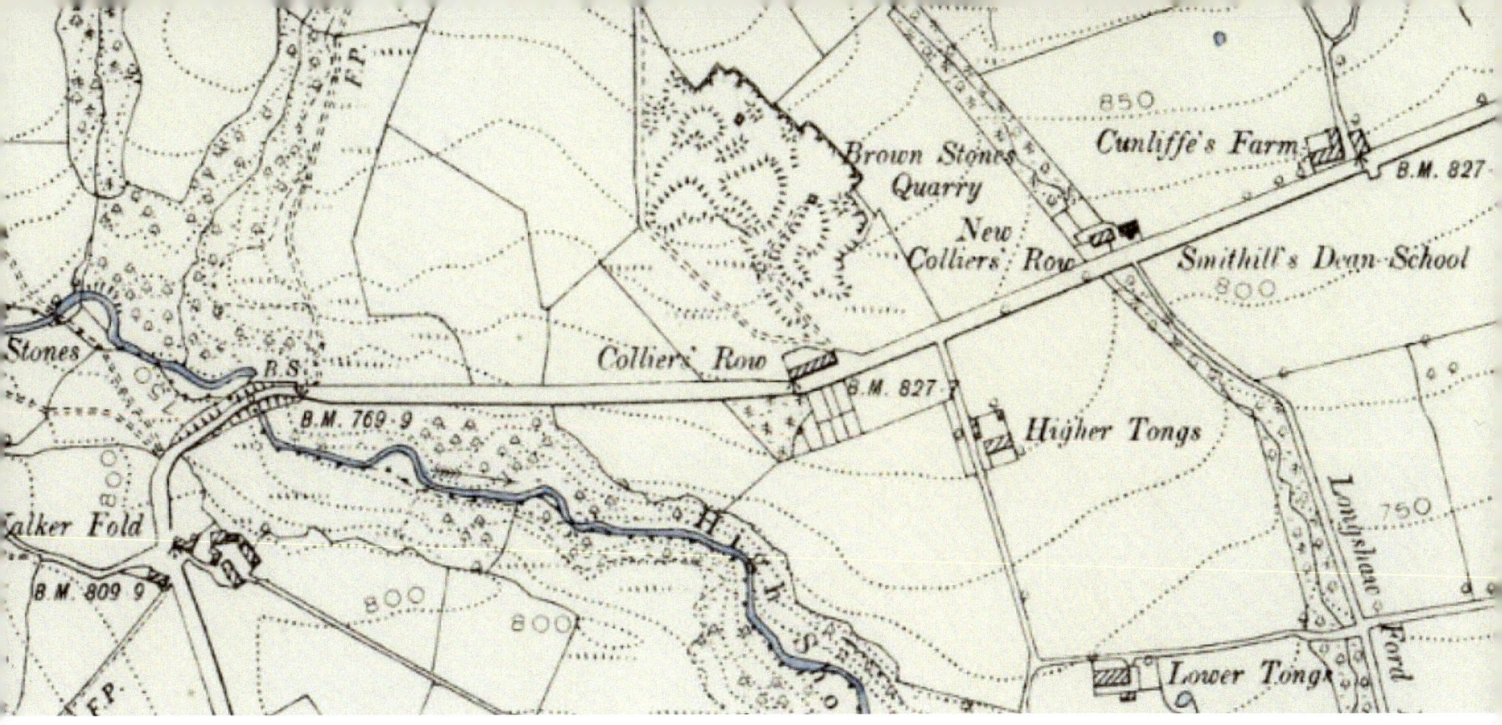

Ordnance Survey six-inch map, 1892. Courtesy National Library of Scotland.

Old and New Colliers Row in the Censuses

Colliers Row Road was named after two rows of cottages which were commissioned by the Ainsworth family. In 1841 the occupations of the families' heads of household were mainly coal miners, probably working in the nearby Ainsworth mines off Coal Pit Road. The majority of wives and siblings also worked in the mines, the cotton mills or the bleach works. One of the women, Ann Ince, who was unusually the head of a family, worked as a coal miner, though this was forbidden after the Mines and Collieries Act 1842. Also living on Colliers Row Road were a stone quarryman, a blacksmith, a bleacher, an agricultural labourer, and a school master, who may have been teaching at Colliers Row School built that year.

Old Colliers Row. Photograph © Margaret Clough, CC BY-SA 2.0.[1]

Following an accident at a Barnsley colliery in 1838 where twenty-six children died, Queen Victoria commissioned an enquiry into the working practices of mining, particularly the employment of women and children. In 1842 the Children's Employment Commission (Mines) produced a report that shocked society. Not only did children as young as five or six work underground pushing and pulling tubs filled with coal, but women and girls wore trousers and worked without top garments in front of their male colleagues. It was possibly the workwear issue that prompted such swift regulation. Many coal mine owners opposed changes to the law however, managing to secure small amendments to the Bill which passed on 1 August 1842.

'Scenes in coal mines in England: The trapper'. Vintage engraved illustration, *Magasin Pittoresque*, 1843. Shutterstock/Morphart Creation.

In 1851, again the majority of the heads of families were coal miners. Alongside these were a plasterer and painter, a blacksmith, a farm labourer, a carter, and a school mistress who was born in London. By 1861 there were only three miners and one of these was retired. However, there were now three quarrymen living there as the demand for building stone grew. There was also a train driver, a dyer of cotton cloth, a wood cutter, a farm labourer, a farm handyman and the plasterer and painter.

In 1871 stone quarrymen and stone masons predominated. Four others worked either in the cotton mills or the bleach works. There was one pipe fitter and the plasterer and painter was still plying his trade. The picture looked similar in 1881, with four stone quarrymen, the same coal miner and coal carter and three people working in a bleach works, one of whom was female.

Nearing the end of the century, in 1891 there were two stone quarrymen, the coal miner and coal carter, a general labourer, a labourer in a bleach works, a pensioner, and a school mistress from Dublin employed by the Ainsworth family. By 1901 only five of the properties on Colliers Row were occupied and the census that year recorded two finishers in the bleach works, a joiner, two quarrymen, and a widow. Again in 1911 only six of the cottages were occupied, and occupations were a field drainer on a private estate (presumably the Ainsworths), a steam fireman, a stone mason, a flyer maker, a retired farmer (from Hampsons Farm) and a widow, Alice Dearden.

New Colliers Row.
Photograph
©Tony Greenwood.

Snippets from Old Colliers Row

One story that has been told recently about the inhabitants of 2 Old Colliers Row in 1902 is quite interesting and was told to me in the Ainsworth Arms. The Taylor family lived at No. 2 and head of the family John Taylor was a stone quarryman. He lived with his wife and seven children, two sons and five daughters. Both sons apparently fought in World War I and neither returned. The youngest son, Harry, was killed at eighteen in 1917 in the big German push of that year. The eldest and the unluckiest son, Thomas, fought all the way through the war from the start and was killed on 1 November 1918, only a few days before the end of the war. A savage blow to the family. Bolton was badly hit by zeppelins during this war, and the Taylors would have the full brutality of it brought home to them with the loss of their sons.

Colliers Row School

Peter and John Horrocks Ainsworth were very interested in the education of the children of Halliwell.[2] With this in mind, they utilised a plot of land adjoining the road from Horwich to Belmont on Smithills Dean to build a school.[3] The formal name for the school reflects its position, Smithills Dean School. The school was to be used for the education of both adults and children of the labouring, manufacturing and poorer classes and was tied to the incorporated National Society for the Education in the Principles of the Established Church. It was to be under the direct control of the Ainsworths, and the officiating minister for the time was from Smithills Hall Chapel.

The school was built in three stages. It was begun in 1841 and extensions were added in 1885 and 1898. The dates of the building and its extensions are visible to this day. It was built with coursed and squared stone and a Welsh slate roof. In 1885 a central gabled porch was added. Each side of the porch had an arched doorway and a single window, and four mullioned and transomed windows flanked the porch in the original building. In 1898 a large separate room was added on the left-hand gable. This room also had a tiered mullioned and transomed window. All gables were coped with finials (stone ornamentation), and the Gothic Revival style of the original building was also used in the extensions. In all, there were two rooms inside the school: a large hall, and a smaller room at one end. The school was given Grade II Listed Building status on 26 April 1974.[4]

In 1880 there were approximately eighty children on the school roll, with children split into two groups: three- to ten-year-olds, and older pupils. The children first came to the school from moorland farms and cottages in the

World War I Zeppelin Bombing raid on Bolton, *Bolton Evening News*, 1914. Courtesy *The Bolton News*.

New Colliers Row and Colliers Row School. Courtesy *The Bolton News*.

Pupils of Smithills Dean School in 1900. From the collection of Stephen Tonge.

nearby vicinity. Over the years the catchment area spread and there was even a story about a five-year-old boy who walked every day from Blackburn Road. He did not stay long as it was deemed by the headmaster to be too far and not safe, and he was transferred nearer home.[5] Children came from Barrow Bridge and would walk up Longshaw Ford Road to get to the school. In later years a bus service was arranged to pick up children from Smithills Dean area. The bus was then used to take people from Colliers Row into town to do their shopping. It returned in the afternoon and brought people up to the school, then took the school children home. I was told by a former pupil who travelled to the school from the top of Halliwell on this bus that several times when the snow was too deep, they had to abandon the bus and walk the rest of the way.

Conditions in the school were pretty rudimentary compared to today. In the early days it would have been heated by a stove. The heat was vital in maintaining the temperature in the school, as well as being useful for drying the clothes of children who had to walk a long distance when it was raining. In those days there were no school dinners and children took their own. If it was a lunch that had to be heated up, it was put on the stove on arrival at school.

Prior to central heating schools would be heated using small stoves. Illustration by Sharron Clayman.

There are a number of entries in the old school logs and in the minutes of monthly Governors' meetings about problems with the heating and water over the years which make interesting reading.[6] In the winter of 1893 the weather was very cold and the school was closed on 14 February because severe frost had burst all the pipes, so there was no fire. By this time the school would have been heated by radiators, the pipes coming from a boiler tended by the caretaker who lived in one of the cottages next to the school. In October 1899 the chimney was smoking badly and the school closed. Colonel Ainsworth visited the school on 12 January 1900 but only one child was present. The temperature had dropped to two degrees Celsius in the classroom and the child's classmates had wisely chosen to stay at home. To add to this the chimney was also smoking badly again. Moving on to January 1906, the boiler in the cellar was leaking and a week later the school was again full of smoke and the fire had to be taken outside. It was decided that a new range was needed, and this was purchased early in 1907 at a cost of £11 10s. after a lengthy debate between the school, church and education committee as to who should pay for it.

However, this was only the start of problems concerning heating.[7] The boiler needed urgent repair in February 1907. Which was bad enough, but there was another problem with ventilation as nobody could open the windows! After further problems with the boiler in February 1908 when the school was full of smoke again and a hole burst on the inside of the boiler, the Director of Education Mr Fred Wilkinson ordered the school to be closed the following month so that a new boiler could be installed. The school temperature without the boiler was seven degrees Celsius. The new boiler plus a radiator were fitted on 23 April 1908, again after a lengthy debate about who was to pay for them. The boiler was finally paid for by the local education authority. There were further problems with the boiler in the 1920s when it kept breaking down but there is no evidence to show the purchase of a new one.

Freezing temperatures after snow on Smithills Dean Road. Courtesy Halliwell Local History Society.

An amusing story came to light in 1911 when the caretaker asked the school to buy him a longer ladder so that he could clean the higher windows in the building which he said he was unable to reach.[8] He was told to stand on a box. This he refused to do, and the matter went back and forth again between the school, education committee and the church as they argued who would pay for it. It took two years for this to be sorted out, but he finally got his ladder in 1913.

School life and the weather

One of the factors affecting the education of children over the years was the weather. Snow, winter winds, and plunging temperatures all played their part.[9] As early as 1880, when the average attendance was eighty pupils, severe weather reduced attendance to eight on Monday 6 January. Later in the same year on 24 September only two children were present owing to the wet weather. In 1884 on 1 December, attendance at school was impossible because the road was closed with snow. In February 1893, the weather was very cold, and the school was closed because severe frosts had burst all the pipes.

The snowplough on Halliwell Road after heavy snowfall. Courtesy Halliwell Local History Society.

Four years later in 1897 snowstorms and drifts occurred. On 24 March 1898 the children were given the afternoon off because the weather was too cold to study. In January 1907 there was heavy snowfall and the school filled up with smoke from the boiler chimney. In February 1908 there were bad gales, the school filled up with smoke again, causing the fire to go out which resulted in a lack of heating. In 1910 snow drifts prevented farmers' children from attending school, and in November 1912 there was severe weather which drastically reduced attendance.

Illness and injury

Before antibiotics and other modern medicines became commonplace, illness played a large part in closing schools for both short and longer periods.[10] In February 1913, for instance, a measles outbreak closed the school for two weeks. Over the years many illnesses we seldom hear about today affected children.

There was a child absent from school in 1893 with quinsy, which caused abscesses to form between the tonsils and the throat. In 1897 four children were absent with diphtheria, a bacterial infection leading to breathing difficulties, heart failure and possible death. In December 1907 one child was suffering from rheumatic fever, a complication following bacterial throat infections which could cause painful

Immunisation poster for diphtheria, whooping cough and tetanus. Courtesy Science Museum Group, CC0 1.0 Universal, donated by the Health Education Authority.

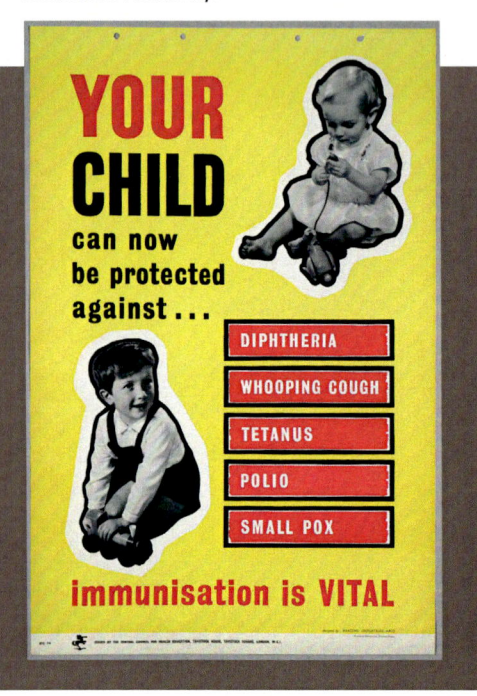

Alongside innovations in industry came advancements in disease control and vaccination. Although there had been known treatments for many diseases throughout history, it was not until Edward Jenner invented a smallpox vaccine in the late eighteenth century that widespread measures began to become available. By 1853 it was compulsory for babies throughout the UK to be administered the smallpox vaccine. n France, Louis Pasteur discovered a cholera vaccine in 1879, and by 1923 a vaccine against diphtheria had been discovered. This was followed by vaccine discoveries for influenza in 1933, tetanus in 1938 and polio in 1955. And although Alexander Fleming discovered penicillin in 1928 it was not until the mid-1940s that antibiotics were commonly used to treat bacterial infections.

joints and heart problems. In June 1920, the school was closed again because of an outbreak of chickenpox. In January 1925 attendance was extremely low because of a flu epidemic, and sometime in 1926, only fourteen out of the fifty-three pupils on roll were present because of an outbreak of whooping cough. And finally, in November 1930, the school was closed for three weeks because of a flu epidemic.

Both children and staff were susceptible to accidents. In August 1919, a pupil fell in the schoolyard when the iron in her clogs got caught in the flags. She cut her head on the school wall and required medical attention. In 1924 the headteacher was scalded by a pan of water which fell on the fire, and in September 1925 a child was run over by lorry on Colliers Row Road and was lucky enough to escape with a cut foot.

Bad behaviour

Extract from a school punishment book showing the name, offence and punishment given. From the collection of Barbara Winder.

An interesting way to understand what life was like in a school is to study the school Punishment Book. This gives a revealing insight into what children were up to in those days.[11] It would seem that in 1898 there must have been some trouble with stone throwing as a lesson was needed on 'stone throwing and its results'. On 22 April 1908, a six-year-old boy was given 'one slight stroke on the hand for striking a girl'. Three months later, two boys were given two strokes for cruelty to a frog and on 2 August 1908, two boys were given two strokes for swearing. A few years later, in June 1921, two strokes on the hand were given for 'disobedience and for robbing birds' nests after being warned'.

Absence due to farm work

Schools may have had poor attendance during the winter because of a variety of problems caused by the weather and malfunctioning heating equipment, but the summer months of school were also susceptible to absence.[12] In July 1898 attendance was poor because many children were kept off school to help with haymaking. Children absent from school at haymaking probably occurred every summer but there is no official recording of this except in 1898, and again in 1904. Although not recorded, other farming activities such as digging the potato harvest probably also caused attendance to fall, and children were always in demand as bird scarers in fields of crops.

Boy digging potatoes in a field in New Brunswick, Canada. Although emigration took children far away from their homelands, the practices for helping at harvests would have been much the same. Courtesy Library and Archives Canada.

Religion

In the early years the curriculum was heavily biased towards religious studies. The school was also used as a Sunday School and was one of the centres of worship attached to St Peter's Church, Halliwell. In the 1920s services were held every Sunday for local people. These services eventually ended but the Sunday School continued in St Peter's Church of England School on Smithills Dean Road. There were regular inspections by clergymen, who also examined the register. On the 12 August 1892 it was reported that, 'grammar has not been well taught'. In June of 1903 a Diocesan inspector gave the school an unsatisfactory report because the teaching of scriptural knowledge was unsatisfactory. By 1908 the Diocesan inspector gave the school a much-improved report on the teaching of scripture, possibly due to the success of questions on the catechism being answered, 'showing careful and reverent teaching'.

School inspections

Continuing the theme of outside inspections, there are a number of entries in the logs detailing the progress, or its lack, of the children.[13] In January 1897 an examiner wrote, 'the children need confidence, and want encouraging by more lessons of a chatty nature'. In March 1898 there was yet another examination to assess progress. And on 20 May that year the older children were examined for the

Labour Certificate so that they could if necessary work part-time. Presumably this was to encourage them to work in the coal mines, as a science lesson on coal was delivered at the same time. In August a report read, 'Good progress has been made. The children are orderly and show increasing intelligence under instruction'. Unfortunately, another report in October 1901 stated, 'The children hardly seem aware they possess the faculty of observation'. By 1903 an examiner found that, 'Standard I cannot do subtractions and gave a poor result on unseen dictation and spelling'.

In early 1904 an inspector from His Majesty's Inspectorate of Schools visited the school and stated there was a problem with the teaching of a wide age range of children in one class, and that a new teacher needed to be employed straight away. His report also said that the timetable was not being followed strictly enough, and that there were no schemes of work for the delivery of lessons. The inspector said the children did not seem able to observe and record their findings in some lessons. In late 1904, another His Majesty's Inspectorate report was submitted, and the Chair of Governors and the Director of Education from Bolton had an urgent meeting with the headmaster - who then resigned! The Chair of Governors recommended a woman be appointed to replace him, and this actually happened. By 1912, a report by His Majesty's Inspectorate said the school was exceedingly good, especially in arithmetic and the work done in the school garden.

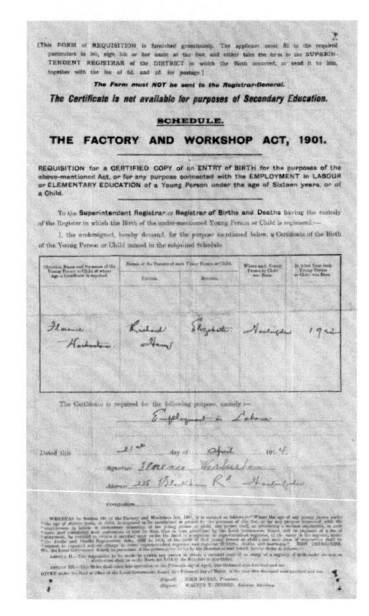

Labour certificates like these, with a copy of the child's birth certificate on the other side, would have been necessary for anyone under sixteen who wished to start work. Florence Warburton had just turned twelve when she signed this, although the Elementary Education Amendment Act 1899 provisions meant she would have remained at school until the compulsory age of thirteen. From the collection of Helena Sanderson.

Following the Elementary Education Act 1870, Six Standards of Education were introduced. These were merit-based standards in reading, writing and arithmetic where pupils were formally assessed throughout England and Wales for the first time. Standard I arithmetic required that a pupil show basic skills in addition, subtraction, and multiplication, while Standard VI required competence in the use of fractions. Not all pupils would achieve all the standards before leaving school, and many left having only achieved the lowest, particularly if they had secured paid work or were needed to help run the home.

The Elementary Education Act 1880 brought in compulsory education for children aged between five and ten, and also decreed that children between eleven and thirteen should reach a satisfactory standard of education before leaving school. This extract from an Exemption Register gives details of which of the Six Standards each child had reached, and where they went on to work. Courtesy Lancashire Archives.

The Curriculum

'Two little girls being taught how to sew', Anna Ancher. Courtesy Skagens Museum/Google Art Project.

From items taken from the school logs and the correspondence related to Colliers Row School, we can see that children were educated in a wide-ranging selection of subjects, all designed to improve their moral and physical wellbeing.[14] On 5 February 1896, eighteen children visited Bolton Museum, this was followed by a lesson on 'good manners'. This suggests that the behaviour of some of the children may have been a little suspect. In 1899 a geography lesson discussed, 'The outlines of the world, British Empire and Colonies'.

In 1901 Ellen Middlemas, the wife of the then headmaster, joined the staff, to 'chiefly exercise management of the use of needles, thimbles etc.'. Incidentally, they lived at Tippett House, which is on the right-hand side of Smithills Dean Road, about half-way up. On 10 November an item in the school log showed, 'Drilled all the under tens for a writing competition'. On 3 June 1903, Colonel Ainsworth came to school to give a drawing lesson.

In 1907 cookery lessons were introduced for the older pupils, and in September of the same year a school library was inaugurated. In 1910, Mr Naylor, the manager of Doffcocker Cotton Mill, showed twenty-five children through the mill to explain the process of cotton manufacture. No doubt many of them would later be employed in the numerous Bolton mills. During Colonel Ainsworth's previously mentioned 1910 visit, he promised a plot of land for a garden and the following year paid for the garden to be rough dug. Parents provided plants for the garden and the children began to grow their own flowers and vegetables. By 1912 gardening was established as a regular subject on the curriculum and over the following years Mrs Ainsworth regularly donated rose trees for the children to plant. Music, art, and games were added to the curriculum in 1920.

The effects of war

Word War I certainly had an effect on the school itself as well as on what was taught.[15] On 25 May 1915 the school was given a Roll of Honour from the Education Office, showing the names of old boys who were serving in the Armed Forces. Later in the year, a sum of 17s. 4d. was paid to the Prince of Wales' National Relief Fund, a fund that supported soldiers' wives and dependants affected by the war, and monthly contributions of 8s. 8d. were paid until the end of the war. In November of the same year, no new desks were allowed because of war requisitions, and in May 1916, the children had to revert to using slates owing to a scarcity of paper. Later that same month, lessons to the juniors on 'The Union Jack' and to the seniors on 'What the Empire means to us' were delivered, and the children sang patriotic songs and saluted the flag.

By 1917 parcels were being made up for prisoners of war and on 9 August a collection of £1 18s. was made for them. In February 1918 one of the teachers took the children to see a tank which was described as a 'weapon to end the war'. In March 1918 twelve eggs were sent for the National Egg Collection (this was a collection started for wounded servicemen in August 1915 and it was estimated that 200,000 eggs would be needed each week). By these collections, the school hoped to make their own small but important contribution.

It must have been a great relief when the war finally ended. On 12 November 1918, the school was closed for the day in recognition of the signing of the Armistice. By 14 July 1919 the children were

Cover of a *Prince of Wales' National Relief Fund* booklet detailing provisions of the scheme. Courtesy Wellcome Foundation.

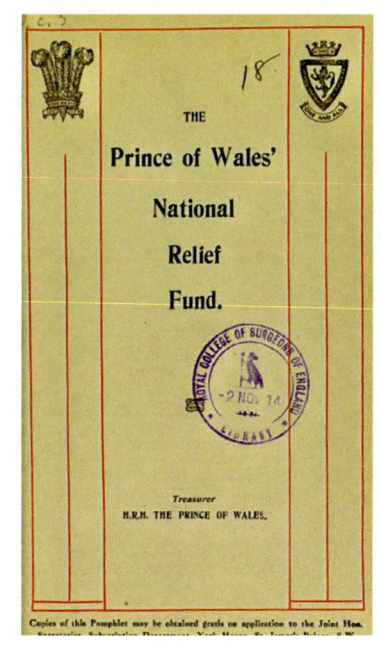

Reverting to the use of a slate after many years of paper would have seemed very strange for pupils during World War I. Photograph ©Dawn Axon.

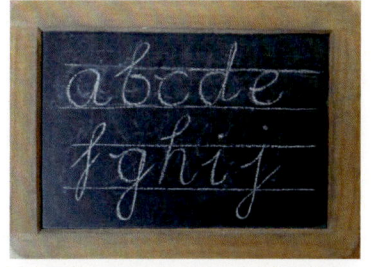

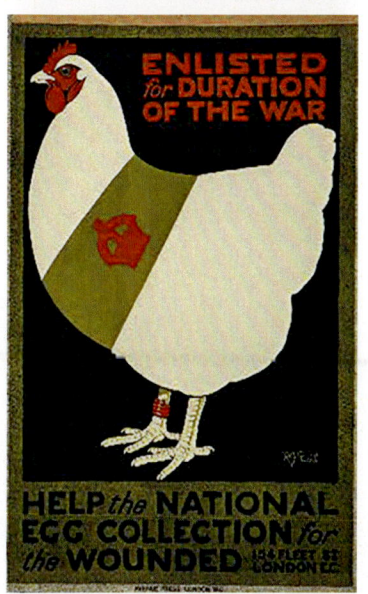

Reproduction of a National Egg Collection poster. From the collection of Helena Sanderson.

singing 'peace songs', and a message from King George V was read to the children on Armistice Day 1919. The meaning of the day was explained to them, and they stood in reverent silence for two minutes at 11 o'clock. A total of fourteen old pupils lost their lives during the war and a memorial was made to record their names. This is buried somewhere in the graveyard of St Peter's Church, Halliwell and unfortunately it appears to be lost. World War I was not the first war to be commemorated, however, as back in March 1899 there had been a holiday for the relief of Ladysmith during the Boer War.

The former Colliers Row or Smithills Dean School today. Courtesy Plucas58, CC BY-SA 4.0.[16]

The last years of the school

Numbers of children at the school began to dwindle by the 1930s, and in June 1934 there were only forty children on roll. This number again reduced when the government ruled that all secondary-aged children be educated in a state secondary school. When regulations decreed only children living on the north side of Moss Bank Way were to be allowed to attend, numbers dropped further.
The school finally closed in July 1971 and the new school, St Peter's Church of England Primary School, was opened and dedicated on 20 January 1973.

The Story of Alice and William Stead

Chapter 17
by Laura Kovaleva

Photograph ©Richard Ash.

In the 1910s, 7 Walker Fold was home to Alice and William Henry Stead and their daughter Vera. Alice and William came from families of engineers and printers, and their life stories will give us a bit of insight into the world of textile production and printing in the late nineteenth and early twentieth centuries.

Alice's life story

Alice and William married in 1904 at All Soul's Church, Bolton. The marriage announcement in the *Bolton Evening News* on 29 September tells us interesting information about Alice's father, James Bootle, revealing his last place of residence as Serpukhov, Russia.[1] James and his wife Ellen married in October 1870, and over the next thirteen years they had eight children, three of whom were born in Russia. Around 1880 James, who worked as an engine fitter, was invited to work in one of the cotton mills in the Moscow region and Ellen followed him, leaving her young children with her sister in England.

At the end of the nineteenth century, there was a boom in textile production in Russia. As noted in the *Cumberland & Westmorland Herald* from December 1882, 'the machinery in Russian mills is almost entirely of English manufacture and is obtained from the principal cotton machinists of Lancashire'.[2] It seems that James Bootle lived and worked in the city of Serpukhov which had become one of the major centres of the textile industry. The Konshin family, who were the major cotton manufacturers in the region, built four mills in Serpukhov and employed around 13,000 people.[3]

All Souls Church, Bolton. Photograph ©Laura Kovaleva.

Factory of N Konshin, Serpukhov, 1890. From the collection of M Zolotarev.

198

Alice and two of her sisters, Ellen and Mary, were born in Russia sometime between 1880 and 1884. In 1885 the family moved back to Bolton where the children were baptised at Holy Trinity Church on 19 August 1885. However, James did not return to England and continued working in Serpukhov where he died in October 1898. It must have been hard for Alice not to be able to share her life with a father she had never seen since early childhood. It was probably no coincidence that Alice called her daughter Vera, the name of Slavic origin meaning 'faith'.

Master Printer from Walker Fold

Four-year-old Vera, living with her parents at Walker Fold Farm in 1911 was probably never short of books, as William was a master printer and the owner of the shop occupying numbers 12 and 14 Bank Street, Bolton. William inherited the printing business from his father James Stead who started as a printer on Manor Street, a continuation of Bank Street. The business was going well, as in August 1871 James was advertising for an apprentice in the *Bolton Evening News*.[4] In 1877, twenty-nine-year-old James married eighteen-year-old Esther Nuttall and a year later their only child William was born.

'Advert for an Apprentice', *Bolton Evening News*, August 1871. Courtesy *The Bolton News*.

'Factory Operatives Exhibition and Bazaar in the Temperance Hall, Bolton', *Illustrated London News*, 2 October 1852. From the collection of Helena Sanderson.

A bazaar and tea party was held in September 1852 to raise funds for the Temperance movement, and featured several thousand items donated by cotton mill workers, both second hand items such as chemises, nightdresses, purses, and even an umbrella, and handmade crocheted items, samplers, and drawings. On the right you can see the banner for the Dean Mills stalls.

Temperance tea meetings or tea parties were a popular event in late nineteenth century Britain. Promoting tea instead of alcohol consumption, they were often held at Temperance Halls and attracted hundreds of townsfolk to take part in a communal tea party, usually with sandwiches and cakes included. The Band of Hope was one of the main organisations teaching young people about the dangers of alcohol, and tea parties became a social phenomenon where whole families could socialise together with the mixing of men, women, and children as well as different ages and social classes.[7]

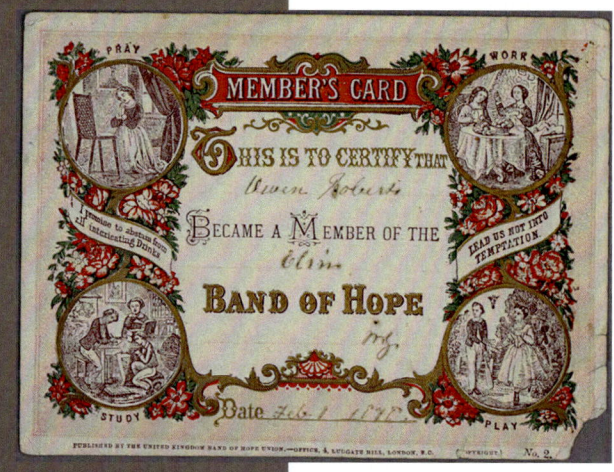

Band of Hope Member's Card, 1870. Courtesy National Library of Wales.

It should be mentioned that at that time a printer's work was not just about supporting family, but was a part of their personal and social identity and status.[5] The newspaper article published in the *Bolton Evening News* on 12 February 1877 illustrates the importance of the printer's role in the community.[6] It tells us about a tea meeting held at the Bolton Moor Temperance Hall by the winders, doublers, and reelers of the Grecian Mills who met to honour Mr Joseph Kay, their overlooker. The central part of the event was the presentation of 'a beautiful illuminated address' written by Mr James Stead to express everyone's gratitude to Mr Kay. Sadly, James Stead's life was cut short, and he passed away in September 1879, leaving son William a printing business, including a letterpress printing machine.

How to Start a Cotton Spinning Mill, published by Stead Printers, 1892. Photograph ©Laura Kovaleva. Courtesy Bolton Council.

Columbian Printing Press, 1813. Photograph ©Richard Ash. Public domain.

Two years after James' death, his widow Esther married Alfred Green, also a printer. Stead Printers kept going and were probably managed by Esther and her new husband. In 1892 a book titled *How to Start a Cotton Spinning Mill* by James Parkinson was published there and was advertised in the *Cotton Factory Times* in February 1892.

William probably learned the trade from his stepfather and by 1901 he had become a printer compositor. In a few years he moved up to the position of master printer employing other workers.

Women in printing

As we already know, William married Alice in 1904, and it was Alice's sister Ellen who was her wedding witness. It is quite possible that Alice and William met through Ellen who worked as a bookbinder in 1901.

Traditionally, women were mostly employed to complete unskilled work in printing. Thus, a great number of women were employed in bookbinding, where they were mainly involved in the process of folding. This process is described by R MacDonald in his book *Women in the printing trades: a sociology study:* 'multiple sheets, fresh from the press, are folded once, twice, three or even four times'.[8] The sheets sometimes had to be cut with a long knife as well as folded. After that, the process of gathering began when copies of the same sheet were placed in piles and the worker 'walks up and down the side of this table collecting one copy of each sheet' and so forming a complete book.

Woman compositor, *West Coast Journal*, 18 May 1870. Courtesy Bancroft Library, University of California, CC BY-SA 3.0.

Things started to change when the Women's Printing Society was established in London in 1878, providing women with an opportunity to learn the trade of printer compositor whose job was 'to set up type - to arrange the separate movable types in required order for printing successive lines of words'.[9]

At first, men looked down with contempt at women compositors and, as noted by one of the newspaper correspondents, they were 'to die off like birds in winter'.[10] However, according to census records, the number of women working as printers in England, Wales, and Scotland increased from seventy in 1861 to 1,430 in 1891.[11]

Bolton town centre showing the top of Bank Street before 1880s. Courtesy Bolton Council.

How to Start a Cotton Spinning Mill published by Stead Printers, 1892. Front cover. Photograph ©Laura Kovaleva. Courtesy Bolton Council.

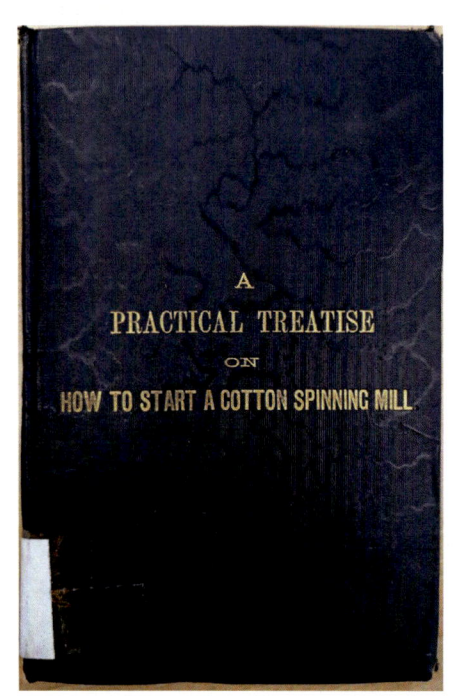

William's printing business on Bank Street was going until at least the late 1920s. Later William and Alice moved to Blackpool where they are recorded on the 1939 Register with William's occupation still a printer.

A brief glimpse at William and Alice's lives at a time when books were printed on letterpress printing machines, and cotton mills shaped the lives of so many people, leaves us wondering where that distant world has vanished. It is fascinating to know that a tiny link between those times and the present still exists. It is a copy of the book *How to Start a Cotton Spinning Mill* published by Stead Printers in 1892 that can be found at Bolton Archives.

The Harts, Emigration to Canada

Chapter 18
by Sam Holt

SS *Canada*, full steam ahead. Original watercolour painting ©Karen Holt.

The history of the Hart family of Walker Fold in the early twentieth century is one of movement across the Atlantic between the UK and Canada. The Third Wave of Canadian immigration began in the latter years of the 1890s and continued through to the early years of the twentieth, peaking prior to World War I. In this period, seven percent of Canadians recorded England as their country of birth, increasing to eight percent by 1921.[1] The opening of the Prairie Provinces; Alberta, Saskatchewan, and Manitoba, brought an influx of British settlers with the promise of cheap and ample farmland. The Harts are an example of such settlers in Canada and between 1910 and 1921 seven members of the family migrated from Smithills to Vancouver, British Columbia, having lived at Walker Fold Farm for over three decades beforehand.

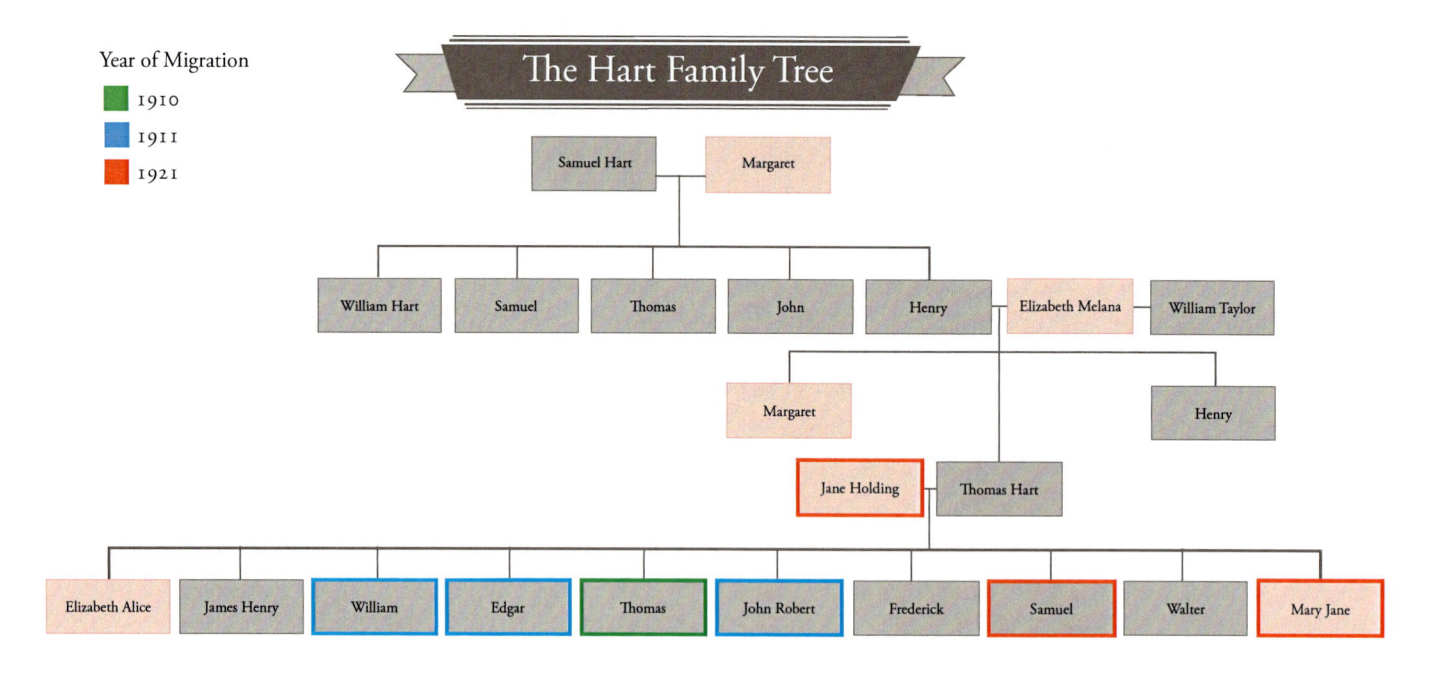

The Hart Family Tree

Year of Migration
- 1910 (green)
- 1911 (blue)
- 1921 (red)

Samuel Hart — Margaret
├── William Hart
├── Samuel
├── Thomas
├── John
└── Henry — Elizabeth Melana — William Taylor
    ├── Margaret
    └── Henry
        └── Thomas Hart — Jane Holding
            ├── Elizabeth Alice
            ├── James Henry
            ├── William
            ├── Edgar
            ├── Thomas
            ├── John Robert
            ├── Frederick
            ├── Samuel
            ├── Walter
            └── Mary Jane

The Harts on Smithills Estate

The Hart family's presence on Smithills Estate can be traced as far back to at least 1836 when Samuel Hart was recorded at Pendlebury's Farm, occupying twenty-two acres, and Jonathan Hart farmed thirty acres at Roscow's Tenement. However, the story of the Harts at Walker Fold begins with Samuel Hart's grandson Thomas, who was born to Samuel's illegitimate child Henry and his wife Elizabeth in 1854. Henry died just two years later at the age of twenty-six and Elizabeth remarried a dyer William Taylor in 1860, Thomas becoming part of that household. He spent much of his childhood at 2 New Colliers Row with his mother, stepfather, and siblings.

Despite being only seven in 1861 Thomas was already working as a doffer in a cotton mill, likely at Dean Mills, removing the filled spindles from spinning frames and replacing them with empty ones. He worked with his sister who was a doubler, operating the machinery that combined two or more strands of cotton to make a stronger thread. In early adulthood, he became a stone quarryman along with his younger brother, a profession he continued throughout his life. Thomas married Jane Holding in 1875 and they continued to live at New Colliers Row with their three children until at least 1881.

Walker Fold and Colliers Row. Ordnance Survey six-inch map, surveyed 1845-47. From the collection of Sam Holt.

The Harts at Walker Fold Farm

By 1891, Thomas and Jane were living at 3 Walker Fold and they would remain there for over a decade before taking up occupancy of No. 5. They were primarily dairy farmers with a herd of sixteen cattle and two horses, all of which were auctioned off after Thomas' death in 1915.[2]

When they began living there Thomas would have had his hands full running a working farm as well as plying his trade as a quarryman. His eldest son James Henry was also working at the quarry, and his daughter Elizabeth Alice was a bleacher, likely at the nearby works. The Harts were then a large family, with Thomas and Jane having a total of seven children living with them, though they were not the only family to be living at Walker Fold during this time.

Walker Fold Farm, bygone days. Original watercolour painting ©Karen Holt.

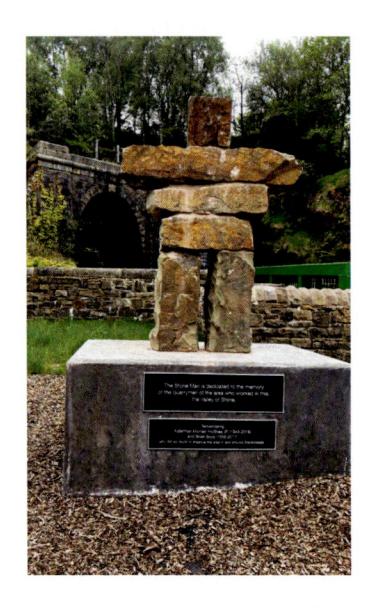

The Stone Man memorial to quarry workers in the Rossendale Valley. Photograph ©Barbara Winder.

'Who pays the quarryman?' relief sculpture in Darwen, approximately 1930s, its title alludes to Greek mythology and misquotes 'Who pays the ferryman?', referring to Charon who ferried dead souls across the river Styx. Photograph ©Barbara Winder.

Line drawing of Walker Fold. From the collection of Henry Lisowski.

Walker Fold had been well-inhabited in the mid to late nineteenth century with several split households almost forming a type of hamlet, but by the time the Harts began living there only three other households were inhabited. The closure of local mines and mills led to an outflux of residents leaving only those employed by the quarry and farming families such as William Lowe's, also landlord of Walker Fold Tavern.

Ten years later in 1901 the Hart family were then one of only two families left, with many of the neighbouring dwellings being derelict. The other family was that of Henry Dearden, the new proprietor of Walker Fold Tavern. The Harts are still farmers primarily with Thomas now seemingly retiring from his quarry work, although his three eldest sons were still quarrymen, most likely at Pilkington Quarry off George's Lane. The other children who were old enough worked on the farm helping Thomas. This included his sons Thomas and John Robert, twelve and ten respectively. The size of the family was still growing with Thomas and Jane having three more children, two sons and another daughter, Mary Jane.

What we see by the time of the 1911 census is quite a stark contrast in the occupational and social class of the residents at Walker Fold. While the Hart family are still present, there are now also two other families living there who seem to represent people of a different status. First there is the family of John Ormrod, an architect and surveyor, who was an avid Whitmanite and a leading figure in the Bolton Whitman Fellowship, with Walker Fold becoming the venue for hosting an annual event celebrating the poet Walt Whitman and his works. We may view the presence of Ormrod and his neighbour William Stead, a master printer, as an indication of the changing demographics of Walker Fold, and another hint to the shifting fortunes of the area as a whole.

Nevertheless, the Harts remain as a farming family with the two youngest sons working on the farm with their father, while another son is apprenticed to a clog and bootmaker, and their youngest daughter is at school. Perhaps more interesting are the fates of those Harts who are no longer present in 1911. Four sons emigrated to Canada prior to the recording of the census in April, their intention being to settle in Vancouver. Their reasons for doing so may be difficult to ascertain, however I do not think it would be unreasonable to suggest that the changes happening across the estate may provide some context to the motivation behind them seeking opportunities further afield.

Migration to Canada between 1910 and 1911: The Hart brothers

The first of the Harts to emigrate was one of the older sons, Thomas. He arrived in Halifax, Nova Scotia via the *Victorian* on the 22 April 1910. At this time Halifax had become a natural transportation hub for those travelling across the North Atlantic thanks to renovations made at Halifax Harbour in 1905 that made the docks much more suitable. These developments coincided with the surge and eventual peak in immigration prior to World War I. To Thomas, it is very likely that Halifax would have seemed a somewhat unassuming port compared to Liverpool where he had started his journey.

Plaque in commemoration of the 'Eagle Street College' or the Bolton Whitman Fellowship at John Ormrod's former home at Walker Fold. Photograph ©Sam Holt.

Walt Whitman (1819-1892). American poet, author, and journalist in 1877 portrait. Courtesy Shutterstock/Everett Collection.

Postcard of RMS *Victorian*. D & W Forrest, Montreal, Canada. From the collection of Sam Holt.

Pier 3 showing parts of Piers 2 and 4, Halifax Harbour, Nova Scotia, 1905. Courtesy Public Archives of Nova Scotia.

From Halifax, Thomas made the approximately 2700-mile journey from Nova Scotia to Vancouver, British Columbia, likely by rail. Such a journey from the shores of the Atlantic to the Pacific Ocean would once have been arduous. However, the development of the Intercolonial Railway of Canada in 1877 and the National Transcontinental Railway in 1885 made the journey across the breadth of the Canadian landmass a relatively comfortable one. By the early 1900s people would be able to travel from Halifax to Montreal via the Maritime Express and then from Montreal all the way to Vancouver via the Canadian Pacific Railway.

Travellers in a Pullman car crossing the plains of Canada circa 1910. Courtesy Shutterstock/Everett Collection.

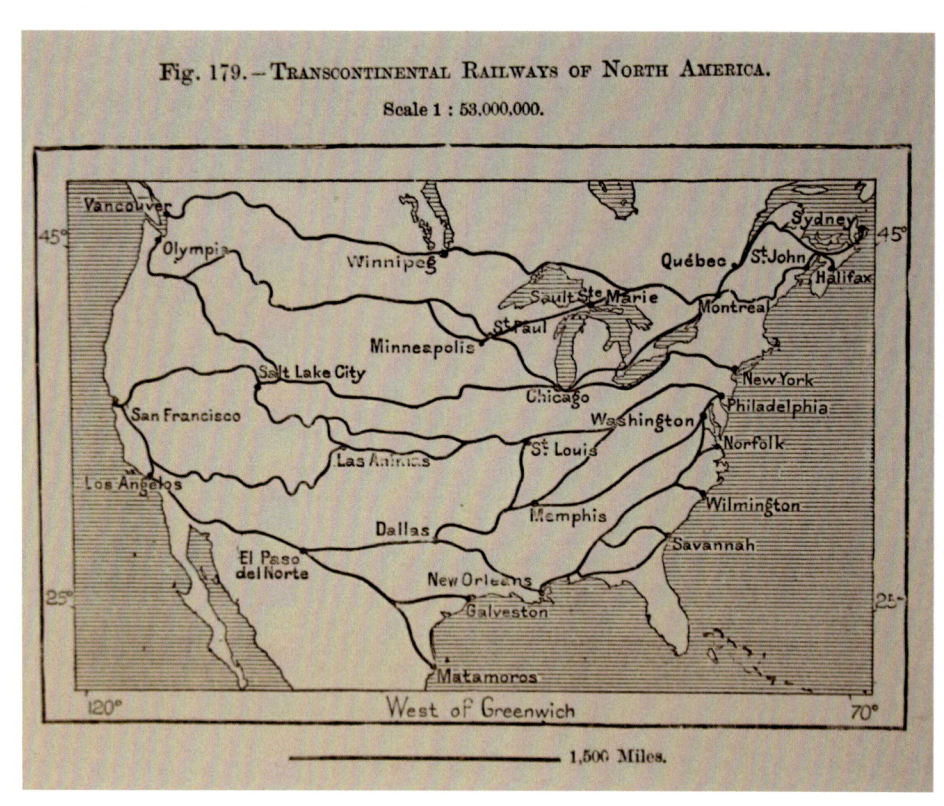

Map showing Transcontinental Railways of North America, 1885. From *The Universal Geography* by Élisée Reclus, edited by A H Keane, published by J S Virtue and Co., London/North America. From the collection of Sam Holt.

A year on from his arrival, Thomas is joined by three of his brothers; William, Edgar, and John Robert, all of whom arrive at St John, New Brunswick aboard the *Empress of Britain* on the 18 March 1911. Travelling with them are William and Edgar's wives, as well as Thomas' betrothed, Mary Ann. Thomas and Mary Ann were married on the 5 April that year and were living in South Vancouver by the time of the 1911 Canadian census. Thomas earned a living as a teamster, someone who drove a team of animals hauling goods. William and John Robert are stonecutters, and Edgar is unemployed. They lived together in Vancouver with William and Edgar's wives, as well as William's three-year-old son, and two lodgers.

The draw of Canada for prospective farmers

Settling in Canada had become an attractive prospect for British migrants with the percentage of UK immigrants to North America heading for Canada rising from fourteen percent in the 1890s to over fifty percent between 1901 and 1911.[4]

It seems likely that British migrants such as the Harts who came from farming backgrounds may have been drawn by the prospect of cheap farmland and the promise of support in securing land from the Canadian government.

The Dominion Lands Act of 1872 made the purchasing of land in the Prairie Provinces extremely affordable, an enticing prospect for tenant farmers and agricultural labourers alike.[5]

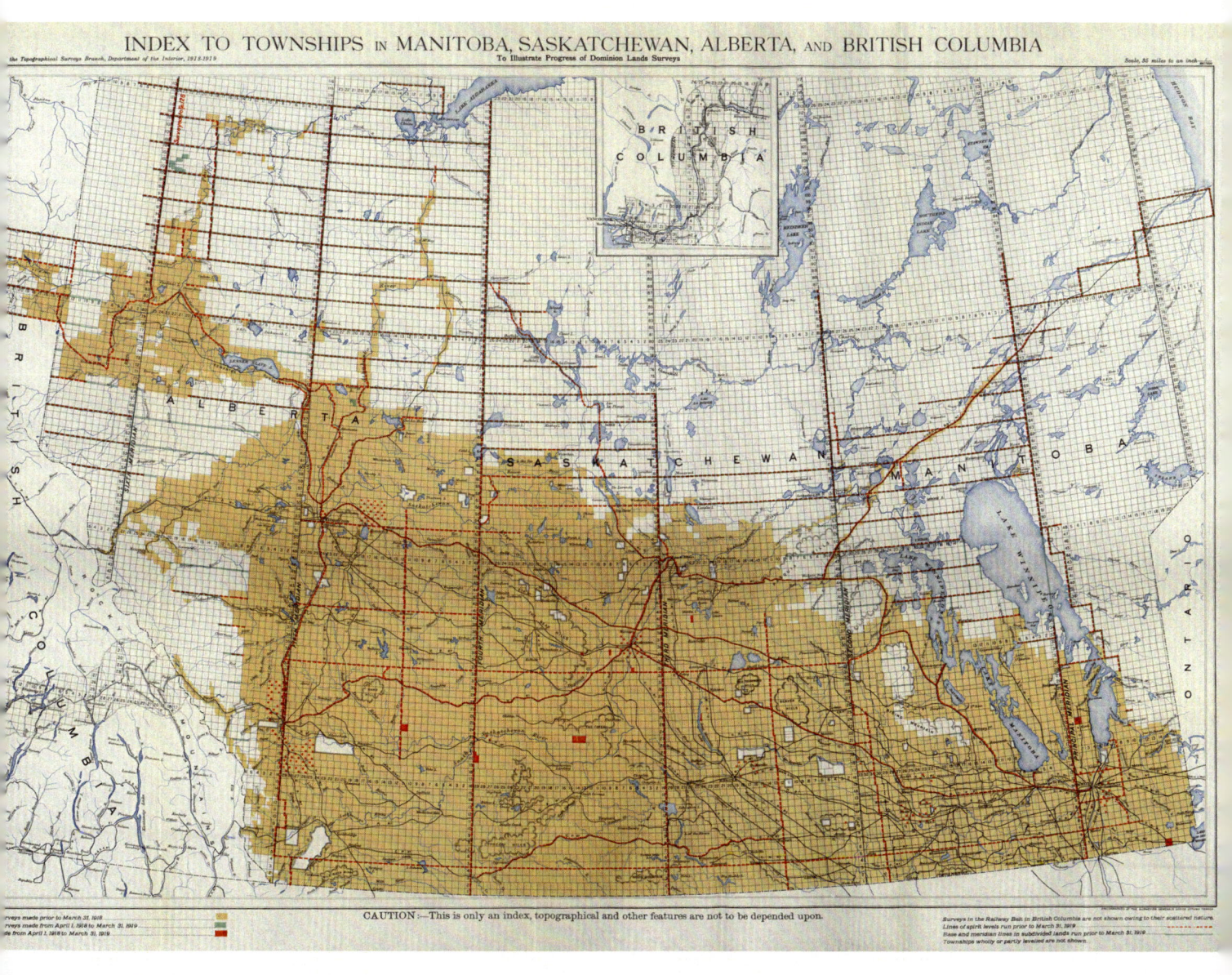

Index to Townships in Manitoba, Saskatchewan, Alberta and British Columbia to illustrate progresses of the Dominion Lands Surveys, 1920. Courtesy Manitoba Historical Maps.[3]

The Canadian government actively recruited emigrants from the UK who had experience working on farms, with the intention that they would be prepared to establish farms or work as farm labourers.[7] An advertisement for emigration to Canada from the *Bolton Evening News* in 1898 shows that both experienced and inexperienced farmers were their chief target demographic. Whilst the advert does prioritise farm recruitment and even goes as far as to gleefully promise, 'FREE GRANTS OF LAND FOR FARMS', it also endeavours to present Canada as a capitalist venture for aspiring entrepreneurs.[8] The Hart brothers seem to be indicative of the type of migrant such advertisements were aimed at: young men who had experience in farming and who were seeking opportunities that eluded them in their hometowns.

Canadian Pacific Railway advertisement promising free land for millions. Courtesy National Archives of Canada, Government Archives TR 15/08, 1893.[6]

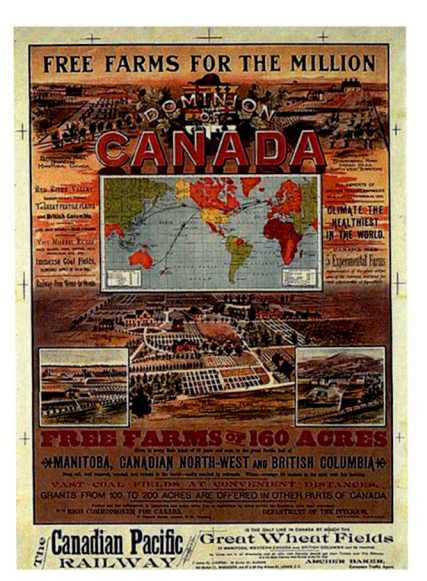

However, the free land provided by the government was not considered to be the most arable and only applied to the provinces of Alberta, Saskatchewan, and Manitoba, although later applying to Peace River County, British Columbia. The fact that the Harts set out for Vancouver perhaps suggests they never intended to seek land from the government. It may have been more attractive for them to either rent or purchase land from the Canadian Pacific Railway which had been granted large blocks of land from the government in 1882.[9] The CPR even supplied and advertised 'ready-made' farms, which were specifically targeted at British immigrants.[10] These farms would most likely have been viewed as a preferable alternative to government land where migrants would be expected to help already established farmers as labourers before starting a farm of their own.[11]

The Hart brothers in Vancouver

Considering that on arrival all four brothers settled in the urban centre that was Vancouver, it would appear they were either not seeking to pursue farming in Canada or they were unable to secure farmland. All listed their intended occupations as farming on arrival, and 'British Bonus Allowed' was also stamped by their names on the passenger lists. This was a commission paid by the Canadian government's Immigration Branch that encouraged steamship booking agents to provide cheap passage for desirable settlers such as farmers and domestic staff. Yet upon their arrival the Harts very much found themselves a part of the majority who worked and lived in towns and cities.

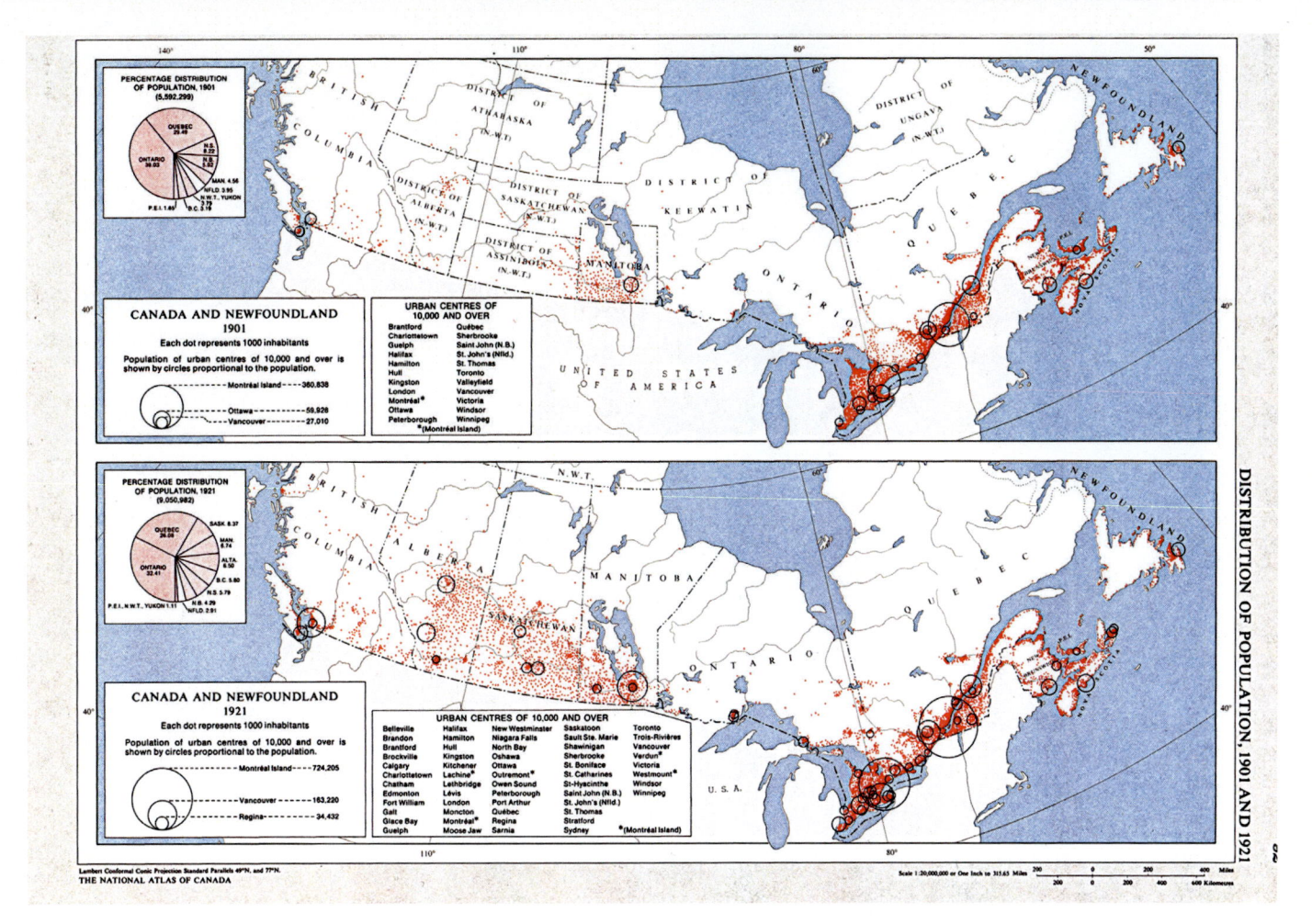

Cropped image showing a collection of two maps showing the distribution of population for 1901 and 1921 by historical region and urban centres. Courtesy *The National Atlas of Canada*, Natural Resources Canada.[12]

According to a consular report, by the time Thomas immigrated in 1910, there were approximately two thousand government sponsored farmsteads left unsettled in the province of New Brunswick, and such policies had only attracted three hundred European settlers the previous year.[13] Although the policy did attract some European immigrants from agricultural backgrounds, the typical UK immigrant to Canada was not a farmer and was living and working in urban areas.

As time passed, some of the Harts seem to have been successful in securing farmland in Canada. Edgar is not listed on the 1921 Canadian census as that same year he returned to England briefly and described his occupation as a rancher on his return ticket. His address is given as R.R.1, Eburne on the arrival manifest, which indicates he was living at a rural homestead. The initials 'R.R.' denote a rural route without a street address. Today Eburne is a built-up area within Vancouver itself. In 1924 he placed an advertisement for the sale of a Jersey Cow in his local newspaper, *The Province,* which lists his street addresses as River Road and No. 2 Road, Vancouver, where he would remain until his death in 1969.[14]

Postcard showing Wholesale District of Vancouver. Novelty Post Card Co., Vancouver, British Columbia. From the collection of Sam Holt.

Postcard of a dairy farm near Victoria, British Columbia, not far from Vancouver, approximately 1910s/20s. The Valentine & Sons' Publishing Co., Ltd. Montreal and Toronto. From the collection of Sam Holt.

Image showing the town of Blackfalds, approximately 1910. Courtesy Blackfalds Archive.

SS *Canada*, full steam ahead. Original watercolour painting ©Karen Holt.

John Robert is another of the brothers who became a farmer in Canada, but he left Vancouver to do so. He married Elizabeth Ann in 1915, and in 1921 they can be found living at Blackfalds, a rural town in Alberta where, like Edgar, he is a farmer on rented land. There he had two daughters before his death at the age of sixty-seven in 1956. His obituary in the *Calgary Herald* gives us an insight into his life after immigrating to Canada, telling us that he lived in Vancouver until 1917, then moved to Blackfalds as a farmer and then later to nearby Calgary where he was employed by the bridge and building department of the Canadian National Railway for over thirty years.[15]

Migration to Canada in 1921: More Harts migrate

Meanwhile at Walker Fold, following Thomas' death in 1915, more members of the Hart family would make the trip across the Atlantic to settle in Canada. Thomas' widow Jane remained in England for another six years after his death before following in the footsteps of her sons and emigrating along with her youngest daughter, Mary Jane. They arrived at Halifax in March 1921 aboard the *Canada* and accompanying them on their journey was Edgar and his wife returning home.

After their arrival, they lived with William, his wife and two children, in Vancouver, very close to where he and his family were living on the previous census. William was a teamster whilst Mary Jane was listed as a saleswoman, likely a store clerk or retail worker, and her mother, now at the age of sixty-seven, was not working.

These two would not be the last Harts to emigrate as later in 1921 Samuel Hart settled in Canada with his wife and infant son, who was just two years of age at the time. They arrived in Quebec on 21 April before moving to Vancouver where the rest of his family was settled, although they do not appear on the census sheet that year.

Thomas and Mary Ann were still in Vancouver in 1921, living about seven miles away from William. They had had a son Henry who was born in 1913 but tragically died that same year at just three months old. Fortunately, they had a daughter in 1917 who was living with them. Thomas was still a teamster, which may perhaps suggest he and William were in business together, but this does not seem to be the case. The census lists the nature of their work, with William working alone on his own account and being occupied with odd jobs. Thomas was a wage earner, recording his yearly earning as $1150, which compared to the double-figure yearly wage a farm labourer could expect to earn in the UK suggests he was doing well.[16]

Immigrants disembarking in Quebec, 1903. Courtesy Shutterstock/Archivist.

The success of the Harts in Canada

Of the Harts who immigrated to Canada most of them remained in the country for the remainder of their lives. Thomas, William, Edgar, and Samuel lived in Vancouver until their deaths, whereas John Robert settled in Calgary. This would suggest that they found a great deal of success in the country, something that eluded many migrants who returned home after a period of time. Both Jane and Mary Jane ended up leaving Canada after emigrating together in 1921, however their destinations were quite different.

An Oregon teamster pictured in 1907. Courtesy Teamsters Archives.

Jane would reside in Canada for over half a decade before returning to England in 1927 aboard the *Montrose* to reside at Hodgkinsons Farm in the Doffcocker area of Bolton. This was not Jane's last trans-Atlantic crossing, she made the journey again five years later aboard the *Duchess of Richmond* from Liverpool to Montreal in 1931, likely to visit her children in Vancouver, and returned via the same liner a year later in 1932. She would pass away three years later in 1935 at the age of eighty-one and is buried alongside her husband at Holy Trinity Churchyard in Horwich.

Transcription: 'In loving memory of Thomas Hart who died March 15th 1915, aged 61 years, also Jane Hart who died April 17th 1935, aged 81 years, also James Taylor who died Dec 26th 1942, aged 66 years, also Elizabeth Alice, his dear wife, who died Oct 25th 1952, aged 76 years, at rest.'

What happened to Mary Jane, the youngest child of the family? At some point after arriving in Canada she married a Robert Lee and then emigrated again but to Australia, however very little is to be found regarding her time there. There is a record in the death index for Victoria, Australia of a Mary Jane Lee dying in 1969 that simply lists her father as 'Hart', which may point to this being the same person, but no further information is given.

Looking back to Smithills

The members of the family who stayed in England remained connected to the Smithills area. Eldest son James Henry was a dairy farmer at Hampsons Farm and then Pendlebury's Farm until his death in 1929, and his son also became a farmer living at Chadwick Close Farm by the time of the 1939 census. Likewise, Elizabeth Alice, the eldest daughter, married farmer James Taylor and lived at Fern Farm in Horwich, and later Bryan Hey Farm on Smithills Estate. Both are buried alongside her mother and father in Horwich. Fred, the younger son who was apprenticed to a boot and clog maker, fulfilled his vocation and became a clogger and bootmaker, relocating to Nelson with his family.

The end of the Third Wave of immigration

The members of the Harts that immigrated to Canada between 1910 and 1921 formed part of Canada's Third Wave of immigration, after which there would be a stagnation in rates of emigration from Britain. A year after the final Hart emigrated the Empire Settlement Act 1922 would be introduced; it was an agreement between the British government and certain Commonwealth countries, including Canada, to allow for the resettlement of mainly agriculturalists and farm labourers, as well as domestic workers.[17] Under the 3000 Family Scheme, British families were offered financing or farm purchases in settlement programmes, placement on Canadian farms and practical instruction in agriculture. British subjects already in Canada could also nominate their relatives, friends, and acquaintances for farm labour or domestic work.[15] The Act ultimately failed to draw British emigrants and by the end of the 1920s, with the onset of the Great Depression, such programmes came to an end.

Love Across the Continents: Putting Down Roots in the New World

*Chapter 19
by Dawn Axon*

Courtesy Library and Archives, Canada.

The Turner Family of Haslams Farm and the Brown Family of Cunliffe's Farm

Stonemason Thomas Turner married Rachel Guest from Twitchells Farm in 1864. They lived at Bottom o' th' Moor but then decided to carry on the family tradition of farming, firstly at Harricroft Farm and then moving into Haslams Farm by 1901. They had five children. Eldest son William lived on Old Colliers Row and was also a stonemason with five children. Daughter Elizabeth married Joseph Brown from Cunliffe's Farm and was farming at Lomax Wives Farm next door, along with their four children. Son Henry was a horse blacksmith, also married with children and living on Chorley Old Road. Youngest children Richard and Edith were still at home and helping on the farm. Life must have seemed settled for Rachel with all her children and grandchildren close by when Thomas died in 1906, aged just sixty-one, leaving her farming alone with her youngest children. The family were at a crossroads.

A wave of emigration in the 1850s had seen some residents of Smithills Estate leaving for Australia. Canada had attempted to lure immigrants; however contemporary accounts do not suggest that Canada was as successful a destination prior to 1900 due to a deep depression.

The *Northern Star and Leeds General Advertiser* in 1844 carried a report that the experience of emigration to Canada to date had resulted in 'much individual hardship and distress, especially in the Emigrant of the poorer class; for on arriving he found himself with little or no money, no friends to assist him in find work, or even to point out in what part of the Province he would be most likely to obtain it'.[2] Many had travelled, lured by the offer of free passage, and the North American Land Agency reported that 'the sufferings which too often befall these people are greater than would be believed'.[3] Farmers were unfamiliar with the land and the seasons, houses had to be built which took time and expense, and many faced starvation before crops were harvested. Emigration to Canada fell by fifty percent between 1842 and 1843 as news reached home. The Agency was one of several set up which purchased huge swathes of land and set forth schemes to ensure a better outcome. They insisted that a man with £100 could better his

'The Last Best West'. Cover of Pamphlet produced by Canada Department of Interior, 1909. Courtesy Library and Archives, Canada.[1]

situation by emigrating to Canada in the future. They proposed that for this amount the Agency would provide passage, a hundred acres of land, three months provisions, tools and the services of a foreman and two labourers to help erection of the dwelling and clearance and sowing of the land.

It is very unlikely that any of the residents of the farms on Smithills Estate had access to £100 in the 1840s, it would have been the equivalent of almost two years' wages for an experienced craftsman, let alone a farm labourer or mine worker. They also perhaps had heard some of the horror stories from those who had ventured out previously. Shipping agencies such as the North Atlantic Trading Companies were paid huge bonuses by the Canadian government to attract agricultural labour whilst not always being totally honest about the prospects.[4]

By the early 1900s, however, the twenty-five-year recession in Canada was over and Rachel and her family began planning a new life away from the estate. According to research by the University of Edinburgh in 2011, approximately 3.15 million people left the UK between 1903 and 1913. The most popular destination was Canada which drew almost half of Britain's emigrants.[5]

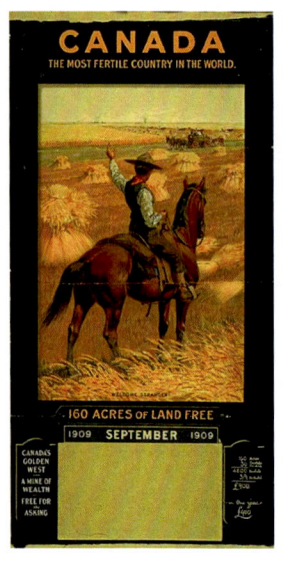

'Canada, The Most Fertile Country in the World'. Courtesy Library and Archives, Canada.[6]

The *Bolton Journal and Guardian* of 20 January 1911 reported that one party of eighteen agricultural workers had been booked to go in March, 'ready for the early-summer work on the boundless plains of Canada…Lantern views, a plethora of literature and stories of remarkable prosperity on the part of the Englishmen who have emigrated after scarcely being able to make ends meet here, have undoubtedly moulded the feelings of disappointed Lancastrians and directed their thoughts to the land of promise'.[7] Colliers and iron turners were said to be needed and particularly joiners, 'as their training gives them knowledge especially useful about the wooden buildings, fences and so on'. The article reported that not many textile workers had emigrated so there was little effect on the cotton trade in Bolton as 'so brisk is local weaving that there is not a single trade union member out of work'.

It must have been difficult for people in Bolton to ascertain whether reports coming from Canada were unbiased. The same article said, 'A Bolton gentleman who has family interests in the development of Canada says he can well understand the flood of immigrants which that giant country is receiving with open arms'. He stated that for the agriculturist with £200 to invest he could have obtained from the government or one of the railway companies a whole farm on what a Bolton shopkeeper would call easy-payment terms, spread over ten years.[8] Many of the farms on Smithills Estate had families who travelled out to Canada around this time. It was quite likely that £200 would equate to three years rental of a farm, so the attraction of owning their own land would be obvious if a tenant could raise the funds for the investment.

Group of Immigrants arriving in Canada, c.1920. Courtesy of Library and Archives, Canada.[9]

Most of Rachel's family made the decision to emigrate to Canada. Eldest son William and her son-in-law Joseph Brown travelled out first in 1911 and then sent for the rest of their family. Rachel travelled out with youngest son Richard, daughter Elizabeth, and Elizabeth and Joseph Brown's five children on the *Virginian* in May 1912. The youngest child Doris was only one month old, very young to make the arduous voyage. William's wife and their four children travelled out to him on the *Empress of Britain*, arriving on 7 December 1912 in St Johns, Newfoundland.

The *Virginian* consumed about 2,500 tons of coal per journey. On her maiden voyage from Liverpool to Canada on 6 April 1905 she broke the Liverpool-Rimouski speed record, as she made it in five days, twenty hours, forty minutes. She and her sister ship *Victorian* remained the fastest liners in the Canadian trade until the new Canadian Pacific liners *Empress of Britain* and *Empress of Ireland* entered the service the following year.

The RMS *Virginian*. Courtesy www.naval-history.net, public domain.

The *Empress of Britain* was built in Glasgow for the Canadian Pacific Railway Company and made her maiden voyage from Liverpool to Montreal on 5 May 1906. She set a new speed record later that year. She carried 310 first-class passengers, over 400 second-class and almost 800 third-class or steerage. Only two weeks after the *Titanic* disaster, *Empress of Britain* also hit an iceberg but with only slight damage. The passengers must have been terrified given that the news of the *Titanic* would be very fresh in their memories.

Commemorating RMS *Empress of Britain*. Postcard. From the collection of Dawn Axon.

'On Board the *Empress of Britain*'. Courtesy Library and Archives, Canada.[11]

In 1912 the *Mercury* reported that the *Empress of Britain* rammed and sank the *Helvetia,* a British cargo ship used to carry coal, in the estuary of the St Lawrence River. Luckily the thirty crew were saved. The bows of the *Empress of Britain* were badly stoved in and her fore compartments filled with water. The Court of Enquiry found that the captain of the *Empress* was culpable.[10] Another near miss.

The family made their home in the Victoria region of Alberta. By 1916 Rachel, now seventy, was listed as living with youngest son Richard, a blacksmith working in a coal mine. Also living close by were William and his family; his two eldest sons were both listed as farmers, aged sixteen and fifteen.

Rachel died soon after this however, aged seventy-two, having spent five years in Canada and seen her family start to make new lives for themselves. William applied to register a homestead in 1921, having lived on the land at Peace River, Last Lake, Alberta since 1918. The house was described as a single dwelling made of wood with four rooms. In the census of that year, they class themselves as Canadians. Richard also applied to register his own homestead with his sister Edith: after the death of their mother neither ever married. The family never returned to England and were all buried locally.

Elizabeth and Joseph Brown and their children remained close to their relatives in Alberta. The 1921 Canadian Census stated that Joseph owned his farm which was constructed of wood with six rooms. Joseph died in 1954, aged seventy-nine and was survived by his wife who lived to the great age of ninety-three. Life would have been hard but the Browns and the Turners obviously remained close. It would appear that they made the right decision to leave the estate to farm in Canada.

When nine-year-old Joyce Cundict's family arrived in Hattonford, Alberta, from England in the spring of 1920, the settlement was a smattering of little log houses, barns and vegetable gardens. This, after weeks aboard a boat across the Atlantic and a train across Canada, would be their new home.
'Our family was poor, like everyone else'. They lived a pioneering life; she and her sister Nora helped to milk the cows, clean the barns, and plough the fields. When Joyce's mother was pregnant with her third daughter, her father carried their nearest neighbour across a flooded creek to act as a makeshift midwife. School was in session only during the summer and the nearest schoolhouse, a one-room log cabin, was a three-mile, mosquito-infested trek away. 'The other children thought we had the measles, we were so covered with mosquito bites'. Groceries, meanwhile, arrived once a month. When Joyce's father made the trip into town, he would bring back, among other things, coal oil and a hundred pound sack of flour. Once, when the oil leaked on the return trip, 'we endured a long month with the most horrible-tasting bread'. Those flour sacks came in handy, too; they held most of the family's clothing.[12]

The Southerns of Roscow's Tenement

Another of the families from Smithills Estate who emigrated to Canada were the Southerns who farmed Roscow's Tenement in 1901. Richard and Mary Southern had six children, two girls and four boys.

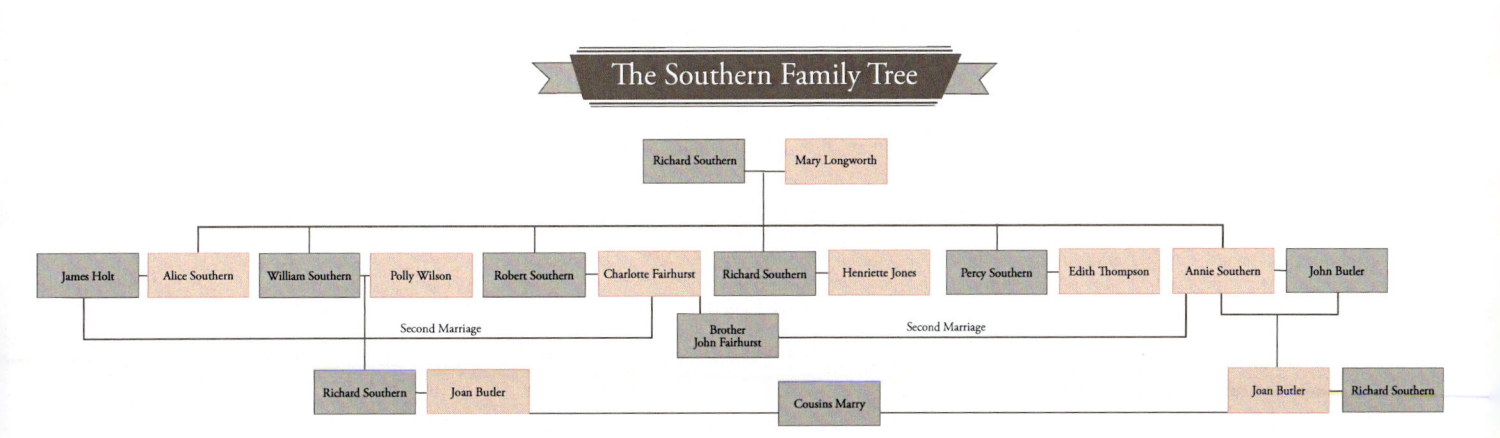

The Southern Family Tree

Richard Southern — Mary Longworth

- James Holt — Alice Southern
- William Southern — Polly Wilson (Second Marriage)
- Robert Southern — Charlotte Fairhurst (Brother John Fairhurst)
- Richard Southern — Henriette Jones
- Percy Southern — Edith Thompson (Second Marriage)
- Annie Southern — John Butler

Richard Southern — Joan Butler

Cousins Marry

Joan Butler — Richard Southern

Richard Southern Senior outside Roscow's Tenement Farm. Courtesy Halliwell Local History Society.

Oldest brothers William and Robert were the first to leave from Liverpool in August 1903, travelling to Brandon, Quebec on the *Lake Champlain*. They are both described as farmers and second-class cabin passengers. William left behind his wife and their one-year-old daughter. He must have come back fairly shortly afterwards however, because they had three further children all born in Bolton between 1905 and 1910. Maybe this was just an early reconnaissance voyage by the brothers. William did not return to Canada but like the Turners and the Browns, the rest of the Southern family did decide to emigrate around 1911.

Father Richard aged forty-six, wife Mary, and their younger sons, Richard, twenty-six, Percy, twenty-one and daughter Annie, eighteen, departed on the *Empress of Britain* from Liverpool to St Johns, New Brunswick on 8 April 1911. The passenger list detailed that all the family were going to Canada for life. They were all listed as farmers, even Annie. Their entries were stamped with 'British Bonus Allowed' stating their intention to farm. Eldest daughter Alice and her husband James Holt and their four children also travelled out on the *Empress of Britain* the following week.

There is evidence that members of the family returned to Britain for several visits over the years, but these voyages were not without danger. The *Empress of Ireland* sunk on her return journey to Liverpool on 24 May 1914 when she collided with another ship on the St Lawrence River in the fog. The liner sank in only fifteen minutes when most of the passengers and crew were asleep and there was a loss of more than a thousand lives. This was more than on the *Titanic* where 817 were lost and the *Lusitania* where 786 were lost. The *Empress of Ireland* had enough lifeboats for all but there was no time to launch them.

Commemorating the sinking of Empress of Ireland. Postcard. From the collection of Dawn Axon.

Those lost included 134 children, and 124 members of the Salvation Army on their way to London for a conference. Of the 420 crew on board, 172 perished, many from the Liverpool area. The ship is sometimes called the *'Forgotten Empress'* as so few people know of her fate. This could be because the story of the *Titanic* was seen as more dramatic as it was on her maiden voyage that she struck an iceberg, and there were celebrities aboard. In contrast, the *Empress of Ireland* sank after hitting another ship in a river on a voyage she had done many times before. Other events of the time worldwide would have been uppermost in people's minds too as war was looming. The sinking of the *Lusitania* caused outrage as it was an act of war. The once opulent vessel has never been raised but in 1999 the wreck was awarded 'historical and archaeological property' in Quebec law to prevent any salvage and there is a museum dedicated to the ship close to the wreck.[13] There is also a display in the Liverpool Maritime Museum.[14]

Richard Southern Senior & Mary Southern. Courtesy Douglas Wiberg.

By 1911 Richard Senior was a farmer living in Vancouver with his labourer sons Richard Junior and Percy. Having seen his family settled in Canada, he died on 5 February 1915 in Vancouver.

Unlike Richard's eldest son William, younger son Robert Southern returned to Canada after the original reconnaissance trip. He married in Vancouver in 1911 to Charlotte Fairhurst, one of a pair of sisters who were both weavers and travelled out to New Brunswick in 1911. Against both the ladies' names their reason for travel was detailed 'to be married – farming'.[15] The two couples lived together in 1911 in Point Grey, British Columbia. One man was described as a teamster, the other a labourer.

Sadly, Robert's Canadian adventure was cut short by World War I. He signed up on 31 March 1916 as a Private in the Canadian Overseas Expeditionary Force, British Columbia Regiment, and was killed in action eighteen months later, on 15 August 1917 in France; his remains never found. His name is inscribed on the Vimy Ridge Memorial in Calais. Charlotte was now a widow.

Vimy Ridge Memorial, France, commemorating Canadian Troops lost in battle. Courtesy iStock/hstivr.

Four days after the UK entered the war they accepted Canada's offer of 25,000 troops. Canadian forces took part in many of the major campaigns, including Gallipoli, Passchendaele, and Ypres. Over 11,000 Canadians who were posted as missing presumed dead during battles in France are commemorated on the Vimy Ridge Memorial. More than 66,000 Canadians died during the war and 172,000 were wounded. Seventy Canadians were awarded the Victoria Cross for 'most conspicuous bravery in the presence of the enemy'.

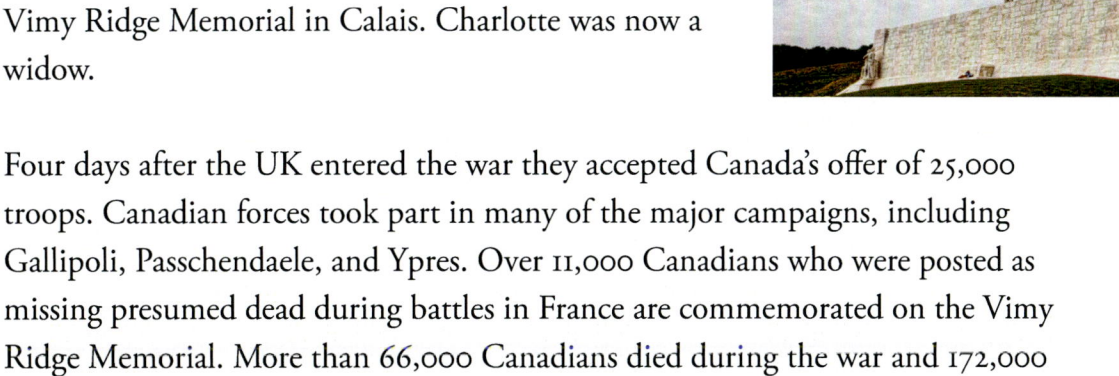

Canadian Recruitment Poster. Courtesy Library and Archives, Canada.[16]

Canadian troops had a reputation for bravery. Many enlisted because of their British roots, fighting on behalf of their country of birth, but many who considered themselves British at enlistment came home considering themselves true Canadians, proud to have been adopted by a country who trained hard fighting troops that seldom failed to take their objective, regardless of the cost.

There was to be more sorrow. Alice, her husband James Holt and their children were listed as living in Strathcona, Alberta in 1916 where James was a dairyman. Alice died in 1918 during the global influenza epidemic which is estimated to have killed at least fifty million people. Mortality was high in the twenty to forty age group, and with no vaccine to protect against it, or antibiotics to treat secondary infections, isolation, quarantine, use of disinfectants, face masks, and limits to public gatherings were the only options to control the spread.

Now a widower, James married Charlotte, his wife's sister-in-law, whose husband had been killed in the war. Three years later James was a farmer in Richmond on his own property, sharing the house with his new wife and the five children they had between them. Maybe he married Charlotte so they could look after their children together, having both lost their spouses? James died in 1959 aged eighty-three, though it is not known if Charlotte survived him.

By 1921 Richard Senior's widow Mary was fifty-seven and living with daughter Annie who had married John Butler in Vancouver in 1913. He had emigrated from Portsmouth in 1890 when he was one year old and became a dairy driver earning $1500 per year. It appears she was the only sibling not to marry someone that they knew from Bolton. They had a daughter Joan in 1917. John died in 1937, and the following year Annie remarried - to Charlotte's brother John Fairhurst! It all makes for a very complicated family tree!

Annie Fairhurst (Butler) (Southern). Courtesy Douglas Wiberg.

Living next door to the Butlers in 1921 was Percy and his wife, also from Bolton. Both families lived in four-roomed houses constructed of wood which they rented for $15 per month. Percy was described as a landscape gardener who had earned $1150 in the previous twelve months. To put that into context the average wage for an agricultural worker in the UK was between 14s. and 22s. per week, or approximately £50 per year.[17]

Matriarch of the Southern family, Mary Southern, died in Vancouver on 1 March 1931, aged seventy-seven, having seen all her children married (at least once!) and settled.

The Southerns who travelled to Canada appear to have prospered, but it is likely these brief snapshots do not tell how hard life was. It would appear not all immigrants made it into farming; many, like John Butler, found work as teamsters or drivers. These drivers fulfilled a vital role in the growth of trade across Canada and America, however life was hard and they were often exploited.[18] By 1903 a union had been formed across the continent to fight for their rights. By 1912, when members of the Southern family would have been in the trade, the Union was fighting for social justice and was pioneering in its adaptation to the use of motor vehicles. The horses or teams which had been such faithful companions however would be the symbol of the Union to this day.[19] The Union fought for standardised contracts and benefits such as reduced hours and increased pay. It was also one of the first to recognise the importance of women in the workplace and demonstrated early openness to racial equality, being able to boast, 'Teamsters know no color line'.[20]

My own great aunt and her family travelled to Canada in 1920 and she wrote home that when they got to their destination there was 'nothing there' and but for the help of the Salvation Army they would not have survived the terrible cold winter.

They sent family photographs home from Drumheller, Alberta and my family were said to be very worried for them. My great uncle was a teamster who froze to death in his wagon when stranded in the snow in winter.

Mary Southern (née Longworth). Courtesy Douglas Wiberg.

Hettie Elliott and family on porch in Drumheller. From the collection of Dawn Axon.

Hettie Elliott & baby prior to emigration. From the collection of Dawn Axon.

Early Teamster in Canada. Courtesy Maggie Land Blanck & family.

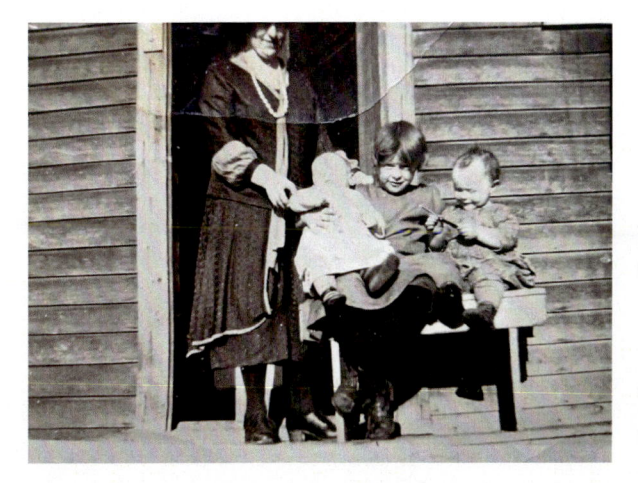

Main Street, Drumheller, Canada. Courtesy Glen Lundeen at Prairie-towns.com.

What of Richard and Mary's eldest son William Henry Southern, known as Harry? Whilst he was the first to travel to Canada with his younger brother Robert in 1903, he returned to his wife in Bolton.[21] There seems to have been something about Canada that did not appeal to him. On his return he found work as a twister in a cotton mill, operating the machinery that twisted threads together to make yarn, but he was still not happy with his life. With most of the family now intent on life in Canada, thoughts must have again turned to further lands. Another country was advertising for farm labourers and William immigrated to New Zealand, leaving his wife and children in Halliwell, on the *Tongariro* in 1910. He arrived in Wellington on 22 September 1910, listed as a farmer.[22] The *Bolton Journal and Guardian* of 20 January 1911 reported that 'odd emigrants go to New Zealand and Australia, for health reasons rather than the fascination of the almighty dollar'.[23] Had William been put off by the cold weather in Canada when he went on his reconnaissance trip and did the warm weather of New Zealand seem more attractive?

Inhabitants of the estate also travelled to North America. In 1850 this journey would have taken around ten days and cost about £4. In comparison the journey to New Zealand would have taken between seventy-five and a hundred-and-twenty days and cost at least £15. Often the passengers never saw land and conditions could be poor. By the 1890s most voyages were by steamer and conditions had improved. Although cabins were lit by electricity and heated by steam, third-class passengers had to provide their own bedding and utensils, and their diet was still poor.

When William and his family emigrated the route would have been around the Cape of Good Hope, probably stopping to take on coal at Tenerife, Cape Town and Hobart, but the 1914 opening of the Panama Canal further speeded up voyages. The weather however could not be changed and produced constant challenges, from storms to incessant sun, and sea sickness was inevitable. In 1911 William was listed in New Zealand as a labourer and Polly and the four children joined him, travelling steerage. They arrived on 8 January 1912 aboard the *Somerset*. They boarded on 22 November 1911, so the journey still took over six weeks.

Previously the high cost of passage made travel to New Zealand unaffordable but the resumption in 1904 of a government assistance scheme, where the government of New Zealand and the shipping companies both contributed to a reduced fare scheme, opened up emigration again. The scheme was limited. The Prime Minister of the time W F Massey said suitable emigrants were 'people of the right class – steady, industrious, respectable people'.[24] Farmers wanted labourers and middle-class families wanted domestic servants. Immigrants had to provide evidence of some capital and a certificate of health and character. Once established, they could nominate all their family members for assisted passage. Shipping companies and the government advertised in British newspapers; the shipping companies being paid £1 per passenger, whether on assisted passage or able to pay their own way.

In 1907 New Zealand became a Dominion within the British Empire. There had been a great depression up to 1910, but then there was a period of steady growth. Almost 37,000 assisted migrants arrived in New Zealand between 1904 and 1915 with the peak being in 1913, just after Polly arrived to join William.[25] Polly is shown on the electoral register of Brooklyn, New Zealand of 1914 in her own right. Though women would only get a restricted vote in the UK in 1918, New Zealand was the first self-governing country in the world to give all women the right to vote, twenty-five years earlier in 1893. In 1917 William is described as a labourer and army reservist. In 1928 he was described as a foreman but by 1938 he was retired, living with Polly in Onehunga. Polly died in 1961, aged eighty-two and William died in 1962, aged eighty-four, leaving their five children.

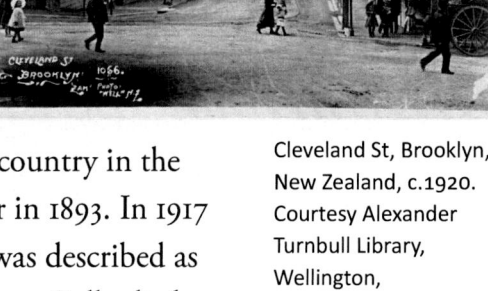

Cleveland St, Brooklyn, New Zealand, c.1920. Courtesy Alexander Turnbull Library, Wellington, New Zealand, Ref: 1/2-047010-F.

New Zealand was to further cement its place as the leader of women's rights when Elizabeth Yates was elected the first female mayor in the British Empire on her election in 1893. She had travelled from Scotland in 1853, married a master

Elizabeth Yates, Mayor of Cleveland, 1893. Courtesy Archives New Zealand Te Rua Mahara o te Kāwanatanga.

mariner who became active in local politics and was mayor between 1888-1892. She shared his interest in local politics and debate, and she was elected mayor the day after the general election in 1893, receiving congratulations from Queen Victoria. Not everyone was happy though, meetings were often disrupted as her fellow councillors attempted to block her, but despite only being in office for a year she succeeded in liquidating the borough debt, upgraded roads, footpaths and sanitation, and reorganised the fire brigade. She returned briefly to council office but never ran for mayor again, nonetheless a remarkable achievement for the time.[26]

Though William was the only sibling to choose New Zealand, there was however a further link between the branches of the family. In 1937, William and Polly's eldest son, Richard, travelled from New Zealand to Canada to marry his cousin Joan Butler, the daughter of Annie Southern and John Butler. Richard and Joan returned to live in New Zealand and raised their family there. The Southern family may have travelled far from Roscow's Tenement, and finished their story on two different continents, but they remained close and, like many families from Smithills Estate, produced generations of hardworking people for their new countries.

Modern day Onehunga, New Zealand. Courtesy iStock/RexEllacott.

Advertisement by New Zealand Shipping Company. From the collection of Dawn Axon.

References

Chapter 1

Two Lads: The Myths and Legends

1. William Yates Map of Lancashire, 1788 http://library.lancs.ac.uk/maps/Map5R1788.jpg [accessed 21 November 2021]
2. https://www.heritagegateway.org.uk/Gateway/Results_Single.aspx?uid=9350d095-c6cd-498a-b0b5-a84cb6825804&resourceID=19191 [accessed 7 September 2022]
3. Hampson, Thomas, *History of Blackrod* (Wigan: *The Observer* Office, 1882) ch. 1; Whitaker, John, *The History of Manchester in Four Books: The History of Manchester, Book the First, Containing the Roman and Roman-British Period* (1771)
4. Miller, Ian and Bill Aldridge, *Discovering Coccium: The Archaeology of Roman Wigan* (Oxford: Oxford Archaeology Ltd, 2011)
5. Irvine, William Fergusson, *A Short History of The Township of Rivington in The Country of Lancaster with Some Account of The Church and Grammar School* (Edinburgh: Ballantyne Press, 1904), p. 156
6. Irvine, p. 8
7. Baines, Edward, *History of the County Palatine and Duchy of Lancaster* (London, Paris, And New York: Fisher, Son, & Co., 1836), p. 48
8. Lancaster University Library, Map 5R, Lancashire Historic Maps, 1788
9. Smith, Robin, *My Theories of Two Lads* (Bolton: Horwich Heritage), p. 9
10. *Bolton Evening News,* 2 November 1979
11. Smith, Robin, p. 6
12. Redding, Cyrus, *The Pictorial History of the County of Lancaster* (London: George Routledge, 1844), p. 281
13. https://www.heritagegateway.org.uk/Gateway/Results_Single.aspx?uid=9350d095-c6cd-498a-b0b5-a84cb6825804&resourceID=19191 [accessed 7 September 2022]
14. 'Moors cairn arises again', *Bolton Evening News,* 31 January 1988
15. *Bolton Evening News,* 31 January 1988
16. 'Mystery of the yo-yo landmark', *Bolton Evening News,* 17 November 1988
17. Pilkington, John, *History of The Pilkington Family of Lancashire, and Its Branches, From 1066 to 1600,* 3rd Edition (Liverpool: C. Tinling & Co. Ltd, 1912), p. 268
18. Pilkington, p.269
19. Redding, p. 281
20. Hampson, Thomas, *Horwich Its History, Legends And Church* (Wigan: *The Observer* Office, Wallgate, 1883), p.37
21. Bagley, J.J., A.G. Hodgkiss, *Lancashire A History of the County Palatine in Early Maps* (Neil Richardson, 1985)
22. Geoffrey Saxton Map of Lancashire, 1577 http://library.lancs.ac.uk/maps/Map2G1577.jpg [accessed 21 November 2021]
23. http://www3.lancashire.gov.uk/environment/oldmap/speed/speed.jpg [accessed 21 June 2022]; William Yates Map of Lancashire, 1786 http://library.lancs.ac.uk/maps/Map5R1788.jpg [accessed 8 July 2022]
24. Billington, W.D., *The Ancient Halliwell Cross* (Bolton: Halliwell Local History Society), p. 2
25. Billington, W.D. and M.S. Howe, *Smithills Hall*, Revised Edition (Bolton: Halliwell Local History Society, 2010), p. 17
26. Billington, 2010, *Smithills Hall*, p. 12
27. Clegg, James, *Annals of Bolton* (Bolton: *The Chronicle* Office, 1888), p. 13
28. Bolton Archives and Local Studies, ZMM/12/1, Papers of Marie Mitchell, Aelle & Smithills Hall
29. https://www.newadvent.org/cathen/05326a.htm [accessed 5 March 2022]
30. https://en.wikipedia.org/wiki/Ecgbert_of_York [accessed 16 March 2022]
31. Bolton Archives and Local Studies, ZMM/12/1
32. Winstanley, John, *Trench Book of Noon Hill Excavation* (Bolton Archaeological Society, 1958)
33. Fletcher, M., *The Bronze Age Complex on Cheetham Close: A New Survey* (1984), p. 7
34. http://chorleyhistorysociety.co.uk/articles_01/sys2286.htm [accessed 2 October 2021]
35. Harrison, William, *An Archaeological Survey of Lancashire* (Westminster: Nichols And Sons, 1896), p. 12
36. Smith, Robin, p. 7
37. Smith, John, *Two Lads* (Bolton: Horwich Heritage), p. 1
38. http://chorleyhistorysociety.co.uk/articles_01/sys2286.htm [accessed 20 December 2021]
39. Clegg, J., *Annals of Bolton. History, Chronology, Politics* (Bolton: *The Chronicle Office, 1888)*, pp. 62, 63
40. https://www.wiganarchsoc.co.uk/how.html#Roman [accessed 8 May 2022]
41. Hampson, 1882, p. 6
42. 'Blackrod: Its History, Its Church, and Churchyard', *Wigan Observer,* 25 March 1882, p. 7
43. Smith, John, p. 3
44. Rawlinson, John, *About Rivington* (Chorley: Nelson Brothers Printers, 1969), p. 83

Chapter 2
Poaching on Burnt Edge, 1630 and 1864

[1] Lancashire Archives, QSB 1/75/60, HORWICH – pursuit of game by setting-dogs on Horwich Moor, 1630
[2] Lancashire Archives, QSB 1/75/61, HORWICH – pursuit of game by setting-dogs on Horwich Moor, 1630
[3] 'Poaching at Horwich', *Bolton Chronicle,* 10 September 1864, p. 8, col. 3
[4] https://commons.wikimedia.org/wiki/File:Desportes,_Chienne_Blanche.jpg

Chapter 3
Chadwicks Close Farm

[1] Bolton Archives, ZJA/1, Plan of Smithills, belonging to Sir Thomas Barton, by William Senior, 1620
[2] Bolton Archives, ZZ/55/36, A Plan of Smithells Demesne, the property of Edward Byrom Esq. by Hugh Oldham, 1769
[3] Bolton Archives, ZZ/365, Quitclaim: Elizabeth Cundliffe, widow of Stephen Cundliffe of Halliwell, and John Cundliffe the younger of Halliwell, 1766
[4] Lancashire Archives, QDL/S/43, Halliwell Land Tax Assessments 1780-1832
[5] 'Shocking Occurrences', *Bolton Chronicle,* 21 January 1843, p. 3, col. 3
[6] 'Assaulting a Publican', *Bolton Chronicle,* 13 January 1855, p. 5, col. 4
[7] 'Cowardly and Savage Assault on a Sergeant of Police', *Bolton Chronicle,* 29 May 1858, p. 5, col. 3
[8] 'Farms to be Let', *Preston Herald,* 15 February 1885, p. 8, col. 4
[9] Bolton Archives, GBO/11/3/16, Smithills Valuation List 1922
[10] Bolton Archives, ABZ/119/2, Smithills Hall Estate Survey 1948

Chapter 4
Women and Work from the Late 1780s to the Early 1850s

[1] Valenze, Deborah, *The First Industrial Woman* (Oxford: Oxford University Press, 1995)
[2] Overton, Mark, *Agricultural Revolution in England* (Cambridge: Cambridge University Press, 1996)
[3] Purvis, June, (ed.) *Women's History Britain, 1850-1945* (London: UCL Press, 1995), p. 27
[4] Valenze, 1995
[5] Purvis, 1995, p. 70
[6] Styles, John, 'The Rise and Fall of the Spinning Jenny: Domestic Mechanisation in Eighteenth-Century Cotton Spinning', *Textile History,* 51:2 (2020), 195-236 (p. 202)
[7] Valenze, 1995
[8] Purvis, 1995, p. 70
[9] http://www.lancashirehistory.org/lecturettes-01.html [accessed 4 July 2022]
[10] Jones, William, *Bolton's Industrial Heritage* (Cheltenham: The History Press, 2006), p. 24
[11] Valenze, 1995
[12] Purvis, 1995, p. 69
[13] Jones, 2006, p. 24
[14] https://commons.wikimedia.org/wiki/File:Webmaschine_in_Tirolervolkskunstmuseum.JPG [accessed 4 September 2022]
[15] Styles, 2020, p. 198
[16] Styles, 2020, p. 206
[17] Berg, Maxine, *The Age of Manufactures, 1700-1820* (London: Routledge, 1994), p. 238
[18] Berg, 1994, p. 251
[19] Berg, 1994, p. 240
[20] https://local-heritage-list.org.uk/greater-manchester/bolton [accessed 4 July 2022]
[21] Phelps, A., R. Gregory, I. Miller and C. Wild, *The Textile Mills of Lancashire The Legacy* (Lancaster: Oxford Archaeology North, 2016), pp. 2, 20
[22] Jones, 2006, p. 26
[23] Billington, D. C. and C. Walsh, *Barrow Bridge* (Bolton: Halliwell Local History Society)
[24] Jones, 2006, p. 28
[25] Phelps, A., Gregory, R., Miller, I. and Wild, C. (2016), p. 24
[26] O'Connor, D., 'Barrow Bridge: A Model Industrial Community of the Nineteenth Century' (unpublished manuscript, Bolton Industrial History Society, 1971), p. 13

[27] Berg, 1994, p. 251

[28] https://www.historytoday.com/working-woman%E2%80%99s-place [accessed 12 June 2022]

[29] Parliament. House of Commons (1834) Report from Dr. James Mitchell to the Central Board of Commissioners, respecting the Returns made from the Factories, and the Results obtained from them (HC 167 XIX). London: House of Commons

[30] Martin, B., 'Leonard Horner: A Portrait of an Inspector of Factories', *International Review of Social History,* 14.3 (1969), 412-443

[31] https://ecclesoldroad.uk/person/robert-gardner/ [accessed 8 June 2022]

[32] https://en.wikisource.org/wiki/Dictionary_of_National_Biography,_1901_supplement/Bazley,_Thomas [accessed 8 June 2022]

[33] 'Dean Mills', *Illustrated London News,* 25 October 1851

[34] *Illustrated London News,* 1851

[35] O'Connor, 1971, p. 63

[36] *Illustrated London News,* 1851

[37] https://ecclesoldroad.uk/person/robert-gardner/ [accessed 15 July 2022]

[38] Jones, 2006, p. 100

[39] Stone, Sheila, 'Barrow Bridge, Bolton, Lancs: An attempt to create a model industrial community in the 19th century' (Unpublished undergraduate dissertation, University of Southampton, 1979), p. 30

[40] http://www.weasteheritagetrail.co.uk/Resources/some-old-job-titles-from-the-textile-industries/index.htm [accessed 8 June 2022]

[41] Liddington, J. and J. Norris, *One Hand Tied Behind Us* (London: Virago, 1978), p. 86

[42] Liddington, 1978, p. 85

[43] https://lancashirepast.com/2019/05/25/moss-bank-house-and-ainsworth-bleachworks-halliwell-bolton/ [accessed 5 July 2022]

[44] Valenze, 1995, pp. 106-111

[45] Liddington, 1978, pp. 27, 220

Chapter 5
Who Killed George Henderson on Winter Hill?

[1] 'Inhuman murder and robbery', *Bolton Chronicle,* 17 November 1838, p. 2, col. 2

[2] 'The Horwich murder', *Bolton Chronicle,* 6 April 1839, p. 2, col. 3

[3] 'The alleged murder near Bolton', *Liverpool Mail,* 4 April 1839, p. 5, col. 1

[4] Holding, David, *Murder in the Heather* (David Holding, 2017)

[5] Jones, Bill, *The Ainsworths of Smithills Hall* (Bolton: Friends of Smithills Hall)

[6] 'Robbing Gardens', *Bolton Chronicle,* 9 June 1838, p. 3, col. 4

[7] 'Another mid-day murder in this neighbourhood', *Manchester Times,* 17 November 1838, p. 3, col. 2

[8] 'Assault by a watchman', *Bolton Chronicle,* 26 May 1838, p. 3, col. 5

[9] 'Highway Robbery', *Bolton Chronicle,* 22 August 1846, p. 2, col. 3

[10] 'A new policeman', *Bolton Chronicle,* 19 August 1843, p. 2, col. 4

[11] 'Singular case of burning', *Bolton Chronicle,* 7 February 1852, p. 5, col. 3

[12] 'Assaults', *Bolton Chronicle,* 17 December 1836, p. 3, col. 3

[13] Holding, David, *Murder in the Heather* (David Holding, 2017)

[14] Holding, 2017

[15] 'The late murder', *Bolton Chronicle,* 24 November 1838, p. 2, col. 5

[16] *Liverpool Mail,* 4 April 1839

[17] *Bolton Chronicle,* 17 November 1838

[18] Bolton Archives, AB/24/1/1, Bolton Watch minutes, 20 December 1838 – 6 June 1839

[19] 'Horrid murder on Horwich Moor', *Blackburn Standard,* 21 November 1838, p. 2, col. 2

[20] 'Highway robbery', *Bolton Chronicle,* 22 August 1846, p. 2, col. 3

[21] Davies, Roy, *Stumped: The Story Behind the Memorial on Winter Hill* (Bolton: Horwich Heritage, 2021)

Chapter 6
Jack O' Nandies

[1] Heaton E. R., *The Heatons of Deane: The varying fortunes of a Lancashire family over 850 years.* (Aberystwyth: Cambrian Printers Ltd, 2000), p. 128.

[2] 'Brutal treatment to a cow', *Manchester Courier and Lancashire General Advertiser,* 6 July 1844, p. 6, col. 3

[3] 'Obstructing the Inspector of Weights and Measures', *Bolton Chronicle,* 20 September 1845, p. 4, col. 7

[4] 'A Singular case – Manslaughter', *Bolton Chronicle and South Lancashire Advertiser,* 19 December 1846, p. 3, cols. 3-4

[5] 'Result of Avarice', *Manchester Courier and Lancashire General Advertiser,* 3 March 1847, p. 7, col. 5
[6] Southern, C., *Changing face of Bolton.* (Hendon Publishing Co Ltd, 1975), p. 59
[7] 'Bad meat', *Manchester Courier and Lancashire General Advertiser,* 12 October 1850, p. 8, col. 3
[8] 'Character. Inspector of Nuisances wanted at Heaton', *Bolton Chronicle,* 18 February 1860, p. 5, col. 3
[9] https://commons.wikimedia.org/wiki/File:Scant_Row,_Bolton.jpg

Chapter 7
The Sutcliffes, Handloom Weavers at Walker Fold

[1] Bythell, D., *The Handloom Weavers: A Study in the English Cotton Industry during the Industrial Revolution* (Cambridge: Cambridge University Press, 1969), p. 1
[2] Bythell, 1969, p. 3
[3] Bythell, 1969, pp. 58-59
[4] https://britishheritage.com/history/history-british-cotton-industry [accessed 18 July 2022]
[5] https://victorianweb.org/painting/fmb/paintings/14.html [accessed 21 July 2022]
[6] https://www.wcml.org.uk/our-collections/working-lives/cotton-workers/ [accessed 30 June 2022]
[7] Taylor, A. J., 'Concentration and specialization in the Lancashire cotton industry', *Economic History Review,* I (1949), p. 118
[8] https://www.lancastercastle.com/history-heritage/further-articles/the-lancashire-riots/ [accessed 3 August 2022]
[9] Gooderson, P. J., *A History of Lancashire* (London: B. T. Batsford Ltd, 1980), p. 137
[10] Gooderson, 1980, p. 138
[11] Bowley, A. L., *Wages in the United Kingdom in the Nineteenth Century: Notes for the Use of Students of Social and Economic Questions* (Cambridge: Cambridge University Press, 1900), pp. 110-112
[12] Ashton, T. S., *The Industrial Revolution, 1760-1830* (London: Opus Books, 1947), p. 11
[13] Bythell, 1969, pp. 144, 257-263
[14] J.S., *Summer Evenings with Old Weavers.* (Manchester: Abel Heywood, c.1870), pp. 55-56
[15] Bythell, 1969, p. 142
[16] Clarke, A., *Moorlands and Memories.* (London: Tillotsons Ltd, 1920), p. 29
[17] Lancashire Archives, Q/EL/1, Electoral Registers, Bolton 1850
[18] Bythell, 1969, p. 267
[19] Clarke, 1920, p. 308
[20] J. S., c.1870, p. 9

Chapter 8
Slack Hall and Newfield

[1] 'Advertisement', *Bolton Chronicle,* 11 August 1860, p. 12, col. 6
[2] Heaton, E. R., *Heatons of Deane, the Varying Fortunes of a Lancashire Family over 850 Years* (E. R. Heaton, 2000), pp. 222-226
[3] 'Statutory Notice', *Bolton Chronicle,* 15 December 1860, p. 4, col. 3
[4] 'To Be Let', *Bolton Chronicle,* 2 October 1858, p. 1, col. 5
[5] 'Medical Relief For The Poor', *Bucks Herald,* 22 December 1860, p. 6

Chapter 9
Lost Cottages on Winter Hill: Newspaper Hall and Black Jacks

[1] Bolton Archives, ZAL 280 & 912, John Albinson, Plans of Horwich Moor intended to be Inclosed, 1813-1815
[2] Partington, Solomon, *Winter Hill Right of Way: The Defence Committees Vindication* (Bolton: Tillotson and Son, 1896)
[3] Clayton, David, *Murder in the Heather* (Bolton: Halliwell Heritage, 2017)
[4] Partington, 1896
[5] Partington, 1896
[6] Waugh, Edwin, *Sketches of Lancashire Life* (London, Liverpool and Manchester: Simpkin, Marshall, and Co., 1857)
[7] Partington, 1896
[8] 'Bolton Trades Council's Picnic', *Bolton Evening News,* 27 July 1903, p. 4, col. 2
[9] Transcript of Witness Statements at 1897 Trial. Derek Billington, Halliwell Local History Society.
[10] Transcript of Witness Statements at 1897 Trial. Derek Billington Halliwell Local History Society.
[11] Heaton E. R., *The Heatons of Deane: The varying fortunes of a Lancashire family over 850 years.* (Aberystwyth: Cambrian Printers Ltd, 2000)

[12] Bolton Archives, ZZ/55/36, A Plan of Smithells Demesne, the property of Edward Byrom Esq. by Hugh Oldham, 1769

[13] Clarke, Allen, *Moorlands and Memories* (1924) (Littleborough: George Kelsall, 1986)

Chapter 10
The Freeman Sisters, Victorian Laundresses

[1] Malcolmson P.E., *English Laundresses: A Social History 1850-1930* (Urbana and Chicago: University of Illinois Press, 1986), p. 20

[2] Royal Commission on Labour 1893-94

[3] 'Intermediate sessions for the Hundred of Salford', *Bolton Chronicle,* 8 December 1838, p. 2, col. 6

[4] 'Robbery', *The Bolton Free Press,* 17 November 1838, p. 3, col. 5

[5] Malcolmson, p. 26

[6] Loane, M., *The Next Street But One* (London: E. Arnold, 1908), p. 183

[7] Budrikis, S., 'The Life of a Laundress' in *Clogs and Clippers* (2016). Available from: https://clogsandclippers.blogspot.com/2016/09/the-life-of-laundress.html [Accessed 10 June 2022]

[8] Hale, S. J. B., [1840], *The Workwoman's Guide* (reprinted), (London: Legare Street Press, 2021)

[9] Malcolmson, p. 20

[10] *Post Office Bolton Directory 1902-1904*

[11] McCleary, G. F., *The Life in the Laundry* (London: The Fabian Society, 1902), p. 2

Chapter 11
Leaving the Estate Far Behind

[1] National Archives, CO 384/66, Australia: Offices and individuals, 1841

[2] Bolton Reference Library Archive, ZZ7 Correspondence of Thomas Bramwell, April 1840

[3] Bolton Reference Library Archive, ZZ287 Correspondence of Thomas Bramwell, 1850

[4] https://www.theshipslist.com/ships/australia/europa1855.shtml [accessed 12 June 2022]

[5] *Statistics of Migrations, National Tables, Australia* Compiled by Walter F Willcox, Published 1929, now out of print. Stats were also published weekly in the *Sydney Herald.*

[6] https://museumsvictoria.com.au/immigrationmuseum/resources/journeys-to-australia/ [accessed 4 June 2022]

[7] 'The Immigration of 1855', *Adelaide Observer,* 3 May 1856, p. 5

[8] 'Arrivals', *Adelaide Observer,* 3 May 1856

[9] https://museumsvictoria.com.au/immigrationmuseum/resources/journeys-to-australia/ [accessed 4 June 2022]

[10] https://www.theshipslist.com/ships/australia/europa1855.shtml [accessed 12 June 2022]

[11] https://www.theshipslist.com/ships/australia/europa1855.shtml [accessed 9 September 2022]

Chapter 12
Women's Work on Deakins, Lomax Wives, and Holdens Farms

[1] Lieshout, Carry Van, Harry Smith and Robert J. Bennet, 'Female Entrepreneurship in England and Wales 1851- 1911' in *Female Entrepreneurs in the Long Nineteenth Century,* ed. by Jennifer Aston and Catherine Bishop (Cambridge: Cambridge University Press, 1990), pp. 197, 307

[2] Pinchbeck, Ivy, *Women Workers and The Industrial Revolution, 1750-1850* (London: George Routledge & Sons Ltd, 1930), p. 10

[3] Verdon, Nicola, '"…subjects deserving of the highest praise': farmers' wives and the farm economy in England c.1700-1850', *The Agricultural History Review,* 51(2003), 23-39 (pp. 27-28)

[4] Billington, W.D., *Barrow Bridge,* (Bolton: Halliwell Local History Society, 1988), p. 26

[5] Leech, Thomas John, Diary 1880, Recipe 58. Courtesy of Karen Holroyd.

[6] Leech, Thomas John, Diary 1880, Recipe 61. Courtesy of Karen Holroyd.

[7] Leech, Thomas John, Diary 1880. Courtesy of Karen Holroyd.

[8] Higgs, Edward and Amanda Wilkinson, 'Women, Occupations and Work in the Victorian Censuses Revisited', *History Workshop Journal,* 81 (2016), 17-38 (p.21)

[9] Seccombe, Wally, 'Patriarchy Stabilized: The Construction of the Male Breadwinner Wage Norm in Nineteenth-Century Britain', *Social History,* 11:1 (1986), 53-76 (pp. 43-54); Higgs, Edward and Amanda Wilkinson, 'Women, Occupations and Work in the Victorian Censuses Revisited', *History Workshop Journal,* 81 (2016), 17-38 (pp. 20-23, 28-29); Gordon, Eleanor and Gweneth Nair, 'The Myth of the Victorian Patriarchal Family', *The History of the Family,* 7:1 (2002), 125-138 (pp. 125-126)

[10] Verdon, Nicola, '"…subjects deserving of the highest praise": farmers' wives and the farm economy in England c.1700-1850', *The Agricultural History Review,* 51 (2003), 23-39 (p.27)

[11] Verdon, 2003, pp. 33-35

[12] Shortall, Sally, *Women and Farming* (London: Macmillan Press Ltd, 1999), p.74
[13] Pinchbeck, 1930, pp. 11-13
[14] Pinchbeck, 1930, p. 14; Verdon, 2003, pp. 29-30
[15] Pinchbeck, 1930, pp. 8, 11; Verdon, 2003, p. 29
[16] Pinchbeck, 1930, pp. 16, 24, 55; Verdon, 2003, pp. 30-32
[17] Verdon, 2003, pp. 27-28, 32; Pinchbeck, 1930, p. 9
[18] Pinchbeck, 1930, p. 9
[19] Smith, E., *The Compleat Housewife: or Accomplished Gentlewoman's Companion* facsimile edition (London: Literary Services and Production Limited, 1728)
[20] Higgs, Edward, 'Occupational Censuses and the Agricultural Workforce in Victorian England and Wales', *The Economic History Review, New Series*, 48:4 (1995), 700-716 (p. 704)
[21] Hill, Bridget, 'Women, Work and the Census: A Problem for Historians of Women', *History Workshop*, 35 (1993), 78-94 (p. 82)

Chapter 13
Up the Sixty-three Steps to Twitchells Farm and the Brown Cow Beerhouse
[1] Clarke, Allen, *Moorlands and Memories* (1924) (Littleborough: George Kelsall, 1986), pp. 129-130
[2] Clarke, pp. 129-130
[3] 'Beerseller fined', *Bolton Chronicle*, 1 December 1860, p. 8, col. 3
[4] Farrer, William and J. Brownbill, *The Victoria History of the County of Lancashire,* volume V (1911)
[5] Billington, W.D. and M.S. Howe, *Smithills Hall,* Revised Edition, (Bolton: Halliwell Local History Society, 2010)
[6] Research by Chris Speed, Woodland Trust Smithills History Group
[7] Clarke, pp. 129-130
[8] 'Be sold', *Bolton Chronicle*, 24 March 1860, p. 4, col. 2
[9] 'Sales by Auction', *Bolton Chronicle*, 26 August 1865, p. 4, col. 3
[10] 'From Marjorie Kay', *Bolton Evening News,* unknown date. Collection of Tony Greenwood
[11] 'From Frances Davies', *Bolton Evening News,* unknown date. Collection of Tony Greenwood
[12] 'From Richard Quinlan', *Bolton Evening News,* unknown date. Collection of Tony Greenwood

Chapter 14
Violent Attacks on Gamekeepers and a Tragic Love Story
[1] 'Poaching Outrage', *Edinburgh Evening News,* 30 December 1882, p. 7, col. 4
[2] 'A Mad Dog Shot at Heaton', *Bolton Chronicle,* 14 January 1871, p. 6, col. 5
[3] 'Poaching Case', *Bolton Chronicle,* 18 April 1868, p. 2, col. 6
[4] https://commons.wikimedia.org/wiki/File:Ansdell_Richard_The_Gamekeeper.jpg
[5] Munsche, P. B., *The Gamekeeper and English Rural Society* (Cambridge: Cambridge University Press, 1981), pp. 82-105
[6] Munsche, 1981, pp. 82-105
[7] Munsche, 1981, pp. 82-105
[8] Halliwell Local History Society, Smithills Estate Agents Books
[9] 'Outrageous Conduct of a Gamekeeper', *Leeds Times,* 13 September 1873, p. 6, col. 7
[10] 'To The Editor', *Sussex Advertiser,* 21 April 1828, p. 4, col. 5
[11] 'Plague Ships', *Bolton Chronicle,* 24 December 1853, p. 6, col. 2
[12] *Bolton Evening News*, 4 May 1882, p. 7, col. 5
[13] 'Emigration to America', *Carlisle Patriot,* 29 November 1817, p. 2, col. 5
[14] *Cork Examiner,* 7 September 1864, p. 4, col. 6
[15] 'The Sad Suicide in Halliwell', *Bolton Evening News,* 25 June 1884, p. 2, col. 6
[16] Weinberg F., 'Infant feeding through the ages', *Canadian Family Physician,* 39 (1993), pp. 2016–2020

Chapter 15
Horwich Casanova
[1] Interesting Breach of Promise Case', *Belfast Evening Telegraph,* 9 August 1872
[2] 'A Horwich Breach of Promise of Marriage', *Bolton Evening News,* 7 August 1872, p. 4, col. 1
[3] 'A Picnic to Whittle Springs and its result', *Preston Chronicle,* 10 August 1872, p. 2, col. 4

⁴ https://access.bl.uk/item/viewer/ark:/81055/vdc_00000003A39E#?c=0&m=0&s=0&cv=0&xywh=-1914%2C-129%2C5266%2C2564 [accessed 18 August 2022]

⁵ *Bolton Evening News,* 7 August 1872, p. 4, col. 1

⁶ *Bolton Evening News,* 7 August1872, p. 4, col. 1

⁷ Beith, M. A., *No Gravestones in the Ocean: The Immigrant Ship Scimitar 1873-1874* (London: New Generation Publishing, 2019), p. 1

⁸ *Bolton Evening News,* 7 August 1872, p. 4, col. 4

⁹ The National Archives, J 77/237/6699, Court for Divorce and Matrimonial Causes, later Supreme Court of Judicature: Divorce and Matrimonial Causes, 1880

¹⁰ National Archives at Washington, D.C., Microfilm Publication M237, 675 rolls. NAI: 6256867. Passenger Lists of Vessels Arriving at New York, New York, 1880

¹¹ *The Hutchinson News,* 18 October 1889, p. 3

¹² *The Caldwell Advance,* 2 October 1884, p. 3

¹³ *Reports of the Department of Commerce and Labour: 1908* (Washington: Government Printing Office, 1909), p. 457

Chapter 16
Old and New Colliers Row, and Colliers Row School

¹ https://commons.m.wikimedia.org/wiki/File:Old_Colliers_Row_-_geograph.org.uk_-_116151.jpg

² Billington, D., 'Early Schooling in Halliwell', Halliwell History Society https://halliwell-lhs.co.uk/articles [accessed 28 June 2022]

³ 'Memories of Colliers Row School', *The Bolton News,* 12 March 2014; 'More memories of Colliers Row School', *The Bolton News,* 19 March 2014

⁴ https://historicengland.org.uk/listing/the-list/list-entry/1387989

⁵ Bolton Archives, SLB/73/1; 2; 3, Smithills Dean Church of England School, Correspondence

⁶ Bolton Archives, SLB/73/1; 2; 3

⁷ *The Bolton News,* 12 March 2014; *The Bolton News,* 19 March 2014

⁸ Bolton Archives, SLB/73/1; 2; 3

⁹ *The Bolton News,* 12 March 2014; *The Bolton News,* 19 March 2014

¹⁰ *The Bolton News,* 12 March 2014; *The Bolton News,* 19 March 2014

¹¹ *The Bolton News,* 12 March 2014; *The Bolton News,* 19 March 2014

¹² *The Bolton News,* 12 March 2014; *The Bolton News,* 19 March 2014

¹³ 'Colliers Row School – snippets from the school log', Halliwell History Society https://halliwelllhs.co.uk/articles [accessed 20 June 2022]

¹⁴ Halliwell History Society https://halliwell-lhs.co.uk/articles [accessed 20 June 2022]; Bolton Archives, SLB/73/1; 2; 3

¹⁵ Bolton Archives, SLB/73/1; 2; 3; Halliwell History Society https://halliwell-lhs.co.uk/articles [accessed 20 June 2022]

¹⁶ https://commons.wikimedia.org/wiki/File:Collier%27s_Row_School.jpg

Chapter 17
The Story of Alice and William Stead

¹ 'Marriages', *Bolton Evening News,* 29 September 1904, p. 3, col. 7

² 'Russian Cotton Mills', *Cumberland & Westmorland Herald,* 30 December 1882, p. 6, col. 6

³ Mitrofanov, A. 'The Konshin family'. Available from: https://www.miloserdie.ru/article/semejstvo-konshinyhdrugaya-realnost-kupe cheskoj-zhizni/ [Accessed 10 July 2022]

⁴ 'Wanted an apprentice', *Bolton Evening News,* 25 August 1871, p. 2, col. 2

⁵ Greenwood, E. L., Work, *Identity and Letterpress Printers in Britain, 1750–1850* (Manchester: Manchester University Press, 2015), p. 142

⁶ 'Presentation Tea Meeting', *Bolton Evening News,* 12 February 1877, p. 2

⁷ Kennedy, C. H., 'Celebrating Sobriety: The Victorian Temperance Party Scene', [Online] Available from: https://newhistories.group.shef.ac.uk/celebrating-sobriety-the-victorian-temperance-party-scene [Accessed 12 July 2022]

⁸ MacDonald, R., *Women in the printing trades: a sociology study* (London: P. S. King & Son, 1904), p. 4

⁹ MacDonald, p. 2

¹⁰ *Printers Journal,* 5 August 1867

¹¹ MacDonald, pp. 18-19

Chapter 18
The Harts, Emigration to Canada

¹ Dunae, P. A., and G. Woodcock, 'English Canadians' in *The Canadian Encyclopedia.* (Historica Canada, 2018)

2. 'Advertisements Received Late', *The Rochdale Observer,* 9 October 1915, p. 8, col. 7
3. https://www.flickr.com/photos/manitobamaps/2831500218
4. Green, A. G., 'Dominion or Republic? Migrants to North America from the United Kingdom, 1870-1910', *Economic History Review,* LV, 4 (2002), pp. 670-671
5. Canada (1872) Dominion lands act. Ottawa: Brown Chamberlain, Printer to the Queen
6. https://commons.wikimedia.org/wiki/File:Canadian_Pacific_Ry_free_farms_1893.jpg
7. Green, pp. 675-676
8. 'Emigration to Canada', *The Bolton Evening News,* 1 April 1898, p. 4, col. 9
9. Gourlay, S., 'CPR's READY MADE FARMS.' *Alberta History,* (Historical Society of Alberta: Autumn 2019), p. 2
10. 'Ready Made Farms', *The Manchester Courier and Lancashire General Advertiser,* 4 February 1910, p. 12, col. 5
11. Detre, L. A., 'Canada's Campaign for Immigrants and the Images in Canada West Magazine'. *Great Plains Quarterly,* 24(2), (University of Nebraska Press: 2004), pp. 119–120
12. https://commons.wikimedia.org/wiki/File:Canadian_pop_from_1851_to_1921.jpg.
13. 'News in Brief', *The Bolton Evening News,* 27 August 1910, p. 4, col. 4
14. *The Province,* 5 April 1924, p. 20
15. *The Calgary Herald,* 10 February 1956, p. 13
16. Bartlett, E. A., 'Real Wages and the Standard of Living in Vancouver, 1901-1929', *BC Studies* 50(4), (The University of British Columbia: 1981), pp. 6-7
17. Library and Archives Canada. Statutes of Canada. A Bill to Make Better Provisions for further British Settlement in His Majesty's Oversea Dominions, 1922. Ottawa: SC 12 George V, Bill 87
18. Kelley, N., and Michael Trebilcock, *The Making of the Mosaic: A History of Canadian Immigration Policy* (Toronto: University of Toronto Press: 1998), p. 189

Chapter 19
Love Across the Continents: Putting Down Roots in the New World
1. https://www.historymuseum.ca/
2. *Northern Star and Leeds General Advertiser,* 7 September 1844
3. *Northern Star and Leeds General Advertiser,* 7 September 1844
4. http://www.canadahistoryproject.ca/1905/1905-02-immigrants.html [accessed 4 June 2022]
5. http://englishemigrationtocanada.blogspot.com/ [accessed 18 August 2022]
6. https://www.historymuseum.ca/
7. *Bolton Journal and Guardian,* 20 January 1911
8. *Bolton Journal and Guardian,* 20 January 1911
9. https://www.historymuseum.ca/
10. 'Sinking of a British Collier', *The Mercury,* 12 August 1912, p. 5
11. https://www.historymuseum.ca/
12. https://www.macleans.ca/news/canada/what-it-was-like-for-pioneers-in-1920s-alberta/ [accessed 2 January 2022]
13. Pointe-au-Pere Maritime Museum, www.shmp.qc.ca [accessed 3 May 2022]
14. Liverpoolmuseums.org.uk
15. www.theshipslist.com/Research/canadarecords.shtml {accessed 28 February 2022]
16. https://www.historymuseum.ca/
17. https://api.parliament.uk/historic-hansard/written-answers/1925/jul/30/average-weekly-wages [accessed 31 July 2022]
18. https://teamster.org/about/teamster-history/the-early-years/ [accessed 9 March 2022]
19. https://teamster.org/about/teamster-history/transcontinental-delivery [accessed 9 March 2022]
20. www.theshipslist.com/Research/canadarecords.shtml [accessed 12 August 2022]
21. http://www.theshipslist.com/Research/canadarecords.shtml [accessed 14 August 2022]
22. Archives New Zealand, Passenger Lists, 1839-1973
23. *Bolton Journal and Guardian,* 20 January 1911
24. J. S. McBean, 'Immigration into New Zealand, 1900–1915.' MA thesis, Victoria University College, 1946, p.22.
25. https://nzhistory.govt.nz/culture/immigration/home-away-from-home/the-english [accessed 18 May 2022]
26. https://nzhistory.govt.nz/media/photo/elizabeth-yates-first-female-mayor

The platt of Smithilles, also of holdens, Roscos
Richardsons, Harrisons, & walkers farmes belonging to the right Worshipfull Sr Thomas Barton Kn:
Taken by William Senior Professor of the Mathe-
matiques ———— Anno domini 1620 ————

Rosco farme

Great pasture
88 — 2 — 20

great pasture
14 — 2 — 24

HOWDENS farme

quarry

Egbordine — 509 — 2 — 20 — acr: woods Poles

Burnt edge Pasture · 67 — 0 — 10

RICHARDSON: Harrison: and walkers farme

DAKINS

William Senior's map for Sir Thomas Barton, 1620, owner of Smithills Estate.
John Albinson Collection ZAL/1231.
Courtesy Bolton Council.

Gazetteer of Buildings

Bryan Hey
Most likely sixteenth century. Earlier named Bryne, Brine or Brian Hey. Two-storey farmhouse with stone-mullioned windows and some round-headed windows. Barn is a Grade II Listed Building, probably early eighteenth century.

Burnt Edge Colliery (Newfield Colliery)
Developed on Newfield farmland early nineteenth century. Seen as single pit on 1845-47 Ordnance Survey map. Later extended and converted into brick and tile works using clay mined from around coal seam. Further extended at end of nineteenth century. Small lodge built next to colliery buildings to provide water for steam engines. Worked into early twentieth century. Remains of kilns and drying rooms still visible and original pit and air shafts are clear in surrounding fields. Accessed initially by tracks along Burnt Edge until stone slab tramway built 1856.

Chadwicks Close
Situated off Coal Pit Road. Probably part of lands occupied by Samuel Chadwick when Smithills Estate was sold in 1722/3. On 1769 plan recorded as 'lower house' of John Cunliffe, who also leased Green Nook. Thomas Cooper resident from 1802, James Cooper 1813-43. Later tenanted and farmed by Tonge and Shuttleworth families, relations of Coopers.

Cottage i' th' Moor (Black Jacks)
Initially site of Morris' Farm, with Walls Farm close by. Both demolished and Eight Houses built as miners' lodgings, which were also demolished when mines closed. Cottage built c.1841 and demolished 1880s.

Cunliffe's
On Colliers Row Road, one branch of old Bolton and Nightingale turnpike. Previously called Chadwicks according to 1769 Estate Plan. Likely part of land leased by Samuel Chadwick in 1720s. Stephen Cunliffe tenant 1760s, farm later adopted his family name. Divided mid-1800s: one twenty-six acres, one thirteen acres. Smaller part farmed by John and Mary Aston between 1841 and 1871. Larger part occupied by Thomas and Mary Brown and family from 1861. Still farmed by Browns in 1940s.

Colliers Row and New Colliers Row
Built by Ainsworth family to house miners working at Holden's Colliery between 1819 and 1841. Some uninhabited by 1911.

Colliers Row School (Smithills Dean School)
Single-storey building next to New Colliers Row. Original datestone 1841, with corresponding datestones to extensions 1885 and 1898. Gothic Revival style architecture. Closed July 1971. Now a private Grade II Listed Building.

Deakins
Originally included a barn, shippon and farmhouse under one roof. Name alternates in records between Deakins and Dakins. Later converted to a single house. The farm was on Papist Returns and 1620 map when land belonged to Sir Thomas Barton. Current building appears mid-eighteenth-century construction, probably replacing earlier seventeenth-century house.

Dean Gate Farm and Cottage
Nineteenth-century farmhouse built atop earlier one probably eighteenth century or earlier. Originally bisected by what is now Smithills Dean Road.

Dean Mills
Commissioned by Thomas Bazley and Robert Gardner 1838 to replace earlier water-powered mill built by Lord family in 1790s. Steam powered with central engine house. Accompanying worker's model village at Barrow Bridge constructed at same time. Sold to William Callender in 1862, derelict by turn of twentieth century and demolished in 1913. Village remains and forms part of a Conservation Area.

Eighteen Acres
Another late eighteenth/early nineteenth century very small farm on Burnt Edge pasture further up from Pinchems. Probably part of Heaton's Newfield estate. Still occupied as a house in 1911 by Mr Morgan. Later demolished.

Five Houses
A terrace of five houses with small pasture fields built on edge of Wildersmoor, probably by William Garbutt. Garbutt had moved from Shropshire to Wildersmoor to establish his Colliery and Brick Works on Winter Hill. His cottage was both colliery office and beerhouse. Empty beyond 1860s and demolished by end of century.

Gilligant's
Part of huge fourteenth-century vaccary of Egberden, by 1620 known as Egbordine. Earliest record in Halliwell Township book 1746 when William Pendlebury was paid £2 2s. for preventing it being settled, presumably by unlawful trespassers. Known as William Pendlebury's Tenement, he leased it from Edward Byrom in 1762. Thirty acres in 1769. His daughter married Richard Pilkington and they farmed here. Subleased by Benjamin Mayoh 1783-1814.

Green Nook
On 1769 plan of Smithills Estate described as 'John Cunliffe's higher house'. Twenty-nine acres, three roods and twenty-two perches in size, and included a third part of Whimberry Moor. Farmed by Barnabas Dearden 1851-1880.

Halliwell Bleach Works
Early site founded by the Ainsworth family 1730s. Developed in nineteenth century using chlorine gas. Demolished twentieth century. Chimney dated 1860s remains.

Hampsons
Another larger farm enclosed from Egbordine in eighteenth century. Large tenement in 1769 with thirty-three acres rough pasture and thirty acres newly marled and limed field down to Dean Brook at Walker Fold. In early nineteenth century occupied by descendants of Roscow family. Known also as Brownstones.

Harricroft Farm and Farm Cottages
No. 3 occupied by gamekeeper Henry Jennison Peachey when he worked for Ainsworth family.

Haslams
Shown on 1620 map as Haslams Intack (intake). An estate workers' cottage with small nine-acre holding. Haslom family listed on Protestation returns of 1642, and in 1722/3 Robert Haslom listed as renting messuage and tenement when area was sold. By 1814 tenancy had passed to Abraham Walsh with rent of £30 per annum to Ainsworth family. Advertised in 1893 as a 'good Milk Farm', it was managed by Pendlebury's Farm. Also known as Lower Lomax Wives.

Higher Tongs
Built on newly divided land in early nineteenth century. New farmhouse was nearer to new Bolton and Nightingale turnpike than Lower Tongs. Tenanted by Coopers from 1830s. Later Browns, and by 1911 Winstanley family.

Holdens
Remote moorland farm, a fourteenth-century vaccary. Called Holden's Tenement on 1620 and 1769 maps. Originally mainly upper moorland pasture covering fifty-five acres pasture and thirty acres meadows. Farmhouse built eighteenth century. Barn early twentieth century. Eighteenth and nineteenth-century handloom weavers' cottage, later lodging house for miners, then a gamekeeper's cottage.

Holden's Colliery
Ainsworth's colliery at end of old Coal Pit Road. Evidence of coal being extracted on high pasture above Holden's in seventeenth century. Single pits shown on 1769 Estate maps. Group of bell pits in early 1800s, with road access built 1822. Holes left from pits still visible.

Hole Bottom Cottages (Winter Hill Bungalow)
Brick built line of three single-storey cottages, later reduced to two, built by William Garbutt next to his Brick and Tile Works for nephew Gabriel Garbutt, and workers and families. Known in 1830s as Quaker John's. Bungalow last surviving building of small cottages and farms built on Burnt Edge and Wildersmoor. Still lived in until 1950s, later demolished.

Little Deakins
Located across lane from Deakins just outside Estate boundary, originally a farmhouse. Name likewise alternates between Deakins and Dakins. Constructed 1776. The two initials E R on datestone stand for Eatock Robert, a local landowner whose descendants owned Little Deakins and surrounding land. Third symbol linked to Robert's wife Martha who died in 1776.

Lomax Wives
An ancient farm enclosed from Egbordine vaccary to be upper pasture for Bryan Hey Farm. On 1620 map as Wm Lumas ground, a four-acre meadow, which along with Haslams Intack were the upper part of Bryan Hey Farm. Situated beside an ancient drovers' road from west to east Lancashire through Cunliffe's Farm. Improved throughout eighteenth century with records of drainage in 1818. Advertised in 1885 as a milk farm to be let with 'Good Farm Buildings'. Also called Lomas Wifes or Lomax Wifes.

Lower Tongs
Lease granted 1713 by Lord Falcounberg to yeomen Ralph Fogg of Blackrod, and James Smith of Newton. Previously said to be in possession of James Pendlebury. Farm known as Fogg's and Bolton's until Ralph Tong's tenancy began in 1769. He died 1804. By 1806 rated at £9 per annum with loom shop. Henry and Betty Rushton tenants 1814 to at least 1819. James and Mary Sewart at least 1841-1871. John and Mary Taylor occupants between 1881 and 1901.

Newfield
Appears on William Senior's 1620 map. Named from practice of laying land with marl (clay, sand, and lime) which changed heathland to productive farmland, as in new field. Laid out garden behind house in 1847. William Garbutt, who managed Wildersmoor Colliery and Five Houses beerhouse died here, as did his brother.

Old Harpers
Late eighteenth-century farmhouse built following enclosure of Horwich Moor. Mixed use. Part of Heaton family's estate. Open farmyard and barn built into hillside. Still a farm in 1911 occupied by Thompson family. In use during World War II. Now a ruin.

Ouzel Hall (Newspaper Hall/Tar Hall/Slate Delph Brow)
Built in a disused quarry surrounded by coal pits, probably 1820s, as homes for colliers and banksmen. Later replaced by a series of short-term buildings, one of which was a handloom weavers' cottage with five looms. Finally demolished in 1865. Sometimes spelt Ouzle.

Pendlebury's
Datestone 1712. By 1769 Jonathon Pendlebury's Tenement. Twenty-three acres, with marled and limed meadows. The Pendleburys were a large and important Bolton and Salford family in eighteenth century with this branch involved in farming.

Pinchems
Probably late eighteenth/early nineteenth century. Two small pasture fields later expanded to brick and tile works. Airshaft in lower field. Abandoned early twentieth century. Sometimes referred to as Burnt Edge.

Roscow's Tenement
Roscoes on 1620 map and in some censuses. A fold with ninety-one acres of high moor pasture up to ancient Dean Ditch, with thirty acres of meadow. Reduced in size to forty-two acres, probably when moors became enclosed shooting grounds. Datestone 1768, John Makinson and his wife Grace Marsden, probably when barn added. Vineyard in late eighteenth century.

Sheepcote Green
Originally lower house to William Pendlebury's farm at Gilligant's, with a nine-to-twelve-acre pasture. Later accessed through Chadwicks Close and path down to Walker Fold. Earlier known as Sheep Coats.

Sheep House
Built 1712, same year as Pendlebury's Farm. Called James Pendlebury's in 1769, a thirty-acre holding. Farmhouse with attached late eighteenth-century cottages and barn dated 1862. Extended by addition of shippons 1901.

Slack Hall
Substantial stone-built detached farmhouse. Greatly transformed in recent decades, doubling in size. Located on ancient Burnt Edge pasture, once common land till 1815 enclosure. Previously a dairy farm. Access would have been from top of Moor Lane, now Matchmoor Lane. William and Alice Heaton lived here in 1828.

Twitchells
Built by Robert Eatock c.1844. Became known as the Brown Cow Beerhouse. Private house by 1911. Demolished 1950s.

Walker Fold
Established probably sixteenth century, seen on Senior's 1620 map where land is marked as belonging to Walker's, Dakin's and Holden's. At least one cottage built for handloom weavers. Became typical mixed-use fold, with weavers, farmers, and a tavern. In 1911, six cottages with farmhouse. Barn opposite converted into large house facing the road and the row of cottages now just two houses.

Wildersmoor Colliery
Probably in use non-commercially from the seventeenth century. Developed by William Garbutt in early nineteenth. Shallow seams accessed by ladder shafts.

Winter Hill Brick & Tile Works
Developed early nineteenth century by William Garbutt with steam engine, grinding and crushing apparatus, stoves, drying houses, and ovens. Advertised to let along with Hole Bottom cottages in 1849. Taken over by Adam Mason following Garbutt's death, later Joseph Cronkshaw. Remains of kilns and walls of drying houses and offices can be seen.

Lists of Tenants and Occupiers of Halliwell and Smithills Estate 1543-1902

Researched and Compiled by Stephen Tonge

1543 Lay Subsidy for Halliwell
Taxation in Salford Hundred, 1524-1802.
Chetham Society. Vol. 83. (1924)

Andrew Barton Esquyer a commyssyoner	for	lx£	in lands	lij£
Roger Warde	"	xv£	in goods	x^s
Robert Taylear	"	xiij£	" "	ij^s viii^d
Robert Rychardson	"	v£	" "	ij^s
John Rychardson	"	v£		xx^d
Adam Sweteloue	"	"	" "	"
Harre Wodward	"	"	" "	"
John Harper	"	"	" "	"
Charles Leghe	"	lij£	" "	vj^d
Vxor Richard Mershe	"	"	" "	"
Vxor David Mershe	"	xl^s	" "	iiij^d
William Marshe	"	xx^s	" "	ij^d
Robert Marshe	"		" "	"
Elizabeth Mershe	"		" "	"
Cycile Mershe	"		" "	"
Alice Mershe	"		" "	"
William Hallywall	"		" " "	"

1613 – 1656 Early Baptisms & Burials for Smithills
The Registers of the Parish Church of Deane, 1604: 1613-1750.
Lancashire Parish Register Society (1916)

Baptisms

Jervis son of Robert Rocklaie, esquire, of Smithills in Halliwall, formerly parish of Deane
14 October 1613

John son of Christopher Walker of Smithels .... spinster: illegitimate, gentleman..
.. February 1617-1619

Peter son of Ralph Worthington, gentleman of Smithill
13 May 1641

Burials

Richard Lockewood lately of Smithills in Halliwall
28 March 1624

Lawrence Worthington of Smythle
16 Oct: 1641

Alexander Worthington from Smithill gent: 12 Octob: 1656

1642 Protestation Returns for Halliwell
Parliamentary Archives Ref: HL/PO/JO/10/1/95/8

The Protestation Returns of 1641–1642 are lists of English males over the age of eighteen who took, or did not take, an oath of allegiance 'to live and die for the true Protestant religion'. Some of the surnames in this list are found on the 1620 map of Smithills Estate, i.e. (1) 'Richardson, Harrison and Walker farm', (2) 'Howden farm' and (3) 'Rosco farm', as well as parcels of land called 'Wm Lomax ground', and 'Haslam's Intack'.

William Lupton
William Sanderson
Arthur Best
Willm Horrocks
John Allmonde
William Horrobin
Thurstan Coup
James Brearley
Alexander Stones
John Dicconson
Robt Willies
John Turner
Richard Edge
Thomas Whitle
Henery Walker
Thomas Shippton
Richard Astley
John Finie[?]
John Johnson
John Yate
Thomas Richardson†
Thomas Slater
Thomas Longworth
John Whitle
John Whitle
Daniell Whitle

William Bordman
Richard Richardson†
Thomas Bordman
George Smith
Mathewe Warde
Robert Taylior
Robert Taylior
Robert Brooke
Roger Taylior
Roger Taylior
Roger Taylior
Richard Dobson
Thomas Marsh
George Marsh
Adame Sweetlove
Lawrence Sweetlove
Adam Roscowe†
Robert Boulton
Thomas Stones
Raphe Taylior
William Williamson
Henery Williamson
Willm Lythgoe
Charles Haslom†
Roger Makinson
John Cooke

Thomas Bradshawe
Willm Houlme
Thomas Longworth
Richard Woode
Edward Whithe[?]
Francis Watson
James Hampson
Thomas Smith
William Smith
John Asmall[?]
William Houlden†
Ellis Houlden†
William Houlden†
William Lomax†
Richard Lomax†
Robert Haslom†
Adam Haslom †
Thomas Roscowe†
Peter Roscowe†
Andrew Wood
Andrew Wood
Francis Pendleton
Robart Brooke
Edward Edge

† Surname appears on 1620 map of Smithills

1666 Hearth Tax for Halliwell
Source: Taxation in Salford Hundred, 1524-1802.
Chetham Society. Vol. 83. (1924)

Sir Rowland Bellasis	19
Mris Harper	3
Robert Warde	4
Jo. Peake	3
Geo. Smith	3
Wm. Broadman	4
Jo. Johnson	4
Ric. Boulton	3

1678 Poll Tax for Halliwell
Lancashire Archives Ref: QDV13/20

March 8th 1678

S^ir Row: Billyssis K^t. of the Bathe	15-01-00
His foure children	00-04-00
Tho: Waringe 3^li wages	00-04-00
Eliz: Alman 3^li wages	00-04-00
Ann Hune 3^li wages	00-04-00
Jon: Longworth 2^li wages	00-03-00
Jon: Waringe 1^li wages	00-02-00
Margaret Burch	00-01-00
Mary Watmough	00-01-00
John Hulton	00-01-00
Hamblet Partington & his wyfe	00-02-00
Robte Ward & his wyfe & 3: Children	00-05-00
Mary Ward widdow	00-01-00
Geo: Smyth his wife & 3: Children	00-05-00
Mrs Jane Harpur widdow	00-01-00
James Harpur her son	00-01-00
Jo^n: Morres his wyfe & 2 Children	00-04-00
Alice Aspinall widdow	00-01-00
James Aspinall her son	00-01-00
Phinias Aspinall her son	00-01-00
Symon Haydocke	00-01-00
Jo^n: Haydocke his son	00-01-00
Adam Sweetlove Senior	00-01-00
Adam Sweetlove Junior	00-01-00
Tho: Marsh his wyfe & 4 children	00-06-00
Thurston Briggs & his wyfe	00-02-00
Ann Leigh widdow	00-01-00
Rich: Grundye junior	00-01-00
Ann Sweetlove widdow	00-01-00
W^m: Edmund, Ann & Izabell her children	00-04-00
Alex^r Houlcroft & his wyfe	00-02-00
Alex^r Lomax junior	00-01-00
Tho: Whitle junior & his wyfe	00-02-00
Eliz: Whitle widdow	00-01-00
Rog^e Roscow & his wyfe	00-02-00
Will Charneley	00-01-00
Chrofer Isherwood & his wyfe	00-02-00
Martyn Taylor his wyfe & children	00-05-00
Rich: Taylor & his wyfe	00-02-00
Tho: Bordman & his wyfe	00-02-00
Hen: Potter	00-01-00
Jo^n: Hardier	00-01-00
Jo^n: Leigh	00-01-00
Tho: Whitle	00-01-00
Est^r Whitle his doughtr	00-01-00
Rich: Bolton	00-01-00
W^m: Smyth	00-01-00
Tho: Willmson	00-01-00
Raphe Enwisley & his wyfe	00-02-00
Tho: Lighbowne his wyfe & 1 child	00-03-00
Rich: Lomax & his wyfe	00-02-00
Jane Morres	00-01-00
W^m: Holden & his wyfe	00-02-00
Eliz: Roscow widdow	00-01-00
Peter Roscow & his wyfe	00-02-00
Ellis Holden	00-01-00
Law: Brooke	00-01-00
Jo^n: Johnson assessor	00-01-00
Bettey his wyfe & 1 child	00-02-00

```
                                 20-12-00
                                 £   s.  d.
```

We present Jon: Johnson for Collector

Assessed by us
 Henerey Morris
 Sam: Greenhalgh,
 Jon: Johnson

1723 Smithills Estate Tenants
Bolton Archives Ref ZAH/13/7/1
Gerrard Manuscripts - Booklet 2, transcript 4

11th May 1723
Viscount Fauconberg, eldest son and heir of the Right Honourable Thomas Lord Viscount Fauconberg, late deceased and nephew and heir at law of the Right Honourable Thomas, late Earle and Viscount Fauconberg, deceased, of the one part and Thomas Eyre of Stockport, county of Chester, and Thomas Foxley of Manchester, Merchants, of the other part .... doth grant, bargain and sell unto the said Thomas Eyre and Thomas Foxley all that Manor or Lordship or reputed Manor or Lordship of Hallywell, alias Hallewall, and also all that capital messuage or Mansion House called Smithells, farm, garden and curtilage &c.

Tenants mentioned

		Notes
William Pendlebury, one corn mill, late in the occupation of Lawrence Cowpe		
John Leah Dakinsholme	3 parcels of land	
William Makinson Sheep Coat Green	1 parcel of land	*Sheep Cote Green*
Peter Roscoe	Messuage and Tenement	*Roscow's Tenement*
William Holden	Messuage and Tenement	*The present Holdens*
Robert Haslom	Messuage and Tenement	*The present Haslams*
James Lomax	Messuage and Tenement	*Lomax Wives*
Richard Melling	Messuage and Tenement	
John Hampson	Messuage and Tenement	*The present Hampsons*
Alexander Howarth	Messuage and Tenement	*(formerly William Melling's)*
Lawrence Livesay	Messuage and Tenement	*(formerly John Holden's)*
James Pendlebury	Messuage and Tenement	*Probably Sheephouse or Pendlebury's*
Ralph Fogg & James Smith	Messuage and Tenement	*Lower Tongs*
Samuel Chadwick	Messuage and Tenement	*Chadwicks Close or present Cunliffe's*
Simon Haddock	a close or parcel of land	*Later Marylooms*
Thomas Whittle	2 closes or parcels of land	*Ropers Barn?*
John Houghton	a messuage or cottage	
Roger Thropp	a messuage or tenement	
Sarah Boardman	a messuage or tenement	*Boardman's*
Robert Roscoe	a messuage or cottage	
Simon Haddock	a messuage or cottage	
Holland Bradley	a messuage and Tenement	
James Kenyon	a messuage or cottage	
William Smallshaw	a messuage or cottage	
Ralph Rothwell	a messuage or cottage	
Ellen Molyneux	a stable with appurtenances	
John Yates	several houses called Kirkall	
Mr Crook deceased Alexander Walker	a messuage and tenement	

(with many other properties in Bradshaw, Horwich, Sharples, Quarlton, and Wigan)

1790 Land Tax for Halliwell
Land Tax Assessments 1780-1832.
Lancashire Archives QDL/S/43

Proprietor	Occupiers	£	s	d
Roger Dewhurst Esqr.	Himself	1	5	7½
"	Peter Ainsworth	0	16	1½
"	" Moss & Lumwood	0	6	6
"	" Hopes	0	3	0½
"	John Haslam	0	15	9
Mr Peter Ainsworth	Himself	0	6	1½
Revd. Richd. Rothwell	Thos. Poole	1	1	6
Mr Aspinall	John Horrocks	2	12	6
Mr Eskrick	Edwd. Rothwell	1	1	11½
"	Lawe. Fletcher	0	13	4½
Mr Ralph Rothwell	Himself	0	12	2½
Mr Am Fletcher	Wm. Seddon	1	2	9
Mr Pilkington	John Rawsthorn	0	6	1½
Mr Oldham	Peter Haddock	0	5	3
Mr Wm. Makant	Himself	0	2	11
"	Jas. Morris	0	5	10
Mr Jas. Fowler	Himself	0	6	1½
Mr T. Nuttall	Ann Kay	0	6	4½
Mr Jno. Cooper	Himself	0	5	3
Miss Byrom	Roger Walker	0	7	10½
"	Abigail Bromiley	0	4	4½
"	Ralph Tonge	0	8	8½
"	John Makinson	0	7	10½
"	John Pendlebury	0	5	3
"	Jere. Pendlebury	1	4	4½
"	Wm. Hart	0	9	10
"	Nichls. Kirshaw	0	7	0
"	John Rawsthorn	0	16	2
"	Benn Mayoh	0	4	4½
"	Thos. Hulm	0	2	2½
"	Jas. Pendlebury	0	9	3½
"	Jas. Barrow	0	6	7
"	Richd. Wroe	0	6	6
"	Robt. Whewell	0	3	6
"	Richd. Turner	0	3	1
"	Roger Roscow	0	3	6
"	Jo? Cooper	0	1	4
"	Wm. Hart	0	6	8½
"	John Rawsthorn	0	4	10
Oliver Morris	Himself	0	6	6½
Henry Morris	Oliver Morris	0	6	6½
John Wood	Himself	0	14	0
Alice Makant	Herself	0	9	2½
Jas. Brown	John Beswick	0	6	1½
	Wm. Fray	1	1	0
Thos. Aspinall	Peter Greenhalgh	0	7	5½

1801 Smithills Estate Occupiers & Tenants, extract from Title Deed
Halliwell Local History Society Transcript Ref: A774

By indentures of lease and release of 23rd and 24th December, 1801 - the release between the Rev. John Clowes of Manchester, clerk and Rector of St John's Church, Manchester of the 1st Part

Henry Atherton of Lincoln's Inn, Middlesex, Esq and Ann Atherton his wife (then late Ann Byrom, Spinster, and one of the two daughters and only children of Edward Byrom) and Eleanora Byrom of Manchester, spinster (the other of the two daughters and only children of Edward Byrom) of the 2nd Part

William Fox of Manchester, Banker, of the 3rd Part

Peter Ainsworth of Halliwell, Merchant, and Richard Ainsworth of Moss Bank within Halliwell, Merchant of the 4th Part

John Clowes sold 745 acres in the several occupations of

Richard Roe	William Greenhalgh	Ann Cockerill
Major Roe	William Pendlebury	John Shaw
John Makinson	John Turner	James Cunliffe
John Cunliffe	Thomas Bromiley	James Schofied
Roger Roscow	James Pendlebury	Ann Pendlebury
James Barrow	John Rawsthorn	Roger Walker
John Hart	Robert Crompton and Richard Orrell	James Hart

or some of them - in the several tenures, or occupations of

John Makinson	Messrs Pilkington & Turner	Robert Cunliffe
Ralph Tonge	Richard Ainsworth	John Pendlebury
Jonathan Cundliffe	Thomas Bromiley	Roger Walker
William Lomax	John Rawsthorn	Ann Roscow
Thomas Longworth	Major Wroe	James Barrow
Messrs William & Robert Hart	John Shaw	James Schofied
	William Greenhalgh	Richard Lomax
John Turner	Roger Entwistle and John Rhodes	Thomas Rhodes
William Wroe		

as the tenants

1814 Smithills Demesne Rents

Richd. Ainsworth Esqr. Rental Book
Bolton Archives Ref: ZJA/69

Name	Property	Rent	£	s	d
Yourself	A. Holden's	Rack	-	-	-
John Makinson	B. Roscoes	2 Lives	16	-	-
Richd. Pilkington	C. Gillygants	2 Lives	-	-	-
Richd. Pilkington	D. Sheep Cote Green	2 Lives	14	15	-
Yourself	E. Green Nook	Rack	-	-	-
Robt. Cunliff	F. Chadwick Closes	1 Life	6	-	-
John Ainsworth	G. Walker Fold	Rack	26	-	-
Jas. Schofield	H. Walker Fold	2 Lives	5	-	-
John Roscoe	I. Brownstones	Rack	75	-	-
[blank] Walsh	K. Lomax Wives	Rack	-	-	-
Abm. Walsh	L. Haslams	Rack	30	-	-
Widow Rushton	M. Fogg & Bolton's	Rack	44	-	-
Wm. Settle	N. Chadwicks	Rack	79	-	-
Abigail Bromley	O. Bryan Hey	2 Lives	21	-	-
Henry Norris	P. Pendlebury's	Rack	120	-	-
Thos. Walsh	Q. Woodlands	Rack	73	-	-
Jermy. Pendlebury	R. Part Sheep Cote	2 Lives	9	1	-
John Pendlebury	R. Part Sheep Cote	2 Lives	8	9	-
Roger Walker	S. Dean yate	2 Lives	18	-	-
Yourself	T. Part of Hall	Rack	-	-	-
Yourself	Stone Delf	Rack	-	-	-
Widow Rawsthorne	U. Water	3 Lives	10	-	-
Widow Rawsthorne	U. Part of Hall	3 Lives	17	5	-
Widow Rawsthorne	X. Mill Farm	3 Lives	30	-	-
Robt. Hart	V. Part of Hall	2 Lives	18	-	-
Thos. Longworth	W. Harrycroft	Rack	124	-	-
Major Roe	W. Harrycroft	Rack	26	-	-
Saml. Wright	Y. Part of Hall	Rack	110	-	-
John Hoyle	Part of Hall	Rack	70	-	-
Widow Ashworth	Part of Tongs	Rack	82	-	-
John Dearden	Small Factory Walker Fold	Rack	3	-	-
Messrs. Lords	Ground Rent	Long Term	36	-	-

1819 Smithills Demesne Rents
Rich[d]. Ainsworth Esqr. Rental Book
Bolton Archives Ref: ZJA/69

Name	Property	Rent	£	s	d
Yourself	A. Holdens	Rack	-	-	-
Tho[s]. Walsh	B. Roscoes	2 Lives	105	-	-
Yourself	C. Gillygants	2 Lives	-	-	-
Yourself	D. Sheep Cote Green	Rack	-	-	-
Geo. Prest	E. Green Nook	Rack	60	-	-
Ja[s]. Cooper	F. Chadwick Closes	Rack	40	-	-
John Ainsworth	G. Walker Fold	Rack	25	-	-
W[m]. Bolton	H. Walker Fold	Rack	21	-	-
Yourself	I. Brownstones	Rack	-	-	-
Yourself	K. Lomax Wives	Rack	-	-	-
Ab[m]. Walsh Senr.	L. Haslams	Rack	31	-	-
Widow Rushton	M. Fogg & Boltons	Rack	53	-	-
W[m]. Settle	N. Chadwicks	Rack	79	-	-
Abigail Bromley	O. Bryan Hey	2 Lives	21	-	-
Henry Norris	P. Pendleburys	Rack	130	-	-
Jerm[y]. Pendlebury	R. Part of Sheep Cote	2 Lives	9	1	-
W[m]. Stones	Q. Woodlands	Rack	76	-	-
John Pendlebury	R. Part of Sheep Cote	1 Life	8	9	-
Roger Walker	S. Dean yate	2 Lives	18	-	-
Yourself	T. Part of Smithills	Rack	-	-	-
Yourself	Stone Delf	Rack	-	-	-
Widow Rawsthorne	Water	3 Lives	10	-	-
Widow Rawsthorne	U. Part of Smithills	3 Lives	17	5	-
Widow Rawsthorne	X. Mill Farm	3 Lives	30	-	-
Yourself	V. Part of Smithills		-	-	-
M[rs]. Hart	House		7	-	-
James Alker	W. Harrycroft		75	-	-
Major Roe	W. Harrycroft		30	-	-
Yourself	T. Part of Smithills		-	-	-
Yourself	U. Walls Farm & Part Morris's		-	-	-
John Roscoe	I. Lower Part of Brownstones		61	10	-
Henry & Major Morris	M. Part of Tongs		60	-	-
Yourself	Small Factory Walker Fold		-	-	-
Mess[rs]. Lord & Noble	Ground Rent		36	-	-
Peter Dearden	House Walker Fold and Cow House		5	15	-
Peter Lord	House at Higher Bank		12	12	-
Marg[t]. Greenhalgh	Cottage at Smithills Hall		4	4	-
Rich[d]. Seward	M. Part of Ashworths		39	-	-
Ralph Knowles	C. Part of Gillygants		65	-	-

1869-1870 Smithills Estate Rental
Ainsworth Family Papers
Bolton Archives Ref: ZAH/13/3/18

Yearly Rent

Proprietor	Occupiers	£	s	d
R. Ainsworth Son & Co	Bleach Works	4,950	-	-
	Bryan Hey Lodge	50	-	-
	Cross Lives	14	-	-
	Sheephouse Farm	100	-	-
	"Eight Houses"	8	-	-
	Mill Meadow	2	-	-
R. H. Ainsworth Esq. Land,	Horwich	22	10	-
	Horwich Close	11	-	-
John Martin	Holdens Farm	110	-	-
James Dearden	Eighteen Acre	8	-	-
William Knowles	Roscoes Tenement	90	-	-
Amos Matthews	Gilligants Farm	50	-	-
James Fairhurst	Sheep Cote Green	36	-	-
Barnabas Dearden	Green Nook	41	16	-
Ralph Tonge	Chadwicks Close	40	16	-
Henry Dewhurst	Hampsons	70	-	-
John Sewart	Lomax Wives	35	15	-
John Gee	Haslams	45	-	-
John Eckersley	Bryan Hey	100	-	-
Thomas Brown	Cunliffes	81	-	-
Mary Aston	Cunliffes	40	-	-
Thomas Cooper	Higher Tongs	60	-	-
James Sewart	Lower Tongs	46	-	-
John Taylor	Pendleburys	125	-	-
Isaac Taylor	Dean Gate	77	-	-
Joseph Walker	Tippett Farm	75	-	-
Self	Park land	-	-	-
William Knight	Land for road near Walkerfold	5	-	-
Thomas Brown	Quarry	10	-	-
George Dewhurst	Quarry	10	-	-
Gardner & Co (	Callender & Sons)	152	6	6
Rep[ves]. of Benj[n]. Wood	Chief	1	8	
Daye, Barker & Co	(Thos. Walmsley) Chief	5	-	-
Ebenezer Naylor	Harricroft	153	13	8
Rev[d]. J. Shepherd Birley	Moss Lee	29	-	-
James Ainsworth	Walker Fold	17	10	-
Robert Wareing	Walker Fold	25	-	-
William Makant Esq,	Gilnow	440	-	-
Lewis Murton & Co.	Water Privileges	2	-	-
North Union R'way	Gilnow	24	-	-
		£ 7,143	15	2

Cottages   *Yearly Rent*

Proprietor	Occupiers	£	s	d
Thomas Ainsworth	Walker Fold	3	-	8
William Ainsworth		3	-	8
Edward Entwistle		3	18	-
Richard Ainsworth		3	5	-
William Wilkinson	Old Colliers Row	8	9	-
James Brown		5	4	-
James Greenhalgh		5	4	-
Jane Smith		5	4	-
James Morris		5	4	-
William Hornby		5	4	-
Jane Mather		3	5	-
James Leigh	New Colliers Row	5	4	-
William Taylor		5	4	-
James Neild		3	5	-
Sarah Farnworth		5	4	-
Matt^w. Fairhurst		3	5	-
James Taylor	Sheephouse	5	4	-
Esther Norris		5	4	-
Jane Freeman	Dean Gate	6	10	-
Joseph Walch	Park Cottage	-	-	-
Joseph Pilling	New Springs	5	8	4
George Harwood		5	8	4
John Livesey	1 Dean Road	5	4	-
John Livesey	Stable	3	18	-
Alice Pilling	Park Cottages	8	6	10
Thomas Openshaw		5	10	6
Daniel Green		6	10	-
John Porter		7	16	-
Emanuel Marbeck	Beech Cottages	7	16	-
Mary Walch		6	10	-
John Williams		2	8	-
Richard Mather	Smithills Mill	5	11	-
Joseph Heaton		5	4	-
John Settle	House, Smithills Mill	10	-	-
John Settle	Cottage, Smithills Mill	4	6	6
James Lawson	Temple	5	4	-
Elizabeth Hamer	Harricroft	6	10	-
Henry Peachey	Harricroft	-	-	-
W^m. Longworth	Smithills	-	-	-
Settle	Lodge Gates	-	-	-
		£ 191	2	10

Bleachworks, Farms and Ground rents		7,143	15	2
Cottages		191	2	10
		£ 7,334	18	-

ccliii

1902 Ainsworth's Estate Tenants
Bolton Archives Ref: ZAH/13/3/13

*'Smithills Estate Office, Bolton
30th August, 1902*

Dear Sir,

*Col. Ainsworth desires me to inform you that, to commemorate the Coronation of King Edward the VII, he has decided to invite his
Tenants and their Wives to visit the Royal Lancashire Agricultural Show at Preston during Guild Week.*

With that object in view, and in order that you may attend the Show on the day which may best suit your convenience, I am directed by him to enclose Postal Orders herewith value 22/- to cover expenses, and hope you may have a very enjoyable day.

*Yours faithfully,
   Joseph Walch'*

Fred[k]. Dunsbie	Moss Lea, Astley Bridge
Robert Brown	Harricroft, Astley Bridge
George Clegg	Harpurs, Smithills
Wright Fairhurst	Hill Farm, Halliwell
Edward Jones	Johnson Fold, Smithills
Alfred Dearden	Lower Pools, Smithills
Lot Howarth	Sheephouse, Smithills
Mr[s] Blundell	Dean Gate, Smithills
Edmund Holden	Bryan Hey, Smithills
Jos. Kershaw	Pendleburys, Smithills
Mrs Lonsdale	High Tongs, Smithills
James Taylor	Lower Tongs, Smithills
Thomas Turner	Haslams, Smithills
William Holmes	Lomax Wives, Smithills
John Brown	Cunliffes, Smithills
George Hold	Hampson, Smithills
John Thomason	Gilligants, Smithills
E. Hilton	Sheepcote Green, Smithills
Jno. Shuttleworth	Chadwicks Close, Smithills
Rich[d]. Southern	Roscoes Tenement, Smithills
Joseph Wheatman	Holdens, Smithills
Thomas Hart	Walker Fold, Horwich
Henry Dearden	Walker Fold, Horwich
Alfred Wagstaffe	Deakins, Horwich
James Thompson	Little Deakins, Horwich
John Lee	Hole Hill, Horwich
[blank] Thompson	Old Harpers, Horwich
Thomas Hindley	Eighteen Acre, Horwich
Samuel Thompson	Hole Bottom, Horwich
Peter Livesey	

Nineteenth and Early Twentieth Century Legislation

Government and Local Government
- 1832 Representation of the People Act (also known as the Great Reform Act) – created wide ranging change to Parliamentary constituencies; first piece of legislation that explicitly barred women from voting
- 1888 Local Government Act – created county councils and was the first move away from historic counties corresponding to areas of local government

Factories
- 1802 Health and Morals of Apprentices Act (aka Factory Act 1802) – this was the first piece of factory legislation and improved conditions for pauper apprentices
- 1819 Cotton Factory Act – banned children under nine from working and limited the hours of nine to sixteen-year-olds to twelve hours a day
- 1825 Cotton Mills Regulation Act – 1819 Act was widely unenforced, this Act aimed to tighten up regulations
- 1831 Labour in Cotton Mills Act – banned night shifts for those under twenty-one; seventeen-year-olds now limited to a maximum of twelve hours a day
- 1833 Factory Act – forty-eight hours maximum per week in textile mills for nine to twelve-year-olds, with a maximum of eight hours a day; thirteen to seventeen-year-olds limited to working twelve hours a day
- 1844 Factory Act – nine to twelve-year-olds in textile mills limited to working six-and-a-half hours a day with three hours schooling; women banned from night work; women and thirteen to seventeen-year-olds limited to working twelve hours a day; introduced safety measure such as fencing off machinery
- 1847 Factory Act – 'Ten Hours Act' restricted women and thirteen to seventeen-year-olds to ten hour working day, with a maximum of sixty hours a week. Again, this was in textile mills
- 1867 Factory Extension Act – brought all factory legislation together and extended legislation to cover all factories employing fifty or more people
- 1878 Factory Act – replaced all previous factory legislation; banned children under ten; ten to thirteen-year-olds maximum of a half day shift; fourteen to eighteen-year-olds and women no more than fifty-six-and-a-half hours per week in textiles, and sixty in nontextiles
- 1891 Factory Act – banned children under eleven; banned women working within four weeks of confinement
- 1901 Factory and Workshop Act – banned children under twelve; thirteen-year-olds could work full time

Mining
- 1842 Mines and Collieries Act – banned women and girls from working down mines; banned boys under ten
- 1850 Coal Mines Inspections Act – introduced inspectors of coal mines in order to reduce accidents
- 1860 Coal Mines Regulation Act – improved safety rules and raised age limit from ten to twelve for boys
- 1872 Coal Mines Regulation Act – requirement for pit managers to have professional certification
- 1881 Mines Regulation Act – enabled Home Secretary to hold inquiries into accidents

Chimney Sweeping
- 1834 Chimney Sweeps Act – banned apprentices under ten, and employment of children under fourteen unless apprentices
- 1840 Chimney Sweeps Act – banned those under twenty-one from entering flues; banned apprentices under sixteen
- 1875 Chimney Sweepers Act – introduced certification for chimney sweeps, and ended the use of child sweeps which had continued despite earlier legislation

Health and Welfare
- 1834 Poor Law Amendment Act – a major overhauling of legislation that had been in place since 1601; workhouses became the only legal way poor people could apply for relief (note however opposition in textile districts)
- 1848 Public Health Act – after an outbreak of cholera, this act established Central Board of Health
- 1872 Public Health Act – established sanitary authorities in rural and urban areas
- 1875 Public Health Act – medical officers and sanitary officers introduced

Education
- 1841 School Sites Act – facilitated buying of land to build schools; enabled the application for grants to educate poor children
- 1870 Elementary Education Act – all children between five and thirteen were entitled to be educated by the State; children ten and over could leave if a number of the Six Standards of Education had been achieved (in Bolton it was all six)
- 1873 Agricultural Children Act – prohibited employment of children under eight; aimed at encouraging school attendance
- 1880 Elementary Education Act – effectively made education compulsory
- 1891 Elementary Education Act – introduced free education for children
- 1893 Elementary Education (School Attendance) Act – minimum leaving age raised to eleven; penalties for employing school-age children
- 1899 Elementary Education (School Attendance) Amendment Act - leaving age raised to thirteen

Agriculture
- 1883 Agricultural Holdings Act – improvements for tenant farmers
- 1906 Agricultural Holdings Act – gave tenants the right to a written tenancy agreement

Index

A
Ainsworth, John Horrocks, 67, 178
Ainsworth, Peter
    bleach works, 66
    building of roads, 108
    death, 166, 168
    influence over trial, 82, 83, 85
    interest in education, 187, 188, 194–195
    problems with poachers, 74, 77, 81, 86
    suppression of alcohol sales, 117
Ainsworth, Richard
    bleach works, 66, 124–125
    blocking paths, 115–116, 118–120, 123, 161
    Bob's Smithy, 160
    death, 67
    suppression of alcohol sales, 117
Albinson, John, 19, 24
alcohol, *see* beerhouses, public houses and temperance
America, 170–173, 181-183, 226
animal cruelty, 88, 191
Anti-Corn Law League, 62
Archaeology, 19, 28, 29, 32-35, 37, 121
Arkwright, Kath, 71
Atkinson, Chris, 32
Australia, 135–141, 214, 217

B
Baines, Edward, 17
Barton, Thomas, 23, 43
Bazley, Thomas, 61, 62, 64
beacons, 38–39
Beamish, Alexander Arthur, 168
beerhouses, 49, 71–73, 115, 116–117, 126, 155–163
Berry, Andrew, 126
Billington, W D, 24, 146
Black Jacks, 115, 124–127
Blair, Stephen, 83
bleach works, 66, 67, 124–125, 145, 146, 158, 160, 161, 205
Bob's Smithy, 89, 160, 161
Bolton and District Archaeological Society, 28, 29
Bolton Union Workhouse, 91, 107
bookbinding, 201
Bootle, family, 198–199, 201
Bradshaw, John, 43

Bramwell, Thomas, 135–136
brick works, 105, 108
Bright, John, 62
Bronze Age activity, 28–30
Brown family, 217, 219–221
Brownlow, Christopher, 49
Bu'Lock, Dr John, 28
Burnt Edge, 43–45, 118
Burrell, Benjamin, 71, 76
Butcher, Mr, 88
Butler family, 224, 228
Byrom, Edward, 47

C
cairns, 16–41
Callender, W R, 64
Canada, 204, 207–215, 217–226
Carr, Anthony, 180
carting, 108–109, 121
Cartwright, Edmund, 96
census data, 144–152, 181, 185–186, 206
Chadwick, Samuel, 47
Chadwicks Close Farm, 47–52
chapels, 25, 27
Chartism, 102
children
    born outside marriage, 85, 129, 178, 204
    emigration, 136, 138, 139
    farm work, 55, 191, 206
    illness, 190–191
    mill work, 61, 65, 97, 205
    mining work, 21–22, 106, 185
    plaiting work, 110
    working conditions, 67, 193
Chorley Historical and Archaeological Society, 28, 29
Clarke, Allen, 99, 155–156, 158
Clayton family, 146
Coal Pit Road, 118–120, 123, 124
Colliers Row School, 161, 187–196
commercial travellers, 71, 126, 173
Constantine, Mary, 145, 146
Cooper family, 48–50, 65
co-operative shop, 64
Corliss, James, 74, 77–78
Cottage i' th' Moor, 124–127
Crompton, Ellis, 180
Crompton, Samuel, 57, 95
Crompton, Wright, 78, 80

Crosby, Alan, 44
Cross, Mary, 73, 84
crosses, stone, 24, 27
Culshaw family, 108–109
Cundict, Joyce, 221
Cunliffe family, 47–48
Cunliffe Farm, 217
Curwen, David, 168

D
Darwen, Joseph, 130
Davis, Enoch, 136
Deakins Farm, 144, 145, 148, 152, 156
Dean Gate Farm, 129–132, 166
Dean Mills, 58–64, 145, 158, 205
Dearden, Henry, 206
deaths
    burial mounds and barrows, 28, 31
    children, 174–175
    funerals, 119, 166
    James Cooper, 48–49
    murder, 70-86
    suicide, 173–174
    Two Lads memorial, 20–23
Dewhurst family, 150–151
Dickinson family, 120
Disraeli, Benjamin, 64
Ditchfield, Elizabeth, 108, 109
divorce, 181
Doffcocker Cotton Mill, 194
domestic service, 107, 150–151
drapery industry, 70–71
dressmaking, 145–146

E
Eatock, Robert, 177–183
Eatock family, 145, 152, 156, 159, 178–180, 181–183
Eccles, Ephraim, 103
education
    adult, 63–64, 187
    Dean Mills Institute, 63–64
    religion, 187, 192
    schools, 63–64, 143, 144–145, 161, 187–196
Eighteen Acres Farm, 88–89
Elliott family, 136, 139–141
emigration
    America, 170–173, 181–183, 226
    Australia, 135–141, 214, 217
    Canada, 204, 207–215, 217–226
    children, 136, 138, 139, 221
    New Zealand, 226–229
Entwistle, Mary, 71, 75
Entwistle, William, 44–45, 71
Escricke, Henry, 56
evictions, 118, 120

F
Fairhurst family, 152, 159–160, 224
Fairhurst, Thomas, 45
farming
    Canada, 209–212
    children's work, 55, 191, 206
    dairies, 94, 143, 148–149
    Newfield, 105–113
    Smithills Estate, 106
    supplement to textile work, 99, 101, 106
    women's work, 54, 143–153
Fielding, Richard, 161
Five Houses Beerhouse, 71, 71–73
Fletcher, James, 72, 74–75, 77, 78
Fletcher, William, 84
footpaths, 115–117, 118–120, 123, 161
Freeman family, 129–133, 136

G
gamekeeping
    conflict with poachers, 165, 166, 167, 168, 169
    duties, 165, 167–168
    housing, 160, 161
Garbutt, William, 72–73, 74, 75, 89, 120
gardens, 17
Gardner, Richard, 61, 64
Garnett family, 140–141
Gilligant's Farm, 119, 124
Gordon-Stewart, W R, 126
Green Nook, 48, 52, 169
Greenhalgh, Alice, 89–90
Greenhalgh, Thomas, 79–80, 83
Guest, Henry, 178
Guest family, 159, 217
guns
    access to guns, 73, 74
    licencing, 84
    shooting parties, 72, 73

H
Haddock family, 132
Halliwell, Joseph, 75–76, 81
Halliwell Bleach Works, 66, 67, 145
Halliwell Local History Society, 71
Hamer family, 125
Hampson, Thomas, 16, 22, 37, 38
Hardman, John, 78
Hargreaves, James, 56, 95
Hart family, 204–215
Haslams Farm, 217
Hearst, Mary, 107
Heathcote family, 137
Heaton, Lambert, 80
Heaton, Mary, 170
Heaton family, 88–91, 91, 106–107, 120–121, 123
Henderson, George, 70–86
Holdens Farm, 144, 150
Holdens Farm coal working, 121, 123
Holdsworth family, 161
Holt, James, 222, 224
Hornby, William, 150
Horner, Leonard, 61, 64
Horrocks, Roger, 78, 78–81, 82, 83
Horwich Locomotive Works, 112
Hulton, Adam, 43, 44
hunting
    poaching, 43–45, 73, 80–81, 86, 167, 168
    shooting parties, 72, 73, 74, 77–81, 165

I
Ince, Ann, 185
Ince, Bartholomew, 78
industrialisation, 94–99, 102, 105, 112, 133
inquests, 70–71, 75
Ireland, Isaac, 78, 79
Irvine, William Fergusson, 17

J
Jackson family, 52
Jardine, William, 70
Jones, Bill, 78

K
Kay, John, 94–95
Kay, Joseph, 200
Kingsmill, Sir John, 21
Kirkman family, 107

L
Lambert, Matthew, 73, 74, 84
Lambert, Mrs, 71
Lang, John Dunmore, 136
laundry work, 129–133
Leech, Thomas John, 147
Leverhulme, Lord, 19, 37, 86
Little Deakins Farm, 178–179
lodgers, 107, 108, 161
Lomax, Sarah, 75
Lomax Wives Farm, 144, 146, 151, 217
Longworth family, 143, 148
Lord, Robert, 58
Lowe, William, 206
Luddites, 97

M
Malcolmson, P E, 130
maps
    Bartholomew 1914, 25
    Christopher Saxton 1577, 23
    John Albinson, 24
    John Speed 1610, 23
    Lancashire 1787, 18
    murder trial, 121
    Ordnance Survey, 23, 45, 63, 123, 124, 159, 160, 185, 205
    Smithills Estate, 14, 47, 48
    William Senior, 23, 156
Meake, John, 44
Merrifield, William, 138
Middlemas, Ellen, 194
Milton, Reverend, 67
mines
    Australia, 136
    children's work, 21–22, 106
    Holdens Farm, 121, 123
    Newfield Colliery, 105, 108
    Winter Hill, 21–22, 30, 32–33, 158
    women's working, 185
Morris family, 124, 125

N
Naylor, Mr, 194
Neolithic activity, 31
New Colliers Row, 204
New Zealand, 226–229
Newfield, 105–109, 113

Newhouse family, 170, 173–174
Newspaper Hall, 115, 115–123
Norman, William, 79
Norris, William, 43

O
Oakley family, 110–113
Ordnance Survey, 23, 45, 63, 123, 124, 159, 160, 185, 205
Ormrod, John, 206–207
Orrell, Mr, 74
Ouzel Hall, 118, 120, 123

P
Peachey, George, 107, 169–174
Peachey, Henry, 45, 126, 165–166, 170
Peachey, Walter, 174–175
Pendlebury, Eleanor, 177–178, 180–181
Pendlebury, Frederick, 180–181
Pendlebury's Farm, 204
People's Charter, 102
picnics, 77, 155, 161, 163, 177
Pilkington, James, Bishop, 20–21
Pilkington, Leonard, 21
Pilkington, Lieutenant-Colonel John, 21
Pilkington, Richard, 19
Pinchbeck, Ivy, 150
poaching, 43–45, 73, 80–81, 86, 167, 168
police forces, 79–80
Poor Law, 111
Pound House Cottage, 170
poverty, 91, 97, 107, 111, 135, 150, 168–169
Prince Albert, 63
printing industry, 199–202
prosecutions
    animal cruelty, 88, 89
    assault, 50, 169
    breach of promise, 177–180
    highway robbery, 83–84
    mass trespass, 115–116, 123, 125
    murder, 70, 71, 75–77, 81–83, 121
    poaching, 43–45, 167
    rotten meat, 90
    theft, 130
Prosser, Leslie, 35
public houses
    Ainsworth Arms, 49
    Black Dog Inn, 71
    Bob's Smithy Tavern, 89–90
    Brown Cow, 159
    Doffcocker, 50
    licencing, 72, 116–117, 156
    Moor Gate Inn, 73
    Old Cock Inn, 71
    Twicham Arms, 156
    Volunteer Inn, 50
    Wagon and Horses, 180
    Walker Fold Tavern, 206
Pye, Thomas, 119

Q
quarries, 186, 205, 206, 217

R
Radcliffe, Thomas, 72
Rasbotham, Dorning, 17
Rawlinson, John, 40
recipes, 147
Redding, Cyrus, 22, 27
Reddish, Sarah, 68
religion, 26–27, 85, 187, 192
Reynolds family, 115–120
Ridgeway, Joseph, 18–19
Ridings, John, 78, 79, 80
Rivington Hall Farm, 177
Romans, 16, 35–39
Roscow's Tenement, 204, 221, 222
Ross, Ellen, 150
Russia, 198–199

S
Saxon activities, 24–28
Saxton, Christopher, 23
Schofield, Margaret, 89
Schofield, Thomas, 88
Scholes, Mary, 181
Scottish drapers, 70, 71
Seddon, John, 43
Seddon family, 50
Senior, William, 23, 47, 156
Settle, John, 49
Sewart family, 65, 145, 146, 166
sewing, 145-146, 150
Shaw, Frederick, 108
Shuttleworth family, 50–51
Sixty-three Steps, 155–164

Slack Hall, 105, 106, 110–113, 120
smallholding, 94
Smith, John, 19, 34
Smith, Robin, 18, 19–20, 33, 39
Smithills Dean School, 187–196
snow, 189–190
Southern family, 221–228
Speed, John, 23
spinning, 55–56, 59, 94–95
Sproat, Alexander, 126
Stead family, 198–202, 207
stonemasons, 217
Stott, John, 80
Stott, William, 81
Sunlight Soap, 132
Sutcliffe, James, 55
Sutcliffe family, 93–103
Swinglehurst, James, 102–103

T
Tar Hall, 120, 121
Taylor, Mr, 76–77, 82
Taylor, Robert, 48
Taylor family, 186
tea houses, 155, 161, 163
temperance, 159, 199–200
textile industry, 54–68
    Dean Mills, 58–64, 145, 158
    domestic spinning, 55–56, 59
    drapery industry, 70–71
    dressmaking, 145–146
    handloom weaving, 55, 93–103, 106, 116
    mills, 58–64, 96–99
    Russia, 198–199
    women's work, 50, 54–68, 94, 97, 110, 144–146
Thompson, F W, 123
Thompson family, 144–146
Thornley family, 144–145, 152
Tinsley, Ann, 178
Tonge family, 50, 51
Towler family, 160
transport
    carting, 108–109, 121
    emigration, 135–141, 171, 207–208, 213, 219, 222–223
    hazards of ships, 138, 139, 219–220, 223
    merchant navy, 179–180, 182
    mines, 108, 123
    schools, 188
trespass, 115–116, 118–120, 125
Turner family, 217, 218–221
Twitchells Farm, 155–163, 217
Two Lads, 16–40, 43
Tyrer, Mary, 181

V
Verdon, Nicola, 146, 150

W
Wagstaff family, 146, 148
Walker Fold, 55, 93–103, 198, 204–207
Walsh, Joseph, 120, 126, 168
war, 186, 195–196, 223–224
watchmen, 78–80
Watson-O'Hara, John, 169
Waugh, Edwin, 116
weaving, 55, 93–103, 106, 116
Whewell, Thomas, 58, 72, 75
Whitaker, John, 16, 37
Whitehead family, 125–126
Whitman, Walt, 206, 207
Whittle family, 70, 73–77, 84, 85
Wigan Archaeological Society, 37
Wilkins, Mr, 76, 82
Wilkinson, Fred, 189
Winstanley, John, 28, 29, 35–37
Winstanley, Margaret, 152
Winter Hill
    archaeology, 32–35, 121
    description, 22–23
    houses, 115–117
    mass trespass, 115–116, 123, 125, 166
    mines, 21–22, 30, 32–33, 158
    murder, 70–86, 121
    trespass, 161
    Two Lads, 16–40, 43
Wolstenholme, George, 74
women
    domestic work, 65, 130, 143, 148, 150–152
    education, 143, 144–145
    employment opportunities, 68
    farm work, 54, 143–153
    laundry work, 129–133
    mine work, 185
    mistreatment of, 89
    New Zealand, 227–228

   printing and bookbinding, 201
   school teaching, 193, 194
   suffrage, 68
   textile work, 50, 54–68, 94, 97, 110, 144-146
   widows taking over businesses, 47, 50, 146, 159, 180
workhouses, 91, 107, 111, 135

Y
Yate, James, 43, 44
Yates, Elizabeth, 227–228